THE BRAHMA KUMARIS AS A 'REFLEXIVE TRADITION'

Drawing on primary research on the Brahma Kumaris World Spiritual University, a millenarian New Religious Movement of Indian origin, this book examines the status of tradition in the contemporary world through a critical engagement with the recent social theory of Anthony Giddens on the emergence of a post-traditional society. Walliss examines both the ways in which forms of tradition not only persist but also flourish in the contemporary world and also the manner in which such traditions are drawn on and (re)created by individuals in their ongoing construction of self-identity. Illuminating some of the difficulties encountered when social theory is applied to 'the real world', this book also offers a way of theorising about the status of contemporary religiosity that does not refer directly to the notion of secularisation.

I0896542

ASHGATE NEW CRITICAL THINKING IN RELIGION, THEOLOGY & BIBLICAL STUDIES

The *Ashgate New Critical Thinking in Religion, Theology & Biblical Studies* series brings high quality research monograph publishing back into focus for authors, international libraries, and student, academic and research readers. Headed by an international editorial advisory board of acclaimed scholars spanning the breadth of religious studies, theology and biblical studies, this open-ended monograph series presents cutting-edge research from both established and new authors in the field. With specialist focus yet clear contextual presentation of contemporary research, books in the series take research into important new directions and open the field to new critical debate within the discipline, in areas of related study, and in key areas for contemporary society.

Series Editorial Board:

Other Titles in the Series:

John Hick's Pluralist Philosophy of World Religions
Paul Rhodes Eddy
The Rhetorical Word
Theo Hobson

The Brahma Kumaris as a 'Reflexive Tradition'

Responding to late modernity

JOHN WALLISS
University of Warwick

Routledge
Taylor & Francis Group
LONDON AND NEW YORK

First published 2002 by Ashgate Publishing

Reissued 2018 by Routledge
2 Park Square, Milton Park, Abingdon, Oxon OX14 4RN
711 Third Avenue, New York, NY 10017, USA

Routledge is an imprint of the Taylor & Francis Group, an informa business

A Library of Congress record exists under LC control number: 2002074451

ISBN 13: 978-1-138-73047-2 (hbk)
ISBN 13: 978-1-138-73038-0 (pbk)
ISBN 13: 978-1-315-18822-5 (ebk)

Contents

Acknowledgements

This material in this book stems from PhD research that I undertook between 1997 and 2000 within the Dept of Sociological Studies, University of Sheffield. I would like to thank the Department for the fees waiver that made this research possible in the first place and also my supervisors – Prof. Richard Jenkins and Dr. Sharon Macdonald – for their support and advice (some of which I took). The research would also not have been possible without the co-operation of the Brahma Kumaris World Spiritual University at both the local and national level. I would like to thank in particular 'Pam', the local BK co-ordinator, for her assistance during the research. I only hope that I enriched her understanding of her computer as much as she enriched my understanding of the University and its beliefs.

Numerous people have offered comments on the various drafts of this manuscript. I would like to thank in particular David Phillips, Philip Mellor, Judith Fox, Jim Beckford, Eleanor Nesbitt and Wayne Spencer. Their advice has frequently been invaluable and has no doubt improved the finished manuscript although any errors are, as they always say, still unfortunately my own.

Last, but by no means least, I would also like to thank my family for their love and support over this last half-decade whilst I have been embroiled Ahab-like in this project. Love and thanks in particular to Natalie, Heather and Isabel.

Introduction

Responding to Late Modernity

Religion and Late Modernity

In many ways there is a fundamental link between sociology and religion. The central issues within the discipline, the problem of meaning and social order, are intrinsically bound up with religion. For example, religion carries out the 'repair work' when social order breaks down as well as providing the symbols and values that bind a society together (Turner, 1999). Indeed, in some instances different religions may provide symbols and values that can fundamentally divide a society, such as in Northern Ireland or the Balkans.

Religion, or more precisely the study of religion, is also important to sociology as a discipline not only because the 'Founding Fathers' concerned themselves with it (and thus it is of historical interest); but because in doing so they located it as an important feature in the formation and, in some ways, the persistence of modern societies. Thus, for Weber, the this-worldly asceticism of Calvinism was instrumental to the emergence of Capitalist modernity; for Marx, religion (as false consciousness) was one important factor in the persistence of that social order; whilst for Durkheim religion was itself society writ large. Indeed, from this latter position one could perhaps argue that sociology could be seen as religious studies!

Over the course of the last century, however – possibly as a result of the growing academic division of labour, possibly as a result of the belief that western societies are increasingly secular – there was a gradual divorce between sociology and religion. This was manifested in two significant ways. Primarily, mainstream sociology did not address itself to the place of religion in society. Thus, whilst some social theorists have made references to religion (see, for example, Berger, 1990; Gellner, 1992), it is difficult to name more than a handful of social theorists of stature who have addressed religion in any depth. Secondly, the sociology of religion increasingly became a 'theoretical side-show' (Turner, 1999; see also Beckford, 1985), focusing on insular debates such as secularisation or Church-Sect-Cult typologies, and did not address itself to wider debates or, more importantly, relate wider debates within the social sciences to its subject matter. Indeed, in some quarters there was a marked hostility to the 'mainstream' and a keenness to concentrate instead on the perceived strengths of the sub-discipline – such as its emphasis on subjectivism. This ethos was perhaps best summed up in Roy Wallis and Steve Bruce's late-1980s assessment of the British contribution to the sociology of religion:

> It remains for proponents of contemporary sociological 'theory' to display – in the sociology of religion as elsewhere – that obscure and abstract conceptual elaboration, and vague social philosophising, can articulate in a fruitful and revealing way with the

> material of the real world...The enthusiasm for these exercises in sociology is scarcely a guarantee that they will prove productive, there or in the sociology of religion. Indeed the evidence is heavily the other way (Wallis and Bruce, 1989, p. 511).

Nevertheless, in recent years there has been the beginnings of 'partial re-synchronization' between the disciplines in two key ways (Beckford, 2000). Firstly, there is growing interest in aspects of contemporary religiosity within more mainstream work – typically in forms of 'fundamentalism' or religious pastiche and pluralism (see, for example, Bauman, 1997; Castells, 1997). Secondly, partly as a reaction to the above, sociologists of religion and religious studies scholars have begun to explore the relationship between religion and issues within social theory. To give but a few examples, there have been explorations of the 'religious dimension' within the work of contemporary social theorists (see, for example, Carette, 1999; Carette *et al.*, 1999, Vattimo, 1999), responses to the manner in which religion is discussed within social theory (Beckford, 1992, 1996; Mellor, 1993; Walliss, 2001), discussions of the relationship between the 'postmodern condition' and religion at the general level (Flanagan and Jupp, 1996; Heelas *et al.*, 1998; Lyon, 2000), as well as at the level of individual manifestations of contemporary spirituality – see, for example, Lyon (1993) and Heelas (1996e) on the New Age Movement.

On the whole, it is still too early to see whether this exchange will be a fruitful endeavour or whether, in the hands of social theorists, religion will become merely another cultural phenomenon – 'an exotic, playful or curious feature of the present-day cultural kaleidoscope' (ibid., p. 18) – and whether, as a result, little or no attention will be paid to it in its own right. In other words, there is the fear that 'religion has been made interesting to social scientists again – but for questionable reasons' (ibid.). There is also concern over the validity of specific social theorists' discussions of contemporary religiosity and, as a result, the belief that such theories have to be modified – in some cases significantly – in order for them to be of any use to the study of contemporary religiosity.

In this book my aim is to contribute to this growing debate; to build a bridge between the disciplines of social theory, the sociology of religion and religious studies. More specifically, I intend to connect issues within the study of contemporary religiosity to wider debates within the social sciences generally. In doing so, I also hope to both illuminate some of the difficulties encountered when 'abstract conceptual elaboration, and vague social philosophising' is applied to 'the real world' as well as offer a way of theorising about the status of contemporary religiosity that does not refer directly to the notion of secularisation; an approach that does not ask, for example, whether the proliferation of New Religious Movements (NRMs) signals a retreat of the forces of secularisation or whether they should be read as its symptoms. Indeed, stemming from what I said previously about the historical marginalisation of the sociology of religion, I wish in particular to avoid the partisan, and frankly boring, nature of the secularisation debate as it has developed over the last few decades.

More specifically, my aim is to critique the idea of 'tradition' as it is utilised within the detraditionalisation debate through the discussion of in-depth ethnographic fieldwork conducted with a contemporary NRM, the Brahma

Kumaris World Spiritual University. I will argue that within social theory 'tradition' has always been deployed as a binary opposite to whatever is defined as 'modernity' and that if it is to be used at all and mean anything, we need a more nuanced understanding. I hope to provide this through the development of Philip Mellor's (1993) conceptualisation of 'reflexive traditions'. Mellor argues particularly against the view put forward by, amongst others, Anthony Giddens that tradition is inherently un-reflexive and static. While accepting that reflexivity in the late modern world has become more systematic and extensive than in the past, Mellor argues that reflexivity – the constant, ongoing revision of knowledge and social behaviour on the basis of new information – has always to some extent been a characteristic of religious traditions. Moreover, despite the reflexivity within the late modern world, the normative features of traditions still play a significant role. Indeed, 'individuals still choose to place themselves within [religious traditions] in order to structure their belief and activity with reference to overarching norms' (ibid., p. 120).

In this way, this book will be concerned with two 'responses' to late modernity. Firstly, how the Brahma Kumaris have responded to Late Modernity – how they have transformed themselves over the course of the last century – and, secondly, using this as evidence, I will respond to the Late Modernity/post-traditional society thesis. In other words, to adapt Karl Popper's famous analogy, taking the description of the white swan of 'tradition' provided by commentators, my analysis will be an attempt to show that the ones on the particular pond that they discussing are in fact black ones. Having done so, if I may stretch the analogy to breaking point, I then intend to catch one in order to examine close-up how it differs from the swans described.

Structure of the Book

Chapters one and two form the broad theoretical basis of the book. In chapter one I trace the relationship between 'tradition' and 'modernity' within social theory from the 'founding fathers' of the discipline to a range of contemporary analyses. In doing so, I argue that historically, tradition has always been a residual category; a conceptual (and typically unfavourable) binary opposite to what was (usually favourably) described as modernity. Thus, where, for example, modernity was characterised by rationality, progress and was forward-looking, tradition and the traditional were seen as all that was ignorant, dogmatic, superstitious and backward-looking; 'a ghost from the past we must exorcise for history to move forward' to quote Marx (cited in Soares, 1997, p. 10). Having looked at its theoretical antecedents I then turn to Paul Heelas' (1996d) notion of detraditionalisation – the shift from external voices of authority to the voice of authority that comes from 'within' the individual – and examine the 'radical' version of this thesis put forward by three authors in particular: Ulrich Beck on the 'Risk Society' and 'reflexive modernisation', Anthony Giddens on Late Modernity and the emergence of a 'post-traditional' social order and Zygmunt Bauman's theorisation of Postmodernity. Finally, I advance a definition of 'tradition' that is faithful to these authors' work which may form the basis of my critique in the following chapters.

In chapter two I begin to discuss the detraditionalisation thesis in relation to contemporary religiosity through an examination of the New Age Movement. At first glance, I will argue, it would appear that the New Age points to a situation of radical detraditionalisation in that there is an emphasis on the emergence of a 'New Age' as well as, is in varying amounts, the rejection of the institutions and belief structures associated with the 'old' (for example, organised religion, instrumental rationality and scientific materialism). In the place of such external voices of authority, authority comes to lie in the 'self'; truth, spiritual or otherwise, ultimately 'lies within'. However, somewhat contradictorily, central to this transformation of the self and the world is the utilisation, maintenance and construction of a variety of traditions, a situation that points more towards a coexistence between the forces of detraditionalisation and those of *re*-traditionalisation.

This takes three main forms. Primarily, New Agers draw on a variety of traditions as sources of inspiration in the spiritual quest, such traditions providing 'seekers with a spiritual core around which they can orbit, picking up whichever rays of enlightenment they feel hit the mark, or resonate with their own inner truth' (Storm, 1991, p. 191). However, on another level, New Agers may be seen to draw on such traditions as much for justification as for inspiration, justifying certain practices, for example, by linking them with the beliefs and practices of ancient (but perhaps more spiritually advanced) civilisations, such as the ancient Egyptians, Mayans and Celts. As well as such occurrences of 'tradition' utilisation and maintenance, one may also cite incidences of the (re)creation of tradition amongst New Agers. Indeed, many of the traditions drawn on by New Agers are themselves 'invented traditions', in the Hobsbawnian sense of '"traditions" which appear or claim to be old...[but are in fact] quite recent in origin and sometimes invented' (Hobsbawm, 1982, p. 1).

All this, I will argue, points to a coexistence, if not a dynamic interaction, between, on the one hand, what the authors discussed in the first chapter would see as 'tradition' and, on the other, reflexivity. However, according to the radical detraditionalisation thesis, reflexivity and tradition are mutually exclusive phenomena and, going further, according to Anthony Giddens (1990, p. 38), tradition that requires legitimisation or is characterised by reflexivity is not 'real' tradition but rather 'tradition in sham clothing'. Rejecting this view, I argue that Mellor's notion of 'reflexive traditions' offers a more fruitful way of examining this dynamic interaction between 'tradition' and personal reflexivity and, in the following chapters, deploy it as a hermeneutic tool to examine the Brahma Kumaris World Spiritual University along three main axes.

In chapters three and four, I focus on the emergence and historical development of both the University and its theodicy. Central to this will be the claim that the University's world-orientation/response has developed over the seventy or so years of their existence from a position of world-rejection to what I term world-ambivalence (Walliss, 1999). Its early outlook, founded on the visions of its founder, was characterised by the belief that it was necessary to separate from the outside world, a world which, the founder claimed, was soon to be destroyed through war and various calamities. The Brahma Kumaris' task was, he claimed, to undergo 'death-in-life', to renounce their families and their lives outside the group, as a necessary preparation for their lives as deities in the post-apocalyptic kingdom. However, over the course of the last century, this world-rejecting ethos began to give way to a newer one of liberalism towards the world. Where they had originally sought to escape the corruption and, perhaps more importantly, the persecution of the outside world, beginning in the 1950s the Brahma Kumaris began a vigorous internationalisation programme involving various forms of proselytising activity and, more recently, an active involvement with international organisations such as the United Nations and UNESCO. Nevertheless, despite this seeming interest in 'the world', the University's outlook, whilst becoming more world-accommodating or even world-affirming, still retains a strong emphasis on millenarian world-rejection. The University thus operates with what I term an orientation of world-ambivalence. By this I mean that it appears to entail two distinct and unresolved orientations toward the world. Primarily, the University's whole worldview is based on the visions of its founder, the central of these being the end of the world by apparent nuclear holocaust or environmental catastrophe, this been seen as *essential, desirable* and indeed *pre-determined* in the nature of things. However, on the other hand, to cite one writer on the Brahma Kumaris, 'there is the spectacle of a University which has the word "spiritual" written into its very name becoming increasingly involved in frenetic activity on behalf of the world that is deemed to be beyond redemption in its present form' (Whaling, 1995, p. 15). Similarly, as I examine in chapter four, the organisation that once referred to membership as 'death-in-life' now, whilst still speaking in such terms to some extent, offers 'success in life' or 'empowerment in life' to outsiders through courses in, amongst other things, meditation, 'positive thinking', 'stress-free living' and 'self-esteem'.

In chapter five I shift the level of analysis to focus on the University's membership and how this world-ambivalence is manifested amongst those who attend the University's events. In particular, my aim is to examine the different membership patterns found within the University and, in particular, the role that the University's theodicy plays in the social identity of those who attend its events. On this basis, I distinguish broadly between four main 'ideal type' membership patterns on the basis of their respective goal of involvement, their self-conception and, finally, the nature of their social identity.

Instrumental Users are drawn to the University through its courses in positive thinking and stress-free living and are typically seeking a method to alleviate the symptoms of physical ailments or to find a successful means of coping with stress or self-esteem issues. Stemming from this, their self-conception is more materialistic and, indeed, many are often ignorant of the University's basic beliefs despite even, in some cases, their long involvement with it. This is equally the case with the second membership type that I discuss, *Eclectic Users*, although there are important differences between both. Whilst both are motivated by a desire for self-improvement, eclectic users differ from instrumental users by expressing this goal in more spiritual or philosophical terms. For them, relieving stress, becoming more centred or building self-esteem are not ends in themselves, but rather steps on a long term process of self-development or, put in spiritual terms, developing their 'Higher-Self'. Similarly, whilst eclectic users' sense of social identity is again highly unlikely to be influenced by the University's collective identity, unlike with instrumental users, this is not the result of ignorance or a lack of interest. Rather, it stems from their epistemologically individualistic attitude to the various traditions that they draw on, combine and utilise in their spiritual quest. The social identity of the final two membership styles that I examine – *Spiritual Searchers* and *Interpretative Drifters* – in contrast, is more likely to be influenced by the University's theodicy. For these membership types, it takes on the status of an external voice of authority, providing not only a salvational system but also the basis of a spiritual life narrative. As a result, through the process of conversion, biography is reinterpreted in the light of the University's theodicy and there is a merging of personal goals and self-identity with those of the University. In sum, a distinction is drawn between those seeking to improve their *lifestyle* and those, in varying degrees, seeking the spiritual *life*. Broadly this distinguishes between those individuals for whom the Brahma Kumaris' theodicy serves as a lifestyle sector or, at the most, part of their reflexive biography, and those for whom it serves as the basis of biography.

In chapter six, I explore the three main issues that I have raised in the preceding chapters in relation to a single concrete example, the University's millenarianism. This, I will argue, acted as a form of Nietzschian 'imaginary vengeance' against the outside world as a response to the persecution it received from the surrounding community during its early years. Moreover, the manner in which this millenarianism has developed historically closely mirrors the University's changing relationship with the 'outside' world – from one of mutual rejection to one of ambivalence – and continues to provide a fundamental site of reflexivity at both the institutional level and amongst the University's membership.

Turning first to the institutional level, the University manages and 'negotiates' the different (world-rejecting and world-affirming) 'millenniums' that it promotes using two main, related techniques. First, there is the differentiation and organisational separation of those instrumental, world-affirming activities that are open to all and those world-rejecting activities that are reserved for committed members only. For example, an individual may access the University's web page, attend public lectures, the various courses and workshops without having to publicly demonstrate their faith. However, in order to progress to the next stage of membership – the visit to the University's headquarters in Rajasthan during the period where its deceased founder communicates via a trance-medium – they have to not only demonstrate their commitment by following the recommended lifestyle but also, more importantly, be seen to be doing so by the University. This is intrinsically linked with the second technique; the utilisation and negotiation of different metaphors or readings of the University's theodicy at the different events and in the different types of literature in relation to its intended (core or periphery) audience. For example, amongst committed, core members '...the tradition is lived [and expressed] without apology, translation or dilution' (Howell and Nelson, 1998, no pagination). However, on the periphery, the terminology of the New Age is deployed and the University is keen to market itself at *Mind, Body and Spirit* fairs and the like. Here, the destruction of the world prophesied by the University's founder is repackaged as 'the New Age' or 'World Transformation' whilst the University's emphasis on undergoing 'death-in-life' gives way to an emphasis on personal empowerment.

Next, among the University's membership one finds three broad types of explanation of the relationship between the Brahma Kumaris' theodicy and the outside world; these being deployed in different contexts and with different audiences. First, in some instances members will employ a dogmatic distinction between the two sets of beliefs in terms of their absolute truth or falsehood. In other words, they accept the dissonance between what they believe and what others outside the University believe and use it to argue that one is inherently true and the other, by definition, false. Thus, on the one hand there is the false, scientific, historical, archaeological knowledge of the outside world and on the other there is the University's revealed knowledge. This then allows them to argue that what appears to be falsehood to those outside the University is actually the Truth and *vice versa*, although only those within the University are aware of this. Second, in other situations members will present their beliefs as objectively true, not by drawing on the self-authority of the tradition, but by making reference to personal experience, scientific rationalism or other forms of culturally accepted academic discourse. Thus, as in the New Age more generally, certain authors (e.g. Jung, Huxley, Blake, Maslow) and certain theories ('New Science') are 'name-dropped' to support claims regarding self-development and human potential. Finally, in some instances members will argue that ultimately all knowledge is relative and a matter of personal faith. In other words, little or no emphasis is placed on the inherent truth of one position *vis-à-vis* the inherent falsehood of another. Rather, such a distinction is seemingly abandoned in favour of a radical perspectivism where truth exists solely within the eye of the beholder.

In chapter six I also examine another rendition of the University's millenarianism put forward by a group named the Advance Party. This group is made up of predominantly of ex-members of the University and are highly critical of what they allege to be the increasing worldliness and corruptness of the University hierarchy. The University, they claim on their website, has 'become a true Ravan Rajya where pomp and show and grandeur are given preference over true Godly knowledge'. However, at a deeper level the Advance Party's critique is aimed at the Brahma Kumaris' theodicy and the manner in which they allege its millenarianism has been misunderstood and misrepresented. In particular, the Advance Party radically re-interpret this millenarianism in an attempt to return to what they claim to be its lost, 'true' original form. This involves, amongst other things, setting a specific date for the destruction of the world – 2008 – and the emergence of the millennial kingdom – 2036. This level of clarity, however, effectively renders the Advance Party's eschatology liable to the problems that have historically beset millenarian groups who provide a specific date for the apocalypse and who have to then rationalise the non-event afterwards to themselves and the outside world. Drawing on a range of studies on the phenomenon of failed prophecy, I conclude the chapter by speculating on the possibility that a number of prophetic failures may have been instrumental in the University's shift in world orientation and the Advance Party's schism in the mid 1970s. I also offer some possible scenarios for how the University and its millenarianism might develop over the next few decades.

Finally, in chapter seven I conclude by relating the various strands of my discussion of the Brahma Kumaris back to the detraditionalisation thesis. On this basis, I argue that the world-ambivalence that I have discussed in the previous four chapters could in some sense be usefully reframed as a tension – or, perhaps, an ongoing dialogue – within the University between the forces of detraditionalisation and those of tradition maintenance and rejuvenation. Thus, on the one hand, one sees within the University the persistence of tradition as a source of moral and identity-conferring authority whilst, on the other, the manner in which this is becoming increasingly a site of personal reflexivity and *bricolage*. Similarly, one may note the ongoing re-creation of tradition within the University in terms of how it is elaborating on its theodicy in various ways, not least in the development of courses dealing with lifestyle issues.

In conclusion, I argue that the tradition/reflexivity dynamic should be seen less as a dualism and more of a dialectic, and that any attempt – as in the radical detraditionalisation thesis – to analyse this dynamic from the former position is inadequate of presenting more than an analytical caricature. On this basis, I argue that the study of contemporary traditions needs to move beyond the 'either/or' of the detraditionalisation debate and to address instead three important issues: the interaction of 'tradition' and reflexivity within contemporary traditions; the changing nature of tradition in the contemporary world; and, finally, the continuing, if not growing, appeal of a variety of traditions to contemporary individuals.

Chapter 1
Beyond Tradition and Modernity

Modernisation I: Beyond Tradition

History is often viewed as the battlefield between two eternally conflicting phenomena; a dialectical relationship between 'the powers of tradition' and 'the forces of modernity' with the former representing 'negative old-ness' and the latter 'positive new-ness' (Luke, 1996). For instance, in relation to modern art, Lyotard asks,

> What space does Cézanne challenge? The impressionists. What object do Picasso and Braque attack? Cézanne's. What presupposition does Duchamp break with in 1912? That which says one must make a painting, be it cubist. And Buren questions that other presupposition which he believes had survived untouched by the work of Duchamp: the place of presentation of the work (Lyotard, 1984, p. 79).

Likewise Bauman, in his examination of the emergence of the work ethic during early modernity, notes how

> for the pioneers of the brave new world of modernity, 'tradition' was a dirty word. It stood for the morally disgraceful and condemnable inclinations that the work ethic rose up against; the inclinations of the creatures of habit to settle today for what they had yesterday...in fact, for surrendering to a crude, cruel, off-putting and incomprehensible, alien regime (Bauman, 1998, p. 11).

Within the West, the tradition/modernity dynamic not only defines a culture's relationship to the past, but also its relationship to its contemporaries. Where previously Western intellectuals discussed the customs of 'primitive', 'savage' or 'backward' cultures, the terminology has shifted to a discussion of 'traditional cultures' who are undergoing the process of 'modernisation' or 'development' (see, for example, Bauman, 1987). In this way, modernity may be seen as what 'we' are now in relation to what 'they' are now in other cultures and/or 'we' were in the past. More recently, debates in Britain regarding issues such as fox hunting have been fought along these demarcations. Advocates of a fox hunting ban argue that it has no place within a civilised, 'modern' country while its defenders justify it, aside from on utilitarian grounds, under the banner of tradition, as part of the country's 'heritage'.[1]

Likewise, Max Weber (1970) saw 'traditional action' as a form of habitual act that would, with the advance of modernity, become superseded by forms of increasingly bureaucratic 'rational action'. For Marx it was the root of false consciousness, 'a ghost from the past we must exorcise for history to move forward' (cited in Soares, 1997, p. 10). In arguing this, both (despite their obvious theoretical differences) drew on a shared heritage; the view stemming from the Enlightenment that saw tradition as coterminous with the *Ancien Règime* and as the *de facto* binary opposite of the forces of modernity. Where, for example, modernity was characterised by rationality, progress and was forward-looking, tradition and the traditional were seen as all that was ignorant, dogmatic, superstitious and backward-looking (Shils, 1981).

This dynamic has also been a feature of social theory since its foundation in the nineteenth century. The 'founding fathers' of sociology sought to explain both the distinctiveness of their own (modern) age as well as its relationship to past (traditional) social forms. The standard narrative, put forward by Tönnies in 1895, involved a development from communitarian social formations based on shared, usually religious, values and beliefs (*Gemeinschaft*) to modern social forms based on association rather than naturally occurring community (*Gesellschaft*). Similarly, Emile Durkheim theorised the move brought about by the individualism inherent within capitalism as being that of a shift from the mechanical solidarity of traditional societies to organic solidarity. In the former (traditional) state, he argued 'society is everything, the individual nothing' (Durkheim, 1952, p. 336), whilst in the latter there is an interdependence of economic, rather than moral, ties and, most importantly, an emphasis on the individual *qua* individual above the community.

In this way, 'tradition' increasingly became a residual category and, indeed, remained so right through to much contemporary social analysis. Moreover, the narrative of modernity became *de facto* a narrative of the increasing erosion of tradition hallmarked by, to quote Marx and Engels' famous passage,

> [the] constant revolutionising of production, uninterrupted disturbance of all social conditions, everlasting uncertainty and agitation [wherein]...All fixed, fast-frozen relations, with their train of ancient and venerable prejudices and opinions are swept away, all new-formed ones become antiquated before they can ossify. All that is solid melts into air, all that is holy is profaned (Marx and Engels, 1996, pp. 8-9).

This view that tradition ultimately gives way to the forces of modernity, however, becomes problematic when it is remembered that often there is a blurring of the conceptual distinction between 'tradition' and 'modernity'. According to Raymond Williams (1976), the term 'Modern' linguistically stems from the Latin *modo*, meaning 'just now', thereby suggesting that the individual exists constantly within modernity and that modernity is, by very definition, endlessly contemporary. He notes how the current definition of the term, as a contrast with the Ancients, emerged during the sixteenth century and by the nineteenth was used interchangeably with the word 'improved'. Thus, to be modern meant to be an improvement on the past. It would, therefore, appear that modernity, rather than being a fixed point, is probably best conceptualised as a relationship, or more accurately an attitude, of the present towards the past; towards a 'Golden Age' that should be recaptured or a 'primitive state' to be left behind. Hence, the very notion of a dynamic dualism between modernity and tradition is, as we have seen, not modern in the sense of 'new' but rather stretches back to the eighteenth century, or perhaps further, as an endlessly contemporary debate (see Gay, 1997). As Fornäs (1995, p. 18) ironically points out 'for at least the last two hundred years, modernity has been a constantly modern concept – an unusually stable tradition!' Indeed, it is perhaps possible to speak of the 'traditional question of tradition versus modernity'.

Detraditionalisation: Radical v. Coexistence

The notion of detraditionalisation – tradition melting into air in the face of the endless 'forces of modernity' – has continued to be a central theme in social theory over the last century. Paul Heelas (1996d, p. 2) defines detraditionalisation broadly as the 'decline of the belief in pre-given or natural orders of things'. This, he says, involves a shift in the locus of authority from 'without' to 'within'; from 'external', established voices of authority 'which speak with force; which make demands; which cannot be ignored without generating feelings of sin, guilt or fear', to the authority of the autonomous, utilitarian individual (Heelas, 1994, p. 103). While generally accepting the reality of this phenomena, contemporary theorists differ in the extent to which they believe that tradition, and even modernity, have given way to a post-traditional or post-modern world. Proponents of the radical detraditionalisation thesis, for example, have developed the position of the aforementioned classical writers and argued that the traditional has given way completely to the autonomous, utilitarian self within the contemporary world.

This position is based on a set of binary oppositions that are situated on the standard tradition/modernity dynamic discussed previously and theorised in terms of the latter replacing the former through the process of modernisation. Thus, necessity and certainty become superseded by contingency and uncertainty, differentiated culture is transformed into the de-differentiated, fate gives way to choice, and so on (Heelas, 1996d, p. 3; see also Heelas, 1998a). Most importantly, the self, once embedded in the confines of traditional systems of meaning, becomes disembedded through the process of modernisation or postmodernisation, loses its givenness, and becomes something that has to be worked upon, or even created from scratch. In other words, there is a shift from 'self under control' to 'self in control' (ibid.).

In contrast to the 'tradition-free' present postulated by advocates of the radical detraditionalisation thesis, stands the coexistence thesis. This features three broad critiques of the radical thesis: that the past was not 'traditional' in the sense claimed; that modernity/postmodernity is not as 'post-traditional' as claimed; and that detraditionalisation interacts with processes of tradition construction and maintenance. In sum, while not denying that detraditionalisation has taken place to some extent, other authors argue that all individuals, whether living in the past or present, are pulled between the demands of external voices of authority and the internal voices of desire, hopes and expectations (Heelas, 1996d, pp. 7-11).

Within this chapter, I aim to present a critical discussion of the concept of radical detraditionalisation, and the associated claim regarding the emergence of a post-traditional society, with reference to two general positions. First, I will discuss the work of Anthony Giddens and Ulrich Beck, both of whom argue that the contemporary world represents a radicalisation of modernity and the emergence of a post-traditional social order within, rather than beyond, modernity. Second, I will examine the opposing position, developed by Zygmunt Bauman and others, that modernity has ended and that we are witnessing the emergence of a post-modern social formation. I will highlight several analytical themes which are developed by both sets of writers, such as the idea of a post-traditional society and the claim that within late or post modernity the self becomes a 'reflexive project'. I will also discuss the sometimes contradictory ways in which these authors theorise tradition and, in doing so, produce a definition of 'tradition' faithful to these authors' work that may be critiqued in the following chapters with reference to empirical evidence.

Late Modernity and the Modernisation of Modernisation

The work of Ulrich Beck and Anthony Giddens on *Reflexive* or *New Modernity* and *Late Modernity* respectively contains many parallels, a situation made all the more interesting by the fact that, as Lash and Wynne (1992) note, their work developed independently of each other until very recently. Both authors share a preoccupation with notions of risk and reflexivity within – rather than beyond – modernity. In addition, both argue that the contemporary world represents the emergence of a post-traditional society, hallmarked by processes of increasing individualisation and the phenomenon of 'reflexive biographies'. In this section I would like to examine both these arguments in turn.

Reflexive Modernisation

In his seminal work, *Risk Society: Towards a New Modernity,* the German sociologist Ulrich Beck presents, as the title suggests, two inter-linked theses regarding modern society. The first thesis concerns the emergence of what Beck terms the 'risk society'. He begins *Risk Society* by arguing that 'we are eyewitnesses...of a break within modernity, which is freeing itself from the contours of classical industrial society, and forging a new form – the (industrial) "risk society"' (Beck, 1992, p. 9). Within this new social formation, Beck argues, the consequences of classical modernisation – in particular scientific and industrial development – have produced a set of social, political, environmental and personal risks qualitatively different from those produced in the past.

These 'manufactured uncertainties', as Beck terms them, differ from the risks encountered in the past in four main ways. First, risks can no longer be limited in time. That is, whereas in the past dangers could be generally limited to perhaps one generation, new dangers such as nuclear waste or oil spills pose a threat to all subsequent human generations. Related to this, risks can no longer be limited spatially. For example, greenhouse gasses and the potential of global warming can not be limited spatially to the countries producing excessive CFCs, but rather their effects become, as the term suggests, global. Third, as such risks are both global and ahistorical it is impossible to hold a single party accountable for them. We can not, for instance, attribute blame to one single individual or nation for a particular risk in the same way that blame might have been levelled at specific individuals for a mining accident within classical modernity. If the risks that we now face represent an accumulation of centuries of scientific and industrial development, then the causal chain is, if not lost, then at least heavily tangled. Finally, Beck says, as these risks are so huge and because accountability is impossible, their potential outcomes are beyond both calculability and insurability. If, for instance, a particular nation or company could be clearly seen to be behind a particular risk, they would not be able to compensate all those affected, assuming that they could even calculate the scale of the compensation needed. Similarly, it is difficult to see how an insurability amount could be set on, for example, the global effects of a meltdown at a nuclear power plant.

Beck argues that, where industrial society was based around the distribution of products, or 'goods', its successor, while continuing this production, is concerned primarily with the distribution – prevention, minimisation, channelling – of these 'bads'. This problem is exacerbated, however, by the fact that traditional securities and certainties, such as fate and even scientific, instrumental rationality, can no longer be relied on in the negotiation of risk. Indeed, 'scientists are becoming lay persons...[while]...society becomes a laboratory' (Beck, 1998, p. 14). According to Beck, in confronting risks, society is confronted with the outcomes of human actions or omissions. In order to effectively deal with this situation, modernity has to become truly reflexive. Individuals have to be freed from structure so as to shape the modernisation process as well as their own biographies. Just as modernisation tolled the death knell of pre-modern society, Beck sees reflexive modernisation as the (self-) destruction of industrial society, hallmarked by a 'radicalisation of modernity' or, more precisely, a modernisation of modernisation (Beck, 1994a, pp. 3, 4).

For Beck, what he terms 'reflexive modernity' is, therefore, inherently post-traditional. Just as (classical) modernisation 'dissolved' pre-modernity (traditional feudal society) in the nineteenth century and replaced it with industrial society, so it now disintegrates industrial society, replacing it with 'another modernity', this being the risk society or 'Reflexive Modernity'. This view, of the radicalisation, rather than end, of modernity, is shared by Anthony Giddens, who, particularly in *The Consequences of Modernity* and *Modernity and Self-Identity* (Giddens, 1990, 1991), argues that modernity has been both radicalised and globalised, in what he refers to as the contemporary period of Late or High Modernity. In a similar way to Beck, Giddens argues that this social formation is discontinuous with previous forms, largely due to its institutional structure and its dynamism.

Turning first to its institutional structure, Giddens identifies modernity as 'institutions and modes of behaviour established first of all in post-feudal Europe, but which in the twentieth century have become world-historical in their impact' (Giddens, 1991, pp. 14-15). Modernity is, therefore, a set of institutions – industrialisation, capitalism, surveillance and industrialised 'total' war – which produce distinctly 'modern' modes of living and social formations. The dynamism within modernity is, according to Giddens, a result of three key features: the reorganisation of time and space; the prevalence of disembedding mechanisms; and institutional reflexivity. Whereas in pre-modern cultures social relations were rooted in time and space, Giddens argues that the invention of sophisticated methods of reorganising space and time radically changed this situation. Through the widespread use of maps, clocks and calendars, social interactions can now be continued between individuals not limited to similar geographical areas or time zones. This 'emptying of time and space' provides the basis for disembedding mechanisms which then mediate these new social relations.[2] Finally, the reorganising of time and space, combined with these disembedding mechanisms, propel day-to-day life in late modernity further beyond the vistas of the traditional order.

Giddens, therefore, joins Beck in claiming that this latest stage of modernity is a post-traditional order in which radical doubt has become institutionalised. Like Beck, Giddens argues that, despite its critique of the traditional, classical modernity was not strictly speaking truly post-traditional because it utilised varieties of tradition (Giddens, 1994b; see also Hobsbawm *et al.*, 1983). In the post-traditional order of Late Modernity, however, all knowledge becomes hypotheses that may be altered or abandoned in the light of incoming information. Within such an atmosphere of uncertainty and possibility in terms of choice and action, trust and risk become important and, in the absence of fate, all actions and choices involve risk.

This is not to say that Giddens sees tradition as being totally absent from the contours of the late modern world. Indeed, he argues that in many instances it not only exists but actually flourishes as a direct consequence of modernity and its institutional reflexivity. However, to do so it has to become reflexive, as 'to sanction a practice because it is traditional will not do; tradition can be justified, but only in the light of knowledge which is itself authenticated by tradition' (Giddens, 1990, p. 38). But, says Giddens, tradition that requires legitimisation, is not true tradition, but rather 'tradition in sham clothing' (ibid.). Tradition that can not be, or refuses to be, legitimated becomes either 'fundamentalism', an assertion that tradition does not need to be justified, or a 'relic' or 'habit', an act or object that has become routinised and invested with meanings from the past (Giddens, 1994a, 1994b; see also Bauman, 1995). Therefore, the post-traditional order marks a watershed period. It represents the end of the traditional order, and the beginning of a new global social order of 'indefinite space' in which 'social bonds have effectively to be made, rather than inherited from the past' (op. cit., p. 107).

Homo Optionis

One site in which both authors argue that reflexivity and risk have become of paramount importance is in the ongoing maintenance and (re)construction of the individual's biography or life narrative. For Beck, individualisation is inherent in the process of reflexive modernisation as an endless process of disintegration of previous social forms and the reintegration of new ones. This position is based on, what he terms, an 'ahistorical model of individualisation' (see Beck, 1992, chapter 5). According to this model, individuals become liberated or disembedded from traditional (prescribed) social forms through the modernisation process. Such liberation is, however, an ambivalent phenomenon, leading to a sense of disenchantment brought about through the loss of normative security. This sense of disenchantment is only resolved when individuals are reintegrated or re-embedded into new social forms with new sets of norms and values.[3] Just as pre-modern identities and values tied up with the 'Great Chain of Being' were disembedded by classical modernity, so too these are being disembedded by reflexive modernisation. It is a process, he argues, that has occurred in all wealthy industrial countries due to the interaction of three forces: education, mobility, and competition. For example, through education the individual 'becomes the producer of his or her own labour situation, and in this way, of his or her social biography'. Similarly, through mobility individuals 'are removed from traditional patterns and relationships...[and] forced to take charge of their life' (op. cit., pp. 93, 94). Finally, through competition they are compelled to advertise the uniqueness of both their work and themselves.

According to Beck, individualisation, therefore, demands an active contribution by individuals: 'If they are not to fail, individuals must be able to plan for the long term and adapt to change; they must organise and improvise, set goals, recognise obstacles, accept defeats and accept new starts' (Beck and Beck Gernsheim, 1996, p. 27). In the individual's biography, opportunities for and constraints on choice emerge, leading to the necessity for life planning. Indeed, 'the option of not deciding is tending to become impossible' (ibid., p. 116). The individual's biography thereby becomes a 'do-it-yourself', or 'risk', biography; a replacement of the preordained with the attitude of 'until further notice' or a 'vagrant mentality'. In sum, the individual becomes the aggregate of his or her decisions and choices – 'homo optionis'. This is not to say that collective, particularly class, fate is replaced by individualism *per se*, but rather that collective issues become individualised and seen as part of a particular individual's 'reflexive biography'. Unemployment, for example, is removed from the area of the class struggle and becomes an aspect of a particular individual's personal success or failure. The blurring of the categories between macro and micro issues leads individuals into social and political allegiances that are not based on traditional (class) lines, as well as compelling them to choose between different social groups and identities.

Likewise, Giddens argues that the dynamism of modernity, linked with the notion of risk, also extends to the individual's self. Giddens argues that, within the post-traditional order, the self becomes a 'reflexive project'. By this, he means that self-identity is no longer something that is conferred through the authority of tradition but is rather something that the individual produces himself or herself through the use of fashion, various therapies, diets, exercise regimes and so on.[4] These choices within the 'life project' then define the individual. As Giddens puts it, 'What to do? How to act? Who to be? These are focal questions for everyone living in circumstances of late modernity' (Giddens, 1991, p. 70).

Late modernity also marks the emergence of what Giddens refers to as life politics, the natural successor of the emancipatory politics of classical modernity. Both share a concern with liberation from dogma and from constraints on human life, but he says, the former is the politics of life choices as opposed to life chances. It is the 'politics of lifestyle' and, in particular, it is the 'politics' of lifestyle issues formed through reflexive choice. It is an attempt to wrestle power back from expert systems, such as the medical profession, who, in providing ontological security, have sequestered the experience of existential issues such as madness, criminality, sickness/death, sexuality and nature itself from late modern individuals. It therefore represents the 'return of the repressed', manifested through a concern with existential issues such as animal rights, ecology, gender and biological reproduction.

In summary, Beck and Giddens share a preoccupation with beginnings and endings (See Beck, 1994b). Both agree that the classical modern era has finished and has been superseded by a new stage within modernity. This, as I have noted, may be seen as a development of the argument from classical sociology that individuals are increasingly freed up from structures via the process of modernisation. Giddens and Beck develop this narrative to argue that within the contemporary era, reflexive (rather than post) modernisation has resulted in, firstly, the undermining of classical industrial society (structural reflexivity) and, secondly, the acquired ability of agents to reflect on and change their social situation (self-reflexivity) (see Beck, 1994a; Lash, 1994). In other words, just as modernity disembedded pre-modernity, so now reflexive modernisation disembeds modernity, and re-embeds a 'new' – late or radicalised – modernity.

Similarly, Beck and Giddens agree that the self-confrontation of modernity is the motor of this latest phase of modernisation. For Beck, this process occurs when the industrial risk society confronts the risks and hazards engendered via the modernisation process thus far. Risk is, therefore, the skeleton in the cupboard of modernity. Likewise, Giddens argues that late modernity involves the radicalisation of modernity, or a self-critical stage within modernity itself. Moreover, both agree on the consequences of reflexive modernisation. As stated above, this entails two inter-connected theses regarding dis/re-embedding and individualisation. Turning first to the phenomenon of embedding, both posit a three-stage periodisation stretching from pre-modernity, through simple (classical) modernity to, finally, a 'new modernity'. For Beck, the difference between the stages is based on the qualitative difference of risks and hazards contained within each. For Giddens, the distinction between simple and late modernity is based on the institutionalisation of reflexivity. Similarly, as with the classical modernisation argument, both link dis/re-embedding with the freeing up of individual agents from structure. Individualisation is, therefore, seen as an intrinsic aspect of such mechanisms, and *vice versa*. Disembedding mechanisms free the individual from structure, who then reflects on and changes structure so as to bring about further individualisation and modernisation.

Therefore, both, in differing mixtures with regard to institutions and structure, also see the individual as the subject of reflexive modernisation. While Giddens and Beck emphasise institutions and structure respectively, both agree that it is the individuals within them who are the reflexive aspect of the process. Thus, within the risk society, reflexive modernisation alters both the nature of risks, globalising them and, more importantly, personalising them. It also frees up or disembeds the individual so that they may reflect upon and change the nature of industrial society or particular institutions. For both, therefore, individualisation serves an instrumental goal; this being the equipping of agents with the reflexive, cognitive tools to affect structural concerns. Therefore, in contrast to the view of commentators such as Paul Vitz (1977) and Christopher Lasch (1991), individual concerns are not merely a narcissistic end within themselves, but rather the natural pre-requisite for structural change (Jary and Jary, 1995).

Finally, there is also relative consensus that knowledge is the medium of the process. In this context, therefore, reflexivity refers to a cognitive act (Lash, 1994; Lash and Urry, 1994). Whereas risks, for Beck, are side effects and the result of a lack of knowledge, the manner in which they are confronted is through knowledge. Drawing on the work of Habermas, risk society is part of the teleology of modernity as an unfinished project. It is the Enlightenment dream 'of a fully conscious, rational society, able to take responsibility for its development and for its relationship to nature' (Rustin, 1994, p. 394). Giddens, too, sees the radicalisation of modernity as a result of cognitive reflexivity. He paints a picture, especially in *Modernity and Self-Identity*, of social actors reflecting on the revisable nature of all truth-claims, living a life of cognitive action and attempting to deliberate between risk and trust, expert systems and the 'sequestration of experience' in order to affect macro issues.

Postmodernity, Vagabonds and Tourists

Zygmunt Bauman discusses many of the themes raised by Beck and Giddens, although there are important differences in his analysis. Bauman, like Beck and Giddens, argues that the current social formation is radically different from preceding forms. However, whilst both Giddens (1990, p. 46) and Beck (1992, p. 9) dismiss the idea of postmodernity as 'unworthy of serious intellectual consideration' and 'so dark even a cat would hesitate to venture in' respectively, Bauman disagrees.

According to Bauman, where modernity was based around the pursuit of the objective truth of 'legislative reason', postmodernity, in contrast, is based around, indeed is the result of, the acceptance of relativity and the impossibility of objective knowledge.[5] Modernity is, therefore, defined in relation to what the current post-modern age is lacking, namely 'the universal criteria of truth, judgement and taste seemingly controlled and operated by the intellectuals' (Bauman, 1992, pp. 23-4; see also Bauman, 1987). It is, to paraphrase Marx, modernity for itself: fully-developed modernity, emancipated from the 'false consciousness' of legislative reason, and based around the overt institutionalisation of aspects of life, such as contingency, ambivalence and pluralism, that modernity tried to conceal or eliminate.

This ambivalence however, causes a distinctly postmodern ethical problem. The pluralism of authority not only rules out the possibility of there being a universal set of binding norms that every individual could reasonably follow, but also brings to the fore those voices of (pre-modern) authority neutralised or ignored within modernity. Moreover, the enhanced autonomy of the individual means that self-control is replaced by self-determination. It is a world 'composed of an indefinite number of meaning-generating agencies, all relatively self-sustained and autonomous, all subject to their own respective logic and armed with their own facilities of truth-validation' (Bauman, 1993, p. 35). Postmodern individuals are, therefore, given seemingly unlimited autonomy, but are deprived of a universal guide for their decisions.

This indefinite state extends to all aspects of life, particularly regarding the non-givenness of self-identity where 'it is now all too easy to choose identity, but no longer possible to hold it' (Bauman, 1996, p. 50). Identity becomes a focus of risk, something that 'has to be constructed, [even though] no design for the construction can be taken as prescribed or foolproof' (Bauman, 1992a, p. 193), rather than something that is given and then authoritatively confirmed in relation to an external criteria of truth. It is, to use a metaphor, a model kit with no instruction manual that must be continually made, pulled apart and then re-made in different configurations.

The absence of such an 'instruction manual' for self-identity generates the demand for orientation points to guide successive moves. These are provided by agencies within the postmodern habitat that, according to Bauman, may be visualised as a field of randomly scattered, unguarded totem poles that the individual approaches and/or abandons without having to ask for permission. Subscription to a particular totem is achieved through the adoption of its symbolic tokens, this adoption being dependent on, among other things, their material presence (availability) and perceived usefulness (utility). The former condition is met by the pluralism within the postmodern habitat while the latter may be seen as a site of reflexivity on the part of both the totem (in terms of its creation, maintenance and justification) and the agent (in terms of choice). The utilisation of these symbolic tokens and their totemic poles is, Bauman has argued elsewhere, manifested in the phenomenon of 'neo-tribes' (see Bauman, 1991, 1992b, 1992d). These fluid, fragile '*momentary condensations* in the ever flowing stream of seductive choices' perform the function of sanctioning various 'comprehensive and relatively cohesive' privatised lifestyles in response to various existential 'problems of survival'. Membership of a particular neo-tribe is neither obligatory nor coercive but rather dependent on the individual's decision to join and when to leave and more often than not is symbolised merely by 'donning a motley dress or bizarre and multi-coloured hairstyle' (Bauman, 1992c, p. 24).

Another distinction that Bauman makes between modernity and postmodernity concerns changes in the mode of social domination, from Foucauldian repression to the seduction of the consumer culture. Bauman (1992c, 1997) argues that the consumer culture produces a stratifying effect, a 'material hierarachisation of cultural participation', between those with the resources to purchase their choices of symbolic tokens and the growing numbers of, borrowing a term from Garnham, (1982) 'flawed consumers'. Thus, in relation to the construction of identity, Bauman argues that access to and knowledge of symbolic tokens is effectively closed to certain segments of the consumer culture who have to make do with 'an increasingly impoverished, homogenised service' (ibid., p. 289).

A similar point is also made by Beck and Beck-Gernsheim (1996), who contend that life and identity in reflexive modernity is a 'precarious freedom', with individuals, while being 'freed' from tradition, becoming constrained by new ties, such as the labour market or consumerism. Individualism, thereby, somewhat contradictorily hinges on the 'mass consumption of generically designed housing, furnishings, articles of daily use, as well as opinions, habits, attitudes and lifestyles' (Beck, 1992, p. 132). Similarly, new types of personal risk arise, particularly those relating to choosing and maintaining a personal identity. By becoming an object of choice and decision, identity becomes a focus of risk. Despite the dissolution of class-based status and the universal sharing of risks, Beck (1992, p. 110) goes on to argue '*the poorest in the world will be hit the hardest*' with, as Bauman (1992c, p. 25) puts it, 'the resourceful dumping their problems into their weak neighbour's backyards' (see also Bauman, 1992d; Hay *et al.*, 1994; May, 1998; Meštrović, 1998).

These 'structural conditions of reflexivity' are of course also highlighted by Giddens, although his analysis is more optimistic than Beck's and, certainly, more so than Bauman's. While he argues that modernity, radicalised or not, 'produces *difference*, *exclusion* and *marginalisation*' and that, therefore, life chances place limits on lifestyle choices, Giddens believes that this is not to say that lifestyle choices are only open to the affluent (Giddens, 1991, p. 6). Indeed, they may even be constructed 'through the resistances of ghetto life...[and] the direct elaboration of cultural style and modes of activity' (Giddens, 1991, p. 86; see also Giddens, 1994b; Hay *et al.*, 1994). His optimism has been criticised however, most notably by Scott Lash who asks 'outside of the sphere of immediate production, just how "reflexive" is it possible for a single mother in an urban ghetto to be?' (Lash, 1994, p. 120). For example, her choice of whether to work or not is limited by the availability, or not, of a crèche or baby-sitter. Likewise, her choice of free-time activity is limited by the time she can devote to it while still fulfilling 'motherly responsibilities' whilst her choice of where she may live is limited to (often public sector) housing which allow children and/or those on benefit.

Tradition

At the beginning of this chapter I problematised the notion of 'tradition' as it is invoked within much social theory, that is, as something that is defined primarily in binary opposition to whatever is defined as 'modernity' or 'the modern'. Following on from this, I discussed the work of three authors, Beck, Bauman and Giddens, who, whilst differing in some terminological respects, suggest that the contemporary world is characterised by being post-traditional. What, however, do these authors mean when they talk about 'tradition'? If we have entered a post-traditional era, what is it exactly that has been transcended? This is an important question, as my aim in the following chapters is primarily to critique these authors' understanding and utilisation of the idea of 'the traditional'. Throughout the following analysis, therefore, my utilisation of the term will, by necessity, have to remain faithful to the manner in which it has been used by them if I am not to be simply attacking a caricature.

As I noted previously, the use of the term 'tradition' within the detraditionalisation debate has stayed faithful to the early writings of the discipline. In particular, the influence of Max Weber's positing of different forms of legitimacy may be seen to be of particular influence, specifically, his notion of 'traditionalism' as 'the psychic attitude-set for the habitual workaday and...the belief in the everyday routine as an inviolable norm of conduct' (Weber, 1970, p. 296).

Reading Giddens' sociology it is often unclear as to whether he views tradition in this way, as simply static, unthinking and habitual. For example, in his fullest exposition of his post-tradition thesis, *Living in a Post-Traditional Society*, he draws on the work of Edward Shils to critique the 'social glue' thesis, arguing that the view of tradition as 'unthinking ritual, necessary to the cohesion of simpler societies...will not work'. Rather, he says, it should be seen as having an organic character and as being 'necessarily active and interpretative' (Giddens, 1994b, pp. 61, 64). Indeed, more recently, in his 1999 Reith Lecture, he went so far as to argue that the former view of tradition is partly a creation of the Enlightenment and its hostility to tradition and thus represents a 'shadow side of modernity', modernity defining its 'Other' *vis-à-vis* itself. In the lecture he then outlined three common misconceptions about traditions: that they are unchanging, when in fact 'they develop and mature, or weaken and "die"' (Giddens, 1994b, p. 63); that their roots always stretch back 'into the mists of time', when they are often invented and re-invented and evolve over time; and that they are unitary, and do not lend themselves to different interpretations (see Giddens and Pierson, 1998, pp. 128-9).

On this basis, then, traditions should *ipso facto* be seen as reflexive to some extent, in that they involve active interpretation and, through invention and re-invention, change and evolve over time. Nevertheless, Giddens also may be seen to subscribe to the modernist myth he himself exposes elsewhere. For instance, he argues that justified tradition is 'sham tradition' and that 'for someone following a traditional practice, questions don't need to be asked about alternatives. However much it may change, tradition provides a framework for action that can go largely unquestioned' (Giddens, 1990, p. 38; 1999, no pagination).

Likewise, Bauman in *Thinking Sociologically* draws overtly on Weber's work to argue that;

> [an] action remains traditional as long as it is not called to *legitimise* itself; traditional action can do without *legitimation*, that is, it does not require reference to values it is supposed to serve. It goes on repeating itself, by and large according to the same pattern, on the strength of the habit alone (Bauman, 1990, p. 118).

He then, somewhat ironically considering his general thesis, goes on to say that most actions are traditional, that is 'habitual, routine and not reflected on' (ibid.). However, whilst Bauman's argument rests on this view of tradition as habitual, un-reflexive behaviour, like Giddens he also at times appears to offer a different view. Specifically, in one of his most recent works, *In Search of Politics*, he distinguishes between 'custom or habit' and 'the traditional'. This distinction is based on the former being 'unthinking, unreflexive ritual', the result of '*no-choice*', whilst the latter 'is all about thinking, reasoning, justifying – and first and foremost about *choice*' (Bauman, 1999, pp. 132-3). Indeed, he then goes on to defend Giddens' view of the 'post-traditional society' by, somewhat contradictorily, arguing that

> The idea of the 'post-traditional society' is better understood as referring not to tradition running out of fashion, but to a *surplus* of traditions: the *excess* of readings of the past vying for acceptance, the absence of a single reading of history likely to command a universal or near universal trust (ibid.).

In this way, like Giddens, he is arguing paradoxically that the 'end of tradition', in fact, means not the end but rather the transformation – if not the flourishing – of tradition (Giddens and Pierson, 1998, p. 129). However, this then begs the following question, in what way has tradition been 'transformed' and so is different from the tradition of the past? If the answer is that traditions have become reflexive where once they were un-reflexive then what was the motor of this change? How, in other words, can changes occur within traditions when, as both argue, they do not invite the questioning that would potentially lead to change. The 'transformation of tradition' thesis is therefore only tenable if one accepts that traditions are characterised to some extent by reflexivity, the ability to develop and be reinvented through human agency, and that tradition and reflexivity are not mutually exclusive phenomenon.

Finally, whilst Beck speaks of tradition in no place does he overtly define it in the way that Giddens and Bauman do. Having said this, his usage of the term is much more consistent, typically referring to characteristics of the pre-modern world. For example, in *Risk Society* he speaks of the breakdown of the 'traditional world of mores' and the demystification of 'privileges of rank and religious world views' during the nineteenth century (Beck, 1992, p. 10). Similarly, in relation to his previously discussed ahistorical model of individualisation, he describes individuals' '*removal* from historically prescribed social forms and commitments' and their '*loss of traditional security* with respect to practical knowledge, faith and guiding norms' (ibid., p. 128). Likewise, more recently, in his co-authored essay with Elisabeth Beck-Gernsheim (1996, p. 25) in the *Detraditionalisation* volume, he refers to 'the fact that traditional guidelines often contained severe restrictions or even prohibitions on action' and that one is born into such frameworks rather than choosing them *per se*. More specifically, Beck and Beck-Gernsheim speak of 'pre-conscious "collective habitualisations", of matters taken for granted', and of how these are 'breaking down into a cloud of possibilities to be thought about and negotiated' (ibid., p. 30).

In sum, whilst at times Giddens and Bauman appear to be unsure of what they mean when they talk of 'tradition', 'the end of tradition' and so on, in general terms all three authors are in broad agreement about the characteristics of 'tradition' or 'the traditional'. Indeed, one could perhaps argue that all three present what may ironically be referred to as a 'Gormenghastian' view of tradition. That is, tradition is presented in a manner akin to Mervyn Peake's description of life in Gormenghast castle in the classic novel *Titus Groan*. Here Lord Sepulchrave, the Earl of Groan, is instructed daily by the lord of the library, Sourdust, in the traditional acts he must perform to sustain the estate, these being presented in one of many ancient books in which:

> The left hand pages were headed with the date and in the first of the three books this was followed by a list of the activities to be performed hour by hour during the day by his lordship. The exact times; the garments to be worn for each occasion and the symbolic gestures to be used. Diagrams facing the left hand page gave particulars of the routes by which his lordship should approach the various scenes of the operation (Peake, 1980, p. 66).

In Peake's description, tradition is presented as unthinking ritual, laid down and followed to the letter by future generations as an external voice of authority. It is also seen as a functional necessity – a 'social glue' – to sustain the estate. Indeed, when, later in the novel, the library containing all the books of ritual is burnt down by the villain Steerpike, Lord Sepulchrave goes mad and the estate falls into disarray.

Their view of tradition, then, may be summarised in four key points. Firstly, there is the claim, stemming from classical sociology, that tradition is characteristic of pre-modern social forms. Secondly, stemming from this, tradition is seen as a being based in habit, routine, the 'inviolable norm of conduct' and so on. As a result, thirdly, it is characterised as 'unthinking ritual' and, therefore, non- (or perhaps pre-) reflexive. Likewise, traditional action is presented as a form of 'social glue' or, more specifically, a voice or framework of unquestioned authority in regard to matters of, for example, morality, practical knowledge and the individual's existential security. In other words, 'tradition' is the binary opposite to whatever is primarily defined as 'modernity'.

In my following analysis, in order to remain faithful to this characterisation, my use of the term 'tradition' will be used to convey the notion of:

> external 'voices' or frameworks of authority that provide – typically habitually accepted or unquestioned – 'Truths' in regard to matters such as morality, practical knowledge and individual existential security, these frameworks being generally pre-modern in origin and/or non- or pre-reflexive in nature.

Whilst doing so, however, I intend to place the term 'tradition' in metaphorical quotation marks. By this, I mean that whilst I intend to use it, this use will be self-conscious, and primarily aimed at showing up its conceptual and empirical weaknesses. In other words, to adapt Karl Popper's famous analogy, taking the description of the white swan of tradition provided by the three authors, my subsequent analysis will be an attempt to show that the ones on the particular lake that they discussing are, in fact, black. Having done so, if I may stretch the analogy to breaking point, I then intend to catch one in order to examine close-up how it differs from the swans described.

Detraditionalisation and the New Age Religious Life

Within this chapter I have presented the basis of the thesis that I intend to critique in the subsequent chapters. My outline has focused on three key themes: the process of detraditionalisation, instances of choice and pluralism within contemporary (late/post modern) society and finally, as a linking theme, the notion of the self as a reflexive project. Finally, I discussed the manner in which the term 'tradition' is used by Ulrich Beck, Anthony Giddens and Zygmunt Bauman and, drawing out a number of related themes, offered a definition faithful to these authors' work that I intend to empirically 'test' in this book.

In the next chapter, I intend to critically develop these three themes with reference to the coexistence detraditionalisation thesis introduced at the beginning of this chapter. I am going to argue that these themes, as well as instances of processes of retraditionalisation, are all exemplified within what have been termed as 'New Age' spiritualities in three key ways. Firstly, within the New Age there is a strong emphasis on the rejection of 'external voices of authority' in favour of 'the authority of the individual self'. This, therefore, suggests a potential site for the investigation of Giddens *et al.*'s claim concerning the emergence of a post-traditional social order emphasising personal reflexivity above and beyond recourse to 'tradition'. Linked to this, the emphasis placed within the New Age on self-development (in the sense of a 'Higher-Self', or a more mundane calm, relaxed, 'de-stressed' self) may be seen as both evidence of the increased emphasis on the self within 'late modernity' as well as, more importantly, the prevalence of detraditionalised biographies. Both the choice of adopting a New Age lifestyle and the very elements (beliefs and practices) utilised appears to represent a high degree of pluralism of options (spiritual consumables) and choice on behalf of the individual spiritual consumer. Again, this suggests a certain amount of autonomy in regards to individuals constructing a 'reflexive biography' from a range of New Age ideas as well as more secular lifestyle options.

On this basis, then, it would appear that the New Age manifests characteristics of radical detraditionalisation. This may be seen both in regards to the emphasis placed on pluralism and choice and the correlative rejection of 'tradition' and, most importantly, the significance accorded to the self both as a locus of authority and also as a 'reflexive project'. However, somewhat contradictorily, the New Age would also appear to involve both the maintenance of existing 'traditions' (e.g. Buddhism, Western mysticism and esotericism) as well as the construction of 'new' traditions. Thus, notwithstanding the emphasis on the rejection of the 'old' and external voices in favour of the internal voice, within the New Age one sees the utilisation of a variety of what constitutes the 'old' as both sources of inspiration and also, more importantly, as sources of authority. In other words, such 'traditions' not only serve to inspire the spiritual quest by providing it with techniques and metaphors, but also serve in many cases as voices of justification and external authority. The New Age would therefore appear to represent a site of *re*-traditionalisation; the active (re)creation of tradition within the contemporary, late modern, world.

In the next chapter I intend to examine this paradoxical situation by, firstly, discussing how the New Age appears to manifest characteristics of radical detraditionalisation. I will then examine how the role of 'tradition' in the New Age can also be seen to point to a situation of retraditionalisation. Following on from this, I will introduce and develop Philip Mellor's (1993) conceptualisation of 'reflexive traditions' as a hermeneutic tool to examine the roles that 'tradition' plays within the New Age.

Notes

[1] The common sensical view of tradition is perhaps best expressed in statements such as 'it's a tradition around here that we....', 'I couldn't not do it this year, it's traditional!'. In both these statements the key aspect of 'tradition' – that which makes the activity 'traditional' – is that it is something that has been passed down and which involves a form of repetition. And, indeed, this is, in fact, etymologically correct. *Traditio*, as Shils (1981) has noted was a method within Roman law of transferring ownership of private property. According to *the Oxford Dictionary of English Etymology*, *tradere* refers to 'that which is handed down as belief or practice in a community'. Likewise, Gross (1992, p. 8) defines tradition as 'a set of practices, a constellation of beliefs or a mode of thinking that exists in the present, but was inherited from the past', with 'the past' being defined as three generations. In this way, one can argue that the common sensical definition of tradition is etymologically at least correct.

[2] Giddens identifies two forms of these *Abstract Systems* (symbolic tokens, standardised units of exchange such as money) and *Expert Systems* (forms of technical expertise that penetrate all aspects of life).

[3] This in itself is not a new argument but rather a re-packaging of one of the central narratives within social theory, the notion of a 'trajectory of the self'. According to this view, during pre-modernity there was a de-focusing on the individual and an emphasis instead on their place in, for example, the spiritually pre-ordained 'order of things' or 'Great Chain of Being'. However, it is claimed that modernisation dissolved these structures and led to a 're-focusing' on the individual *qua* individual (see, for example, Barfield, 1954; Baumeister, 1986, 1987; Heelas, 1981; Taylor, 1989). Similarly, Beck's notion of individuals becoming disenchanted in the painful transition to modernity is not a new claim but may be found, for example, in Durkheim's (1952) analysis of anomic suicide which he claimed was the result of individuals being insufficiently regulated and integrated into industrial society. Parallels may also be drawn between it and Weber's (1970, 1989) discussion of the 'disenchantment of the world' and the emergence of an 'iron cage' of bureaucratic rationality.

[4] Perhaps the best example of this is the human body which, according to writers such as Chris Shilling (1997) becomes the prime site for the construction of self-identity in late modernity. By this he means that the individual's body becomes the 'canvas' on which self-identity is displayed and that 'its appearance, size, shape and even its contents, are potentially open to reconstruction in line with the designs of its owner' (Shilling, 1997, p. 5). These attempts at reconstructing the body to shape self-identity can be envisaged as a continuum ranging from fashion through diet and exercise regimes to more radical measures such as sex-change operations. All these attempts being filtered through 'expert systems' such as fashion experts, dieticians, therapists and plastic surgeons.

[5] Bauman refers to this latter form as 'interpretative reason' (see Bauman, 1987). More recently Bauman has abandoned his use of the term 'postmodernity', adopting in its place the term 'liquid modernity' (see Bauman, 2000; Bauman and Tester, 2001, conversation 3).

Chapter 2
Reflexive Traditions and the New Age Religious Life

In the closing decades of the last millennium in both Western Europe and the United States of America, there was a massive rise in interest in various forms of 'non-orthodox' spirituality such as Eastern faiths, non-conventional Christianity, and 'New Age' spiritualities. Within a decade, these 'New Age' activities moved from being a marginal 'freak show' to a mainstream activity, affecting many areas of popular culture. For example in the USA, the programme director of the 'Whole Life Expo', Timm Gunns, stated that

> Americans are becoming more open to universal spiritual principles as the old religious structures are breaking down. In the nineties you can pray anywhere. You don't need to be in a place of worship to pay homage to whatever you believe in (Wroe, 1995, p. 18).

While sociological writers such as Finke and Stark (1988, p. 245) dismissed this phenomenon as 'more of an amusement than a religion', resulting from media hype and involving few followers, many Christian commentators expressed concern over these developments. *Christianity Today* went so far as to dub 1995 as 'the Year of the Neo-Pagan' (ibid.).

A similar mood was experienced in the UK. One journalist, for example, writing in the mid-nineties claimed that 'Britain is slipping into mysticism'. He defined this as a move from 'homo economicus', the aggressive individualism of the 1980s, to 'homo spiritualitas', ethical humanism focusing on personal empowerment and enrichment (Kane, 1995, p. 12). Likewise, another, tongue firmly in cheek, stated, that

> ten years ago nut cases (or Americans) discussed crystals and gurus and arcanas. Five years ago it was becoming rather fashionable to do so here, though it was hardly common practice. Now, however, the most normal people are climbing into flotation tanks, becoming Buddhists and wearing mystic symbols around their necks; far from being noteworthy, such behaviour has become rather ordinary (Thompson, 1995, p. 78).

In this chapter I intend to examine these 'New Age' spiritualities in relation to the detraditionalisation thesis. As set out at the end of chapter one, this will take the following form. Firstly, whilst drawing attention to the difficulties encountered when one attempts to define 'the New Age', I will propose an 'ideal type' definition based on some of the recurring themes in the academic literature. I will then discuss how the New Age may be seen to represent a situation of radical detraditionalisation through its emphasis on pluralism and choice and the correlative rejection of tradition in favour of the voice that comes from 'within' the individual. Following on from this, I will challenge this view by showing how the New Age may also be seen to point to a situation of retraditionalisation in the sense of both the maintenance of existing traditions and also the construction of new ones. In doing so I will highlight what to me is the central irony of the New Age. On the one hand New Agers reject the 'old' and external voices in favour of the internal voice, whilst simultaneously drawing on such voices as both sources of inspiration and also, more importantly, sources of authority. Finally, drawing these themes together, I will advance and develop Philip Mellor's notion of 'reflexive traditions' as a hermeneutic tool for the examination of 'post-traditional' spirituality.

The New Age

Attempts to define the 'New Age' meet with almost immediate problems and difficulties. Even before one begins to tackle the issue of defining what is meant by the term, difficulties are encountered regarding the term itself. The first problem encountered is that a number of 'New Agers' are self-consciously backing away from describing themselves as such for a number of reasons. Kenny Kaufman, for example, the organiser of the San Francisco *Whole Life Expo*, prefers the term 'new era of consciousness' because he believes that the term 'New Age' is linked in the public's mind with 'spiritual rip-offs' (Drane, 1991). Carol Riddel of the Findhorn Community and Eileen Campbell share this view and admit that the term is controversial through its association with some trivial activities and sensation seekers (see Button and Bloom, 1992). Linked to this, it is often wrongly associated with 'crusty' New Age travellers and the accompanying moral panic (Heelas, 1996e). A third problem is that although some of its themes may be new to Westerners, many of its core ideas are not new and reflect a diverse spiritual heritage. The Pope, for example, has publicly criticised the New Age, stating that 'it is only a new way of practising Gnosticism' (Heelas, 1996c, p. 17). Similarly, as Palmer (1993) has noted, many of its millenarian themes date back millennia. On this basis, he argues, the New Age may be seen as simply a repackaging in modern language of old ideas that arise naturally with every generation, especially in times of social or cultural stress. Finally, the 'New Age movement' is not strictly speaking a homogenous movement or single organisation or 'Church'. Rather, it is a conglomeration of networks, communities and individuals that are either placed or place themselves, under the term (see, for example, York, 1995).

The next problem encountered is arriving at a satisfactory definition of the New Age as, while there is widespread agreement that it is a blanket or umbrella term, there is disagreement over its exact nature from both those labelled as 'New Agers' and the various commentators. Goodwin (1994), for example, cynically defines it as mainly 'a look and a life style': a loose term for various alternative behaviour emphasising green politics, freedom, contempt for authority and a 'liking for black leggings'. In contrast, the practitioner Eileen Campbell defines it as the practice or an esoteric/spiritual tradition, an interest in forms of therapy, a concern for humanity and the environment and respect for feminine wisdom (Button and Bloom, 1992). However, having said this, a number of themes do recur in the range of material on the subject. Firstly, that the New Age encompasses a wide range of practices and beliefs, such as alternative therapies and philosophies, ecology and 'intuitive sciences', that have their roots in a variety of mystical and spiritual traditions. Secondly, that, stemming from this eclecticism, it is an attempt to break down various boundaries, such as those between nations, religions and, most specifically, those between mind, body and spirit. Thirdly, influenced by its adoption of Human Potential ideas, there is an optimistic belief in personal and global consciousness transformation.

Yet, among academic commentators the inherent diversity of New Age phenomenon is often seen as precluding any neat categorisation. Some, for example, have argued that its organisational features and beliefs defy 'modern' styles of categorisation, such as 'new religious movement' or 'cult' and require a more open-ended definition (see, for example, Lyon, 1993 and Sutcliffe, 1995). Others, attempting to utilise existing models of religious organisation, have argued that it should be seen as either a 'client cult' – a vague relationship between a consumer and a purveyor – or as an 'audience cult' linked by the mass distribution of the written word (Bruce, 1995). Having said this, a number of attempts to satisfactorily define the New Age have been proposed.

Primarily, focusing at the level of what actual 'New Agers' believe or do, attempts have been made to distinguish between the 'New Age', with its emphasis on 'other-worldliness' and human consciousness development, and 'Neo-Paganism', emphasising a 'this worldly materialistic inclination' manifested in concerns for wildlife or anti-nuclear issues (York, 1991, 1994). Similarly, Greer (1995), argues that the New Age embraces two contradictory theologies: 'Patriarchal', evidenced in traditionally 'male' religious and philosophical beliefs emphasising dualism and hierarchy, and 'Ecological', evidenced in 'female' beliefs, such as those found in Neo-Paganism, emphasising materialism. However, the water is muddied somewhat as 'we have pagan New Agers or pagans who identify with the New Age and we also have New Agers who entertain pagan metaphors and even what could be identified as pagan or Gaian beliefs' (York, 1994, p. 16). A similar point is made by Heelas who notes how

> Some paths...emphasise an individuated form of spirituality, the primary locus of God – or the Goddess – being within the individual human subject [while] other paths emphasise the spirituality which runs through all that is natural, and which therefore connects everybody with the cosmic order of things (Heelas, 1993, p. 105).

Problems are also encountered when one attempts to define the New Age through the application of cult or sect typologies. As noted previously, the New Age is not a homogenous movement but includes solitary individuals, informal networks and groups, and formally organised groups. To utilise the terminology of Stark and Bainbridge (1985), the New Age ranges from 'audience cults', to 'client cults', and then on to full blown 'cult movements'. One could muddy the waters even further by asking whether one should consider New Religious Movements as part of the New Age or see the New Age as one amongst many NRMs.

In an attempt to overcome these kinds of problems, Heelas shifts the level of analysis to what may be referred to as the level of individual motivation. This involves postulating a continuum of individual 'world orientation' ranging from the (world rejecting) *Purist* to the (world affirming) *Empowerer*. At the centre of the continuum is what he refers to as the *Best of Both Worlds* individual who believes that 'one can liberate oneself from the baneful effects of modernity whilst living in terms of much of what the good life – as conventionally understood – has to offer' (Heelas, 1996e, p. 31). Similarly, if we were to expand the model, theodicies featuring an 'other-worldly' orientation, such as Gnosticism or Platonism, can be placed at one end while systems emphasising a 'this-world' orientation, such as Neo-Paganism, can be placed at the other. I feel that this approach offers two main advantages over the previous two approaches. Primarily, as the New Age is typically highly individualistic and, as a result, often lacks clear organisational structures, it seems more appropriate to focus at the level of individual motivation. Thus, whilst there may indeed be a number of formalised New Age groups and organisations, the majority of those labelled as New Agers are independent seekers rather than belonging to a specific organisation. Similarly, as will be discussed later in the book, the same beliefs can be adopted with often markedly different levels of seriousness and commitment. On this basis, again, it seems more appropriate to focus on how individuals draw on, combine and make use of the various 'spiritual consumables' on offer. In other words, to continue with the consumption metaphor, whilst the other approaches can tell us what 'spiritual outlets' and 'spiritual consumables' are available respectively, this approach can be used to examine how the individual 'spiritual consumer' utilises these and the ends to which they are put.

Notwithstanding the problems inherent in defining the New Age, it is possible to outline an ideal type set of characteristics based on the recurrence of these themes in both the academic literature, media commentaries and amongst practitioners. While by no means exhaustive, a perusal of the literature from all sides reveals four such recurring themes that could, at the most, arguably form the basis for any proposed ideal type definition or, at the very least, provide a sketch of the phenomenon under consideration. These will then be elaborated in the rest of the chapter:

1. The belief that a 'New Age' is dawning, or has dawned.

2. The rejection, in varying degrees, of external voices of authority, particularly those of organised religion and modernity.

3. An emphasis on the self and an inner directed search for meaning.

4. The drawing on, and the synthesising of, a variety of such traditions, despite the apparent rejection of external voices of authority.

This is by no means a definitive list of characteristics, as the diverse nature of New Age thought and activities makes such a task virtually impossible. However, as will be expanded on below, a number of strands may be drawn out. These, I intend to argue, allow for the empirical investigation of not only the status of tradition in the contemporary, allegedly post-traditional, world but also of the creation of individual reflexive biographies.

Detraditionalisation, Choice and Reflexive Traditions

At first glance it would appear that the New Age points to a situation of radical detraditionalisation as discussed in the previous chapter. Primarily, there is an emphasis on the emergence of a 'New Age' – the *Age of Aquarius*[1] – said to herald the end of the Picean Christian age and the emergence of a pluralistic all-embracing spirituality in the West. For example, William Bloom argues that spiritual factors ('New Age') such as this move from the age of Pisces to Aquarius coupled with cultural factors (which he calls 'New Paradigm') and the 'transformation of consciousness' will lead to a 'New Culture'.[2] Similarly, Philips (1997, pp. 24, 26), writing in the New Age magazine *Prediction*, claims that 'like an oyster, humanity is opening itself to reveal the pearl of a new consciousness...[and that within this "Golden Age of Enlightenment" humans will become]...magicians with the power to create with thought alone'.

Linked to this emphasis on the 'new', there is in varying amounts the rejection of the institutions and belief structures associated with the 'old'. Organised religion, instrumental rationality and scientific materialism come in for particular castigation for failing in their utopian promises and so bringing the world to a crisis situation. Eileen Campbell for example echoes Ulrich Beck to some extent in her argument that 'we have neglected the spiritual and are now reaping the consequences. We put our trust in science, reason and materialism and failed to nourish our souls' (Chunn, 1995, p. 20).[3] Likewise, Herman Slater, the editor of *A Book of Pagan Rituals* claims that 'science itself...seems to have reached a plateau in its discoveries....[and that]...politics has reached a similar impasse'. The reason for this, he argues, is that 'both Marxism and Capitalism were created using the precepts of Christianity, and thus both suffer the same weakness as their parent; inflexibility, dogma, intolerance and hypocrisy'. He goes on to add, 'while we are sad for those who are bemused by Reason, we are deadened by those who see no further than his syllogisms as he turns the eternal wheel of the Great Tautology' (Slater (1988, pp. ii, 3-4). In the place of such external voices of authority, authority comes to lie in the 'self'; truth, spiritual or otherwise, ultimately 'lies within'.[4]

With tradition being rejected in favour of the authority of the individual, this would seem to suggest a situation of radical detraditionalisation as outlined by Giddens *et al.* previously. However, somewhat contradictorily, central to this transformation of the self and the world is the utilisation, maintenance and construction of a variety of traditions, a situation that points more towards the coexistence thesis of detraditionalisation.

For me, the rejection of external voices of authority, when coupled with the utilisation of tradition as the key to unlocking personal potential, is the central paradox of the New Age. Indeed, part of the difficulty in characterising the New Age is that it draws on a variety of different, and often contradictory 'Truths'. For example, an adherent may draw upon and combine the symbolism of alchemy, elements of humanistic psychology as well as Buddhist meditation techniques. This contradiction has been discussed at length by Heelas, who characterised it as exemplifying a *perennialist outlook.* One holding to such a perspective believes that it is possible to use one's intuition, often described in terms of a 'Higher-Self' or 'inner voice', to move beyond the corrupted manifest content of a particular tradition and discover its spiritually pure latent content (Heelas, 1996e). In practice such an approach approximates what Umberto Eco has referred to as 'hermetic semiosis', a kind of interpretative free-for-all characterised by 'the uncontrolled ability to shift from meaning to meaning, from similarity to similarity, from one connection to another'. This is based on the belief that

> to salvage the text [myth or belief system] – that is to transform it from an illusion of meaning to the awareness that meaning is infinite – the reader [the seeker] must suspect that every line of it conceals another secret meaning (Eco, 1990, p. 39; see also Eco, 1992a, 1992b).

Hence, by moving beyond the surface differences of, say, Celtic mythology and 'new science' a particular seeker may discover a shared hidden meaning and utilise this in the creation of their own, personal spiritual message. In this way, traditions do not function as external authorities *per se* but rather provide 'seekers with a spiritual core around which they can orbit, picking up whichever rays of enlightenment they feel hit the mark, or resonate with their own inner truth' (Storm, 1991, p. 191). In the hands of New Agers, these techniques and beliefs become gateways to the self, methods of experiential self-understanding and self-actualisation, rather than intellectual inquiry or faith. This allows for the possibility of spirituality without dogma by circumventing both dogma and theological conflict and penetrating to what is perceived to be the archetypal core of all religions.

However, at another level there is evidence that New Agers draw on such traditions as much for justification as for inspiration. Certain practices, for example, are given a cultural or historical 'pedigree' by being linked with the beliefs and practices of ancient (but perhaps more spiritually advanced) civilisations, such as the ancient Egyptians, Mayans and Celts (see, for example, Bowman, 1993, 1995). This is connected to a re-manifestation of the notion of the 'Noble Savage', the belief that these cultures were 'more in touch' with the core human values that, it is believed, are lacking in contemporary culture. By drawing on this past wisdom is it believed that the future may be transformed. Thus, Philips (1997, p. 25) writes of 'a mysterious journey to humanity's roots and the ancient wisdom' while William Bloom states that 'New Age culture particularly respects the [spiritual] tools and paths of the past and of indigenous peoples' (Perry, 1992, p. 35). Likewise, Herman Slater holds Neo-Paganism to be 'based on valid beliefs from the distant past....ancient sources, restored and updated by scholars from various Pagan groups...[adding that]...different peoples have called the God and the Goddess many names. All the names are the true name, for it matters not what they are called [sic]' (Slater, 1988, pp. ii, 86).

In a similar vein, despite overt hostility towards science what is referred to as the 'new science' of Quantum Mechanics is often used by New Agers to justify ancient beliefs or lend them scientific credibility. New Agers have a 'a love hate relationship with the modern world', rejecting science and still using it occasionally to validate certain teachings.[5] While Slater feels 'sad for those who are bemused by reason' and Button and Bloom (1992) cite science as a 'villain' of the New Age, Danah Zohar (1991) draws on Quantum theory in *The Quantum Self*.[6] Similarly, Laurie Cabot, a practising Witch, defines a Witch as 'a person versed in both scientific and spiritual truths' and states that 'the ancient power of magic is both spiritual and scientific'. She adds with, some chagrin, that 'in recent years I have met many "New Age" people who ignore the need to ground themselves scientifically' (Cabot and Cowan, pp. 7, 14).

As well as such occurrences of 'tradition' utilisation and maintenance, one may also cite incidences of the (re)creation of tradition amongst New Agers. Indeed, many of the traditions drawn on by New Agers are themselves 'invented traditions', in the Hobsbawnian sense of '"traditions" which appear or claim to be old...[but are in fact] quite recent in origin and sometimes invented' (Hobsbawm, 1982, p. 1). For example a number of the contemporary Druidic organisations, although often claiming a lineage back to the Ancient Order of Druids (1781) or the ancient priests themselves, are recent 'inventions'.[7] Similarly, modern witchcraft although again claiming a lineage back to ancient, pre-Christian times was rather an 'invention' of a civil servant, Gerald Gardner, in the 1940s (Luhrmann, 1994; York, 1999). One could also cite the examples of the Theosophical Society and the Hermetic Order of the Golden Dawn, both of whom claimed to be in contact with an ancient 'immortal secret brotherhood' of occult powers (see, for example, Symonds, 1973; Morgan, 1982; Washington, 1993; Barrett, 1996).

Such rediscovering, reinterpreting and reconfiguring elements of numerous traditions involves the disembedding of native traditions from their specific time/space locales of face-to-face communication via forms of mediated or quasi-mediated (mass) communication. Through books, television or the Internet, these traditions may be invoked by individuals from completely different cultures and eras. To take the example of New Age books, Steve Bruce has commented on how all the major publishing houses have their own specialist New Age labels. The New Age ('Mind, Body, Spirit') section of *Waterstones* booksellers in Aberdeen, he has also noted, is fourteen times larger than that devoted to Christian texts.[8] Moreover, the sales of New Age books increased by 150% in the 1970-90 period (Bruce, 1995) and by 75% during the nineties (Alberge, 1998).

This coexistence and dynamic interaction of processes of detraditionalisation and retraditionalisation may also, perhaps best, be evidenced in New Agers' utilisation of tradition in the creation of reflexive biographies. Aside from the emphasis placed on the self in terms of its hermeneutic ability, attention is also paid to its potential as a project. Indeed, the two are inter-linked, with the former providing the basis for the latter. As we have seen, for many New Agers the spiritual quest leads ultimately within to the core of spirituality that is, or manifests as, the individual self. Heelas has coined the term 'self spirituality' to describe this phenomenon. He has argued that, looking at the image of the self presented in the various New Age discourses, 'in the context of our culture, it is impossible to think of a self which is more autonomous or free, more in control or powerful, more responsible, more perfect, more internalised, more expressivistic' (Heelas, 1996e, p. 154).

To discover or develop this inner realm requires the utilisation of techniques often characterised by those outside the New Age as 'spiritual consumables', from yogic classes to dream encyclopaedias, ritual equipment, incense and crystals as well as all the background reading to discover what path actually suits. As the attempt to find one's true path is an on-going process, various techniques or ideas are combined, added to or tried out while others are jettisoned. In this way, the New Ager's quest for spiritual or inner perfection exhibits many parallels with Giddens' conception of the self as a reflexive project. Both are characterised by the ongoing, reflexive construction of a life narrative, through the mediation of expert systems and symbolic tokens outside of the fixed 'sureties of tradition'.

Hence, to paraphrase Giddens (1994b, p. 76), within the New Age choice is obligatory. Options range from shamanism to 'healing the wounds of childhood' weekend courses, from Buddhism to management development, from pre-Christian mystery traditions to UFOs. The individual is confronted by the choice of beliefs and practices spanning the globe (if not further afield) and stretching back millennia. The image of the 'spiritual supermarket' (Lyon, 1993; Bunting, 1996b) or catalogue (Drane, 1991) is often invoked in describing this phenomenon. Indeed, the cover of *The Guardian's* media section featuring Madeleine Bunting's article on this matter ('Shopping For God') shows a pop-art image of man looking in the window of a bright supermarket ('*Religiomart* – Your Spiritual Supermarket') asking 'My God!?'.

Relating this back to the detraditionalisation thesis, four themes emerge that would appear to be manifested in New Age practice: the notions of the totemic poles/neo-tribes, symbolic tokens, the reflexivity of the totem and agent and issues of personal (and global) 'survival'. Firstly, Bauman's (1992c) image of a symbolic totem or tribe that the individual may join or leave at will without making any specific commitment seems a rather apt metaphor for New Age 'membership'. As we have seen, the New Age is seen to be an inherently fluid phenomenon with individuals picking and choosing from a variety of spiritual consumables with a range of seriousness and commitment. For example, Van Hove describes the 'free entrance' into New Age groups and the ethos that 'anyone can join them, for whatever motivation, and can think about it whatever s(he) wants' (Van Hove, 1996, p. 186). Similarly, an Anglican priest cited by Cook (1994, p. 9) bemoaned the attitude that 'people think they can go on a couple of spiritual weekends for instant enlightenment, then bugger off home'.

This is related to, secondly, the notion of a particular totem/neo-tribe's symbolic tokens of belonging. These tokens may indeed be 'motley dress or a bizarre and multi-coloured hairstyle' (Bauman, 1992c, p. 24). However, other types of New Age symbolic tokens may be highlighted, including birthstones, meditation tapes, Native American 'dream catchers' or the New Age book. As discussed previously, due to the growth of forms of quasi-mediated communication, the availability of these products has increased, effectively turning them from a fringe to a mainstream activity. The notion of 'spiritual consumerism' is a familiar one in academic and media discussions of the New Age. For example, Heelas (1996b) speaks of the emergence of 'Spiritual Disneylands', while one journalist writing in the early 1990s warned that Glastonbury was 'in danger of turning into a New Age theme park'. She went on to describe how 'packed hugger-mugger into the tiny streets, New Age-y outlets abound, with fey names such as the *Star Crystal Shop*, *Pendragon*, *Starchild* and, indeed, the *Brigit Healing Wing*, a sort of beauty salon for the soul' (Moir, 1993, p. 8). Similarly, Pat Kane (1995, p. 12) cynically pointed out how the UK tabloid press 'moved instantly to exploit this occult consciousness', citing as examples 'Mystic Meg' providing '*News of the World* readers with a "lucky lottery six-pick wheel" each week, conveniently matching magic numbers to particular star signs', and the manner in which *The Sun* newspaper urged 'readers to rub their lottery ticket "on our psychically charged red dot to increase your chance of the jackpot"'. In this way, it may be argued that although the New Age is the 'religion of your choice', the choice is typically something that has to be purchased.

Thirdly, within the 'spiritual supermarket' that is envisaged, a particular totem must 'sell itself' to potential spiritual consumers through the ceded authority of the scientific expert or the noble savage. This involves a certain degree of reflexivity on behalf of the totem, in its construction, maintenance and even self-justification. Likewise, due to the emphasis on choice within the New Age, individual reflexivity becomes of paramount importance in terms of what practices to adopt, what level of seriousness/commitment to maintain, and the justification (or even abandonment) of certain practices.

While much of the New Age has been seen to appeal to titillation-seeking, consumeristic 'casual part-timers' (Heelas, 1996a), some of those involved are 'serious part-timers', attempting to (re)discover some sense of meaning in their life, whether this be psychological, spiritual or experiential. In some cases this personal goal is often linked to more universal aspirations involving the whole of humanity and/or the world as a living organism. Thus, personal growth and change are often seen as necessary pre-conditions for global change with the 'New Age' dawning when enough individuals have switched consciousness (see, for example, Ferguson, 1982). Notwithstanding the New Age rejection of instrumental rationality and the Enlightenment project, much of this ethos appears resonant Ulrich Beck's Enlightenment-influenced views regarding individuals reflexively affecting the modernisation process. In both the goal is a fully conscious (whether rational or spiritual) society in which individuals take responsibility for themselves, the world and nature through their choices. For example, in relation to the Neo-Pagan end of the spectrum, there is an emphasis on individual responsibility towards the earth in the form of direct action. This may take the form of inner development as a basis for global change, honouring the earth as a living entity through an ecologically-informed lifestyle or celebrating the yearly Solstices and Equinoxes, or through direct action against road-building, the destruction of native habitats and the like. In all these examples, the one central theme is that responsibility for change rests firmly with the individual. Thus, to refer back to the first example, the emergence of the New Age is dependent on, of course, a global consciousness shift but this has as its basis the individual's responsibility for their own development.

Reflexive Traditions

From the above analysis it is clear that there has been widespread characterisation of the New Age as manifesting strong detraditionalising tendencies, both in regards to the emphasis on a New Age, the rejection of tradition, the weight given to pluralism and choice and, most importantly, the significance accorded to the self in terms of its authority and as a 'reflexive project'. Such an approach would, therefore, locate the New Age within late or high modernity and cite it as an example of processes of reflexive modernisation or radical detraditionalisation.

However, I have argued in this chapter that these tendencies when examined more closely, can also be construed to coexist between processes of detraditionalisation and *re*-traditionalisation. Thus, notwithstanding the emphasis on the rejection of the 'old' and external voices in favour of the 'new' and the internal voice, there is the utilisation of a variety of what constitutes the 'old'. Nevertheless, in many ways this is not tradition in the sense discussed in the previous chapter that is drawn on, but rather tradition as filtered through personal reflexivity, identified as the 'Higher-Self' or 'inner voice'. This point is perhaps best evidenced by the incidences of the use of various traditions by New Agers in the ongoing construction of reflexive (spiritual) biographies. In this context, a tradition is displaced from its role of external voice and becomes simply one expert system or symbolic token among many or one aspect of particular neo-tribes' fluid identity.

However, I have argued, at another level this does involve the utilisation of tradition as a voice of authority, specifically in the justification of certain beliefs and practices. This utilisation is particularly marked in relation to the (re)creation of a variety of ancient spiritual traditions and the emphasis placed on the vouchsafed authority of the 'noble savage'. Moreover, despite the emphasis placed on the 'new' and the self in its various guises, both are seen to be dependent on drawing on of such voices of authority for inspiration or authority. In this somewhat contradictory way the present and the self are transformed and future is created through the drawing on of, particularly the authority of, the past (as manifested in the notion of its perennial wisdom). Indeed, in many ways the future is envisaged as strikingly similar to the 'childhood innocence' of the past where, it is claimed, humanity had a closer, more genuine, connection with true spirituality, the environment and each other;

> When the streams flow clear and the winds blow pure, when the sun never more rises unrenowned nor the moon rides in the skies unloved; when the stones tell of the Horned

> God and the greenwood grows deep to call back her own ones, then our work will be ended and the Pagan Way will return to the beloved womb of our old religion...to the nature of the goddesses and gods of paganism (Slater, 1988, p. 4).

All this then would seem to suggest a coexistence, if not a dynamic interaction, between, on the one hand, what the authors discussed in the previous chapter would see as tradition and, on the other, personal reflexivity. However, as will be recalled Giddens argued that reflexivity and tradition are mutually exclusive phenomena and that tradition which requires legitimisation or reflexivity is 'sham tradition'. Philip Mellor (1993; see also Mellor, 1991), who argues particularly against Giddens' use of this term, has critiqued this position with regard to contemporary religious studies. While accepting that reflexivity in the late modern world has become more systematic and extensive than in the past, Mellor argues that reflexivity has always to some extent been a characteristic of religious traditions. Moreover, despite the reflexivity within the late modern world, the normative features of traditions still play a significant role. Indeed, 'individuals still choose to place themselves within [religious traditions] in order to structure their belief and activity with reference to overarching norms' (ibid., p. 120). Thus, reflexive traditions refer to the active, reflexive (re)creation of 'new, dynamic forms for the expression and development of religion within the context of high modernity' (ibid., p. 111).

These two aspects of reflexive traditions, the reflexive and the normative, may also be seen in manifestations of New Age practice. Returning to the theme of reflexivity, it can be seen that New Agers actively create, rediscover or rejuvenate (some might say rehabilitate) a range of traditions. This reflexivity extends further to the maintenance of such traditions, with them being defended, justified or adapted with others on an ongoing basis. For example, in the confrontation with 'science', New Agers may either, aside from 'Noble Savage' arguments, attempt to justify their beliefs with reference to 'cutting edge' research or adapt certain scientific theories to their beliefs. In this way, a particular individual's belief is closer to Giddens' (1991, p. 3) notion of a reflexive hypothesis – a claim 'which may very well be true, but which [is] in principle open to revision and may have at some point to be abandoned' – than of a 'sham tradition'. Similarly, individuals who, for example, reject mainstream religiosity in favour of New Age practices do not embrace nihilism, but rather a set of, albeit probably transient, normative structures in an attempt to answer the existential questions of life. These structures range from the example of the individual who enters into the strict lifestyle of the Gragian Order of 'New Age' monks (see, Thompson, 1994) right through to the individual who may choose simply to embrace the idea of the earth as *Gaia* in order to experience 'something greater' than themselves.

Reflexive Traditions and the (New Age) Religious Life

Within this chapter I have developed the detraditionalisation thesis with reference to the New Age Movement, focusing particularly on the coexistence of aspects of radical detraditionalisation and tradition maintenance. In conclusion, I drew on Mellor's notion of 'reflexive traditions' as a more fruitful way of examining this dynamic interaction within the New Age between 'tradition' and personal reflexivity. As noted, Mellor's use of the term developed out of a critique of Giddens' 'sham tradition' thesis and the contrasting argument that, whilst reflexivity may be more pervasive and radical in the contemporary world, religious traditions have always been to some extent reflexive. In conclusion he argued that a potential method of investigating this phenomenon within religious traditions would be to examine this reflexive/normative interaction along three axis:

> [1: *personal reflexivity*] the relationship of individual reflexivity to overarching normative structures, [2: *intra-tradition reflexivity*] the incorporation of different degrees of reflexivity into collective expressions of traditional normativity, and [3: *inter-tradition reflexivity*] the relationship of these traditions to other collective and individual explorations of normative/reflexive relationships (Mellor, 1993, p. 126).

Within the context of the sociology of the New Age the analysis of personal reflexivity would therefore be concerned with the relationship of the individual to a particular New Age 'tradition' or set of traditions. This would examine the manner in which such structures impinge on their daily life, the manner in which they may be to some degree reflexively reconstructed by the individual as well as the nature of such reflexivity. In contrast the analysis of intra-tradition reflexivity would focus on the somewhat higher level of institutional reflexivity manifested by a particular New Age 'tradition', specifically in regard to its systematic reconstruction and maintenance. Finally, inter-tradition reflexivity, the relationships and interactions between different traditions, may also be analysed in terms of the relationship between the New Age and Orthodox faiths (see Bunting, 1996a) or between orthodox and New Age renditions of the same tradition (see Cush, 1996).

So far my analysis has remained fairly much at the theoretical level. This emphasis shifted slightly in this chapter where I began to explicitly link my theoretical base with a discussion of the New Age Movement as well as introducing a potential hermeneutic tool in the form of Mellor's conception of reflexive traditions. However, in subsequent chapters this balance will shift more in favour of empirical analysis, albeit informed by the arguments developed previously, with an examination of the Brahma Kumaris World Spiritual University (BKWSU or Brahma Kumaris), a South-Asian NRM currently operating within the UK.

Whilst the Brahma Kumaris historically predate the emergence of the New Age Movement, my argument will be that they afford us the opportunity to examine the developments that occur within contemporary traditions and the New Age in particular in two main ways. Firstly, my central argument will be that whilst the Brahma Kumaris may on one level be seen as a neo-Hindu sect, a position developed by Reender Kranenborg (1999), over the last decade the movement has actively embraced many of the aspects identifiable as 'New Age'. This therefore allows me to examine both the historical change and organisational/ideological reflexivity within a particular tradition and also how a particular tradition may re-brand itself in the spiritual supermarket. Secondly, an examination of the Brahma Kumaris' membership, conceived in its widest sense, will allow us to discuss the different levels or types of influence that such traditions play in the lives of contemporary 'spiritual consumers'.

Developing slightly Mellor's three axes or levels of analysis, my own investigation will focus on four inter-linking sites or levels. Firstly, the genealogical[9] analysis of continuities and, more importantly, changes or ruptures within the BKWSU. This will focus on the social conditions of the University's emergence and development, the manner in which and reasons articulated for why elements – such as belief or ritual – have been added or removed over time and the changing relationship between these elements. Secondly, as an extension of this, the examination of current changes occurring within the BKWSU. This will involve describing the changes that are currently occurring within the Brahma Kumaris, analysing the (internal/external) factors that have brought them about and, following on from this, examining of how these are both rationalised and accommodated. Thirdly, shifting the focus of analysis from the macro to the micro level, the examination of the interaction between membership (in its broadest sense) and the BKWSU's normative structures through the use of in-depth interviews and case studies. This will seek to ascertain, firstly, why and to what extent individuals choose to place themselves within the University's normative structures and, secondly, the influence of these structures on the ongoing (re)construction of identity. Finally, partly as an aspect of the analysis of contemporary changes and the analysis of membership patterns, the examination of the different types of explanation or justification used by the BKWSU in its dealings with other traditions and the wider society. Does this involve, for example, simply an assertion of 'formulaic truth', as Giddens would argue, or, rather, a degree of reflexivity? In both cases what sources of authority are drawn on – for example, the experiential realm, divine revelation, scientific discourses – and do these types of explanation and sources of authority drawn on vary in different contexts and with different audiences?

My aims are therefore twofold, to produce an ethnography of the Brahma Kumaris examining, firstly, the interplay of reflexivity and normative structures within the tradition and, secondly, individual's use of the Brahma Kumaris tradition in the construction of embodied, reflexive biographies. This will take the following form. Firstly, I will present an account of the historical development of the University over the last sixty or so years, concentrating particularly on the manner or its inception as well as its organisational development both at home and abroad (chapter 3). Secondly, following from this, I will outline the University's beliefs and demonstrate its 'perennialist' use of primarily aspects of its own native, Hindu spiritual tradition and also, through international development, other world traditions (chapter 4). Thirdly, I intend to explore the membership or attendance patterns of the University (chapter 5), focusing on the different levels of membership and thereby different levels or types of influence of the tradition on individual member's sense of identity. I will then present a discussion of issues raised with reference to the University's millenarianism; in particular, the institutional and personal strategies utilised to deal with the ambivalence or dissonance engendered by the University's world-orientation/response (chapter 6). Finally (chapter 7), I shall conclude with a discussion of the validity of the notions of detraditionalisation and Late Modernity to the study of contemporary (New Age) religious life.

Notes

[1] Aside from being the title of a song from the musical *Hair*, this is an astronomical event caused by the 26,000 year revolution of the Earth on one of its axis. This 'year' is divided into a number of 'months' represented by the procession of astrological constellations viewed in the eastern sky on the day of the spring Equinox. These are said to correspond with great movements of thought, for example, the Greek cult of the minotaur coincided with the Age of Taurus, the Egyptian cult of the ram coincided with the Age of Aries while the birth of Jesus heralded the Age of Pisces (Philips, 1997). Commentators are divided however over whether The Age of Aquarius has already begun, specifically with the 1960s counter-culture, or whether it coincided with the year 2000.
[2] This includes such factors as such as 'new science', 'new psychology', 'new ecological awareness', 'new electronic culture' and 'global village'. See Bruce (1995).
[3] Button and Bloom (1992), for example, point to two 'villains of the New Age'; *scientific materialism*, which is seen to have led to political, economic, ecological and spiritual crisis, and *organised religion* for its persecution of heretical ideas.
[4] Within the literature this 'self' may be referred to as the 'higher self', 'the light of consciousness' (Anderton, 1990), spirit or soul. For example, rebirthing is described as 'the process of getting to know and love your self' by one of it's practitioners, Bob Frissel (Drane, 1991, p. 79), Andrew Weil describes healing as something that occurs naturally from within (Dilner, 1997) while the Gragian Order, New Age monks based in London, emphasise environmentalism and 'developing and exploring one's inner life' (Thompson, 1994, p. 44).
[5] See, for example, Peters (1991) and Perry (1992).
[6] See also, for example, the work of Capra (1992) and Gary Zukav (1998).
[7] For example, The Glastonbury Order of Druids (founded: 1988), The Secular Order of Druids (founded: 1986), The Universal Druid Order (founded: 1988). See Carr-Gomm (1992).
[8] For example, *Penguin* and *Arkana*, *HarperCollins* and *Aquarius*. See Bruce (1995).
[9] In recent decades the genealogical method has been popularised in the work of the French philosopher-historian Michel Foucault (see Foucault, 1991, 1997), who took his inspiration from the work of Friedrich Nietzsche. In my own interpretation the genealogical method is characterised by the examination of the historical trajectory of certain ideas or social structures on the basis of their socio-psychological motivations. For example, Nietzsche's famous Genealogy of Morals (Nietzsche, 1998) was concerned with tracing the origins of the concepts 'Good' and 'Evil' to 'human, all to human' factors.

Chapter 3

From World-Rejection to Ambivalence: A Genealogy of the Brahma Kumaris

> In [the] future, when you see with your own eyes the great destruction which is to take place, you will automatically feel disinterest. On [the] one hand there will be disinterest, and on the other hand you will be filled with excitement about what you are to become in the future. You say that in one eye there is liberation, and in the other liberation in life; so also the destruction is the gate to liberation, and the establishment is the gate to liberation in life...Always remember that for the world it is the time of loss, but for us it is the time of great benefit. The people of the world see only the destruction; but for you, together with destruction, there is also establishment. Always keep in your heart the most elevated thoughts; that the establishment is as if almost accomplished (Brahma Kumaris World Spiritual University, 1996, pp. 11-12, 15).

> We are at a crossroads of human civilisation. On the one hand, things are rapidly disintegrating. That is made bitterly apparent by wars, civil strife, riots, ethnic cleansing, and so on. However, on the other hand, an almost invisible integration involving alternatives and possibilities is putting the pieces back together. Bringing peace back into the social, economic, political and other fibers of society would require looking at peace from two levels: the external and the internal. Peace education, conflict resolution, and all peace initiatives must take seriously the critical connection between individual and world peace. Programs and projects must include an emphasis on individual peace, offering proactive and practical means to peace, beginning with the first step of knowing the inner self (Brahma Kumaris World Spiritual University, 1995a, pp. 29-30).

I would like to begin this chapter by juxtaposing these two statements. Here we have, firstly, a celebration of the destruction of the world and, secondly, a suggestion for peace and conflict resolution which must 'take seriously the critical connection between individual and world peace'. Both these statements were published contemporaneously, the former in a book entitled *Visions of the Future* and the latter published in a book 'in honor of the fiftieth Anniversary of the United Nations' entitled *Living Values: A Guidebook.* Indeed, both these statements were published by the same organisation, the Brahma Kumaris World Spiritual University. In this chapter I intend to discuss the transformations within the Brahma Kumaris that led them from promulgating the former view to, in varying degrees, both views simultaneously, or, to draw on the terminology of Roy Wallis (1984), from manifesting an orientation of world-rejection to what I would refer to as *world-ambivalence* (see Walliss, 1999).

This chapter will therefore be concerned with presenting a genealogical analysis of the Brahma Kumaris from their inception in India in the 1930s to the present day. Its focus will be three developmental stages of, or ruptures within, their world-orientation and organisational structure. These transitions, I will argue, cannot be adequately accounted for with reference to the typologies of Wilson (1969, 1970) and Wallis, hence the development of the notion of world-ambivalence. This shift will be analysed largely in relation to the Brahma Kumaris' changing relationship with the 'outside' world, in terms of how their beliefs developed in relation to both local persecution and then, later, international acceptance. The analysis presented in this chapter will then be further developed in later chapters with reference to the University's beliefs and membership.

Before doing so, however, attention should be drawn to the difficulties and pitfalls in both constructing and relating such a history. Primarily, as Babb (1986) notes, the only source for the University's early years – and in particular the founder's visions – are members themselves and, in particular, Jagdish Chander's (1983) hagiography of the Brahma Kumaris' founder, *Adi Dev*. As a result there is the possibility that many events are related with the benefit of 'spiritual hindsight' or as 'filtered' through the University's theodicy.[1] This point is exacerbated by the fact that for the majority of the University's existence no written records were kept and those that have survived are guarded jealously. Likewise, access to primary sources from other *dramatis personae* in the narrative, for example, the 'Anti' Party or husbands of members, are either non-existent or near-impossible to track down. Therefore, like previous writers on the subject, my sole source for this chapter has had to be Chander's text, albeit supplemented by additional primary sources from within the University and the academic literature pertaining to the Brahma Kumaris.[2]

Spiritual Outcasts

The story of the Brahma Kumaris begins with their founder, Dada Lekhraj, who is seen by members world-wide as 'the incarnation and descent of God, the World Father, into the corporeal world' (ibid., p. 13). Lekhraj was born in Sindh in 1876 into the Kriplani family who were devotees of the Valabhacharya sect. Although he was well-educated, being self-taught in literature and art and able to speak Hindi and English as well as his native Sindhi, Lekhraj chose to become a wheat merchant. After some years, he became a diamond merchant, his business prospered and he became a millionaire, commanding large respect within the community. This was to have an influence on Lekhraj's later spiritual message in two respects. Firstly, it is claimed that his profession gave him 'more than ordinary insight into women's problems' through, when compared with his peers, frequent personal contact with them. Secondly, it also led him into intimate dealings with royalty (Babb, 1986, p. 99). For example, Chander discusses how Lekhraj had a large reputation among the Rajas, Maharajas and British Viceroy and how they 'became his clients and friends'. Not only this, Chander also claims that Lekhraj was a 'close friend' of the king of Nepal and the king of Valaipur and, indeed, given free access to their palaces for his own personal use (ibid., p. 26).

In his spiritual life, Lekhraj was a follower of Narayan and had numerous images of the deity around his house and office. According to Chander, Lekhraj disapproved of how in most images Narayan's consort, Lakhshmi, was presented in a submissive position. Indeed, Chander claims that Lekhraj was so offended that he commissioned a painter to paint a version showing both in an equal status. In addition, he is presented as a devout Hindu, known for his piety, frequent pilgrimages, vegetarianism and teetotal lifestyle. However, it was not until late in life that his true spiritual mission began.

In 1936, at the age of 60, his wife proposed that he should retire and spend the remainder of his life in spiritual pursuits as is the custom in the Hindu community for a man in late life (see Kinsley, 1993). Lekhraj, it is claimed, declined, saying that he wished to work for a few more years in order to double his fortune which he would dispense to the poor and then retire. However, at this time he began reporting frequent visions of the deities Vishnu and Shiva and of the destruction of the world via natural catastrophes, civil strife and, what has been later (re)interpreted as, nuclear holocaust. In the visions, destruction was followed by the establishment of a future earthly paradise completely unlike the contemporary world in which, for the tiny population there would be food in abundance rather than famine, peace and happiness rather than competition and strife, equality rather than sexual inequality and where death would be painless and followed by rebirth.

As a consequence of these and other visions, Lekhraj decided to retire and sell his business to his partner. On his return to his home in Hyderabad, during a lecture by one of his gurus, he quite uncharacteristically got up and walked out. A relative followed him and later reported that Lekhraj seemed to be light and bodiless, glowing red and speaking in a different voice saying,

> I am the Blissful Self, I am Shiva, I am Shiva... I am the Knowledgeful Self, I am Shiva, I am Shiva... I am the Luminous Self, I am Shiva, I am Shiva... I am the Form of Self, the Form of Knowledge, the Form of Light (op. cit., p. 42).

At the time both Lekhraj and his family were puzzled over what the messages were referring to and why he had been chosen as the medium for them. Following this event, he began to act in ways that seemed odd to those around him. He began telling everyone, including his wife and son, that they were souls. After a few days, others, particularly women from the wealthy families of Hyderabad, came to listen to him speak and experienced similar visions themselves.

Lekhraj's message to them was that, as the avatar of Krishna, God had descended into him with a new and important message for humanity regarding the present age. This centred mainly on his original vision of natural disaster followed by a new, glorious age. Later, however, it developed into the belief that he had experienced the truth hidden within the sacred text, the *Bhagavad Gita*, which, he claimed, had become distorted, diluted and full of errors in the 5,000 years since it had been delivered orally. In recognition of his role, Lekhraj told his followers that God had renamed him *Prajipita Brahma* (the Father of Humanity) or *Brahma Baba* while those who joined him became known themselves as *Om Mandli.*[3] At this time a young girl Radha, later renamed Om Radhe in an allusion to one of the gopis favoured by Krishna, joined the group. She was, according to Chander (1983, p. 58), a natural disciple who 'took Baba's [Lekhraj's] message completely to her heart...[,] wedded herself totally to God [and] surrendered her every thought to His direction'. Indeed, her entrance was pre-cognised by members of the group, especially by Lekhraj's wife, who had a vision of Radhe becoming the Empress Lakshmi in the future age, after she, Jashoda, had given her 'the kingdom'. Later Radha was renamed Jagadamba Saraswati after Brahma's consort and the Goddess of knowledge.

Thus, it may be seen that from its foundation, what would later become the Brahma Kumaris World Spiritual University drew heavily upon, and yet radically re-interpreted, aspects of its native Hinduism. This is particularly the case with Lekhraj's own personal mythology which draws heavily on that of Krishna in regard to allusions to the *Bhagavad Gita*, the membership as his adoring gopis (especially the reference to Radhe) as well as making distinct references to other deities such as Brahma, Vishnu and Lakshmi, the consort of Lekhraj's favourite deity Narayan.

However, as with many, particularly novel or unorthodox, new religious movements, Lekhraj's message was not received well universally. Almost from its inception the group was subject to often violent reactions from the surrounding community. Indeed, Chander's account appears to be mainly an exercise in decrying the persecutors whilst simultaneously valorising the purity, blamelessness and innocence of the group in the face of such opposition. Frank Whaling (1995), while not going so far, points out a number of cultural factors which may be seen to have brought about such a societal reaction. Primarily, the group's previously mentioned utilisation of Hindu practices (such as celibacy, teetotalism and vegetarianism), spiritual terminology and texts – specifically the *Bhagavad Gita* – in an unusual manner drew incomprehension and suspicion upon them. As we have seen, the proto-University not only drew exclusively on its native Hinduism, but also heavily reinterpreted it to fit in with its own mythology. Secondly, because of his largely female following, and particularly after an article in *Newsweek* magazine which portrayed Lekhraj as a modern-day Krishna surrounded by admiring *gopis* (cowgirls), the group was seen as a justification for Lekhraj to set up a harem comprising of females from the upper-classes of the community. For example, Howell and Nelson (1997, p. 8) comment on the 'vilification of the movement', while according to Babb

> Lekhraj himself was regarded with deep suspicion...many believed that he was a man of inexhaustible sexual appetite whose real motive was the seduction of his female disciples. One informant, a boy of the time, told of being ordered by his mother to avert his eyes from Lekhraj's ashram as they passed by (Babb, 1986, p. 102; see also Skultans, 1993, p. 48).

Similarly, Dadi Manohan (1996, no pagination) in her oral history of the University also recalls how 'no matter what the people of the [outside] world said to us, it made no difference. They would say you are turning mad...the people of the city had not a good impression of [Brahma] Baba's home and the organisation'. However, once the group's emphasis on celibacy became known, the opposite criticism arose. Husbands would return home from business trips to find that their wives had taken vows of chastity, were intent on turning their homes into temples and wished to live with their husbands in a celibate manner in a similar way to the asexual love practised by, according to Lekhraj, the deities Lakshmi and Narayan (op. cit.).

In reaction to what was perceived to be offensive behaviour by the group, the husbands formed an 'Anti-Om Mandli' group intent on destroying the fledgling movement. The tactics utilised to this end included sending intimidators door-to-door with the message that families would be ousted from their caste if they allowed their wives or children to attend the group's meetings, beating up members, as well as putting pressure on civic leaders and local newspapers to run campaigns in favour of banning the group. Within such an environment of world rejection (that is rejection by the outside world) Lekhraj felt that he could not fully contemplate the messages that God was sending through him and so he travelled to Kashmir to do so. In Lekhraj's absence the group continued to meet regularly, spending time meditating and listening to the daily sermons that he sent from his retreat; these being referred to as *murlis* in reference to the flute Krishna played to call the gopis.

Following his return in October 1937, Lekhraj suggested that a trust of nine women be formed to administer the day-to-day organisation of the group, now renamed *prajipita brahmakumari ishvariya vishvavidyalaya* – the Brahma Kumaris World Spiritual University.[4] Om Radhe, now called Mama (from World Mother), became chief administrator.[5] However, world-rejection continued and, indeed, intensified. On the 21st of June 1938 the 'Anti' Party set fire to Lekhraj's meeting place, causing slight damage but no deaths. As a result, meetings moved to another building which was picketed in August for three days by the 'Anti' Party. The District Magistrate charged those involved, including Lekhraj, with 'disturbing the peace', although after appeal in November the charges were dropped. Effectively driven from Hyderabad, the group, now numbering around 300, relocated to Karachi, purchasing five bungalows to live and meditate in. However, hostility was to arise towards them there also because of a number of female members 'fleeing' from their homes in Hyderabad to join the University in its new home.

The remainder of this period of the University's growth was characterised by a continuation and expansion of its persecution. Chander makes extensive reference to this period and the reader is referred there for details. However, to give a flavour of his account, one may cite the 'Anti' party's attempts to 'pay off' various local ministers and officials to put pressure on the Prime Minister to outlaw the group, the Prime Minister agreeing to 'look the other way' while the 'Anti' party utilised their 'own tactics', the blackmailing/bribing of numerous local newspapers and officials, the presenting of lawsuits by irate husbands for the return of conjugal rights, as well as the hiring of local rowdies to beat up members. However, two inter-linked events may be seen as characteristic of this early period.

Although, according to Chander, the Prime Minister privately supported the movement, in early 1939 he bowed to 'Anti' party pressure and agreed to set up a fact-finding tribunal into the Brahma Kumaris' activities. The Brahma Kumaris 'declined' to attend the hearing tribunal as it was heavily biased against them. According to Chander, the tribunal board consisting mainly of 'Anti' party members who had placed a prohibition on the group employing or speaking to a lawyer, presenting witnesses or even meeting among themselves. In their absence the verdict was given that the University should disband immediately. However, in spite of the verdict, the Prime Minister advised the Brahma Kumaris informally that the Government had no real intention to take steps against them and that they should continue their meetings, albeit while maintaining a low profile, until the protests died down. Nevertheless, in order to put their own side of the story across, the Brahma Kumaris published a book entitled *Is This Justice?* and mailed it, along with other literature, to various international figures both at home and abroad. Angered by this, the 'Anti' Party hired an assassin to kill Lekhraj. Under the cover of darkness, the assassin easily managed to infiltrate the group's compound and entered Lekhraj's bungalow. However, on confronting Lekhraj, who is said to have calmly looked up from his desk at him, the 'bandit' was 'engulfed in a golden miasma. Blinded by the unearthly light', he stumbled and:

> His will to destroy began to weaken. Waves of blissful vibrations overpowered him. He lost the sense of his body entirely. He felt as if he had died and ascended to Nirvana. All memory of his original purpose was washed away. The sword dropped from his hand...[After being captured]...They gave him food and sent him away with the instruction to remember God and to be non-violent (Chander, 1983, p. 155).

From the above account, it can be seen that the University was subject to some degree of local persecution during its early years, ranging from legal attempts to have it outlawed to attempts on the founder's life. This world-rejection, however, may be seen to have affected it then and subsequently in a more subtle way. In a dialectic with its rejection by the outside world it, to use a term borrowed from Roy Wallis (1984), developed as a world-rejecting millenarian organisation, characterised by a strong dualistic vision in both self-image, belief and practice. In this way Lekhraj may be compared with leaders of other millenarian groups – such as Jim Jones of the *Peoples Temple*, Joseph Di Mambro of the *Order of the Solar Temple* or Doe of *Heaven's Gate* – for whom paranoia, exacerbated by actual or perceived external persecution, finds creative outlet in theodical elaboration and the delineation of the elect from the forsaken (see Hall *et al.*, 2000).

During this period of persecution, as Babb (1986) notes, the doctrinal system of the University was formulated with Lekhraj claiming to channel messages from God in his daily murlis. The major theme of these was the necessity of separating from the outside world. Lekhraj told members that they had undergone 'death-in-life' when they joined the University. They had 'died' to their worldly lives and families and been 'reborn' as a member of a 'divine' family. As senior sister Dadi Manohan recalls:

> We had no connection with the old world, with the laukik [physical] relationships. There were no letters written; they didn't write to us, we didn't speak to them and they didn't speak to us. We were detached and lived within our own community...There was no vibration from the old world in front of us and so our lives were very beautiful...We would be sent money or things from our laukiks and we would send them back to our

> laukiks for the first fourteen years. We would return it and say 'we are being nourished by God and Baba' (Manohan, 1996, no pagination).

To signify this they were given new, divinely inspired, names. Again, Indian mythology was drawn on to explain and symbolise the group's enforced, and yet rationalised as necessary, detachment from the external world. Lekhraj told them that the story of Krishna's 16,108 wives, represented symbolically the total number of Brahma Kumaris that there will be 'at the end'. Likewise, the water-polished souls in which form Vishnu is represented (*saligrams*) symbolise the souls of the Brahma Kumaris while the Hindu rosary (*mala*) symbolises Lekhraj's 108 stainless followers. The *Mahabharata* was also heavily reinterpreted, or rather its original, true meaning was rediscovered, so that the Pandavas were the Brahma Kumaris, the Kauravas were the Indian population while the self-destructive Yadavas with their 'magical club' were in fact Western scientists. Indeed, Lekhraj interpreted the thirteen years forced exile of the Pandavas at the beginning of the *Mahabharata* as a forgotten historical *memory* of the exile and persecution of the Brahma Kumaris. This is then explained through the use of the metaphor of memory: it is claimed that these Truths have been forgotten and that the world lives in a state of what Babb (1982, 1986) terms 'spiritual amnesia'. The Brahma Kumaris, in contrast, exist in a state of 'spiritual remembrance'. Thus, whilst the 'true' meaning of Indian mythology has been 'forgotten' by the world, it is 'remembered' by the Brahma Kumaris. Likewise, Lekhraj's true identity (as Krishna in a previous incarnation) has been 'mis-recollected' by the Hindu world but has been 'recollected' by the Brahma Kumaris.

This strong division between the Brahma Kumaris and the outside world was also manifested in the group's daily life which, to use a term from Goffman (1971), represented a form of 'total institution'. Indeed, in many ways the early community recalls Foucault's (1991) notion of a disciplinary system, not least in the case of the Panoptican-like 'message daughters' (*sandesh putris*). For example, spatial distribution was manifested both externally in the sense of the community versus the outside world and internally in the case of the individual's true spiritual self versus their desires (or soul v. body consciousness as it came to be known). Similarly, aside from the emphasis placed on yogic practice, the highly regimented life of the community made a high degree of control of activities possible. Within the community, daily life was strictly organised with mornings spent listening to Lekhraj's murlis and the remainder of the day spent meditating or in other spiritual pursuits. Moreover, often whole weeks were spent in complete silence in order to purify themselves. Within the community, as Babb notes, whilst 'its image of itself was familial...its discipline was quasi-military' (ibid., p. 104) with huge pressures on individuals to conform. For example, message-daughters would have visions of the private delinquencies or secret desires of particular members as well as the divine punishments that awaited them as a result. These delinquents were then summoned before nightly courts in order to confess their weaknesses before Lekhraj and the whole community, although, as Chander points out, this was not for the sake of recriminations but rather to 'help each other towards perfection' (Chander, 1983, p. 176).

Returning to Wallis' conception of the characteristics of a world-rejecting organisation, it is clear that early Brahma Kumaris manifested most, if not all, of these tendencies. Primarily, as I have shown, the University was based upon the belief that the prevailing social order had departed from the life of the spirit and that this would, and indeed will, be rectified by imminent and major world transformation (nuclear war, environmental catastrophes) in which only the spiritually pure (the Brahma Kumaris) would survive. Secondly, within the University an emphasis was placed on a life of service to the message and preparing oneself for the new world through yogic inner control as well as disciplined external organisation. Finally, membership of the University involved 'dying' to one's previous life and being reborn in a new spiritual family, in which one received a new name, dressed in a similar way (a white sari), referred to each other as 'brother' and 'sister' and the founder and his 'spiritual consort' as 'father' (Baba) and 'mother' (Mama) respectively. However, beginning in the 1950s this situation was to change. As with the Padavas, after thirteen years the Brahma Kumaris' exile was coming to an end. It is this intra-tradition development or shift in world orientation, to continue with Wallis' terminology, that I shall now address in the next part of this chapter.

World-Ambivalence

In 1947, Sindh became part of the Islamic state of Pakistan. Whilst, according to, Babb (1986) they were 'unmolested', Chander states that Lekhraj had warned members 'in advance that Hindus and Muslims would beat and kill each other because of their religious intolerance'. Indeed 'when the killing started, it came as no surprise for [them], nor were [they] frightened' (ibid., p. 80). Consequently in 1950 the Brahma Kumaris moved to their current headquarters at Mt. Abu, Rajasthan, the place where, 5,000 years earlier Brahma and Saraswati had done penance. By this point most of Lekhraj's fortune had run out and it seemed that the 'Anti' party would succeed in their tactic of waiting until the University's resources ran out and it broke up (Babb, 1986; Whaling, 1995). Yet this was not to be the case as they received, and most importantly (considering their former reticence) accepted, a large anonymous donation. In addition they began to accept gifts and money from well-wishers and new members in addition to dowries from the families of members who realised that their children would never marry.

The Brahma Kumaris' move to Mt. Abu was therefore associated with the beginning of a somewhat drastic change of world orientation. Where before, largely because of outside persecution, Lekhraj had emphasised isolation and world-rejection, from 1952 he began to emphasise active proselytisation or 'world service' as it came to be known. This was not in itself entirely new for the University. Lekhraj had from the very beginning published numerous pamphlets as well as writing a huge amount of letters to important national and international figures in which he interpreted contemporary events with reference to his revealed knowledge. Rather, this marked an intensification of the process, with seven-lesson courses in the group's teachings being offered to outsiders. To draw on the experiences of Dadi Manohan, again:

> Baba would say 'children from the foreign lands will come'. We didn't even know what a foreign land was. We hadn't been taught in a school, we didn't know what London was, didn't know where America was, we didn't know anything about South Africa. We'd never seen a map. And Baba was sitting there saying 'my children from foreign lands are going to come here and sit' and we'd think 'but *who* is going to come here from foreign lands? Which children are these? How are children from Japan going to come here? We don't speak any foreign languages'...and Baba would say 'these children are mine from foreign lands' (Manohan, 1996, no pagination).

A number of possible reasons for this change of direction may be postulated, none of which by itself would seem to suffice. Firstly, I would argue that the need for money might not have been an overt factor, as not only has the University never made great play of charging for its services, but also, as we have seen, it has always had (at least, potentially) its well-wishers and benefactors. Secondly, to some extent there is the questionable viability of a second generation of a movement of celibates. It follows that unless something goes drastically wrong, a movement of celibates can not grow from within itself, but rather has to, at one point or another, accept outsiders into its ranks in order to continue into a second generation (Babb, 1986). However, as with the financial consideration, this would appear to be a questionable motive when considered in relation to the immanence of Lekhraj's eschatology. Likewise, the desire on behalf of the group to reform the world would also appear to be an unlikely motive. Perhaps, instead a more pertinent factor may have been a change in the reaction of those outside the University. Whereas the Brahma Kumaris' early years were characterised by animosity from the surrounding community, their change of location effectively moved them away and beyond it. Thus, in finding themselves in more hospitable surroundings it is not beyond the bounds of possibility that the Brahma Kumaris let their defences down and began interacting more with the outside world (see Wilson, 1969, p. 371).

In 1952 'World service' began, as would be expected, in quite a low-key manner with friends and relatives of members who had relocated to India inviting members to their areas to discuss their beliefs. This was followed in 1954 with the opening of a centre in Delhi, to be followed soon by centres in Lucknow, Calcutta, Bombay, Amritsar, and Bangalore. This national expansion continued apace and in the same year the Brahma Kumaris made their first official visit outside their homeland to the World Religious Congress in Japan. Visits were made *en route* to Hong Kong, Singapore and Indonesia although no centres were set up. However, this was to follow in the 1970s.

Following the death of 'Mama' in 1965, what Whaling (1995) refers to as 'more sophisticated methods of outreach' began to be utilised, such as divinely inspired exhibitions of artwork being taken around India and displayed at various seminars and conferences. Suspicion still remained of the University among the Hindu community, particularly regarding what was perceived to be the 'un-Hindu' nature of its active proselytising. However, this local critique was beginning to become largely offset by international acceptance and growth. Local hostility would always be a thorn in the University's side but this would become more and more displaced by its attraction to many non-Hindus for whom the charge of being 'un-Hindu' or threats pertaining to caste were meaningless. Having said this, however, as Whaling notes, the Indian-based nature of the University was far from passing. Allusions were, and still are, made to murlis, satsangs and other aspects of Indian cosmology. In this regard, as Kranenborg (1999) has shown, the Brahma Kumaris may be considered to be a Hindu sect. However, following Lekhraj's death in 1969 this balance began to shift.

In the period since Lekhraj's death, the University has, while maintaining much of its original nature, effectively re-invented itself. Generally speaking, this has centred on its move that I have noted towards a more world-ambivalent stance or, to use Babb's terminology from being a 'highly reclusive sect' to 'an aggressively proselytising movement'. In this way, it is possible to point to a number of changes within the University in the intervening years. Primarily, there has been a change of leadership with two women, Dadi Prakashmani and Didi Manmohini, taking over the administration of the University. However, having said this, the University's routines have not altered in any significant sense, which in many ways is the reason for its survival following Lekhraj's death. The daily patterns of meditations, murli readings and spiritual classes were already in place and so there was no apparent confusion or ambiguity of purpose about what should be done on a day-to-day basis. Therefore, in many ways, for the University the death of its founder was, although important, no real organisational problem. Indeed, as we shall see below, Lekhraj's involvement continued apace despite his physical absence. Similarly, international growth continued, led by the University's joint administrative head, Dadi Janki, from the 1970s to the current day. This was facilitated to a great extent by the founding of a centre in London in 1971. From here expansion followed throughout the UK, into mainland Europe and from there to the rest of the world. As a result according to the University there are currently around 450,000 members attending 4,000 centres in 77 countries managed directly from the Mt. Abu. Headquarters.[6]

This is linked with the Brahma Kumaris becoming more active on the world stage generally. The 1980s and 1990s saw the University taking a prominent part at a high level of international affairs. In the 1980s it became affiliated to the Department of Public Information of the United Nations (1980) and gained consultative status with the UN Economic and Social Council (1983) and UNICEF (1988). The early 1990s saw Dadi Janki among those given the title of *Keepers of Wisdom* at the 1992 *Earth Summit* in Brazil while in the following year Dadi Prakashmani was appointed as one of the presidents of the World Parliament of Religions. Also in this era, the University's original centre in London (*Globalgate House*) was demolished and in 1990 work began on what would become the University's new international centre – *Global Co-Operation House* – with funds (£4 million) generated from centres around the world. The centre opened in the following year as did *The Global Hospital* project in Rajasthan, offering medical facilities to the local population. Four years later, a 150-bed hospital wing was added, its aim being to provide holistic care, emphasising physical care within a spiritual environment. In the UK, the *Global Retreat Centre* at Nuneham Park, Oxford was inaugurated in July 1993 to provide a location for spiritual retreats, seminars and courses on meditation, self-management, personal skills and has attracted over 13,000 people since its opening.

For over two decades, the University has organised a series of annual Universal Peace Conferences at its headquarters in Rajasthan. Similarly, in 1986, during the United Nations Year of Peace, the University inaugurated *The Million Minutes of Peace* which raised over one billion 'minutes of peace' from millions of people in 88 countries participating in prayer, meditation and positive thoughts. For this work, the University was awarded one International and six National 'Peace Messenger' Awards. Two years later, as a continuation of this work, it launched the *Global Co-Operation for a Better World* project from the United Nations headquarters in New York and the Houses of Parliament in London which aimed 'to increase communication and co-operation between nations, between communities and between people'. This project involved thousands of people from 129 countries, the results of which, in the form of essays, quotes and paintings, were synthesised into the aforementioned United Nations Peace Messenger publication *Visions of a Better World*.

The University is currently involved in a range of activities on both the international and national level, such as the aforementioned *Global Co-Operation for a Better World* project, the *Sharing our Values for a Better World* project and the UNICEF project *Living Values: An Educational Initiative*. On the national level, it runs training sessions in confidence building and character development within schools, workshops in stress reduction and relaxation in hospitals, homes for the elderly, drug clinics, community centres and prisons as well as meditation and integrity discussion groups for business people.

The University's international expansion has also affected it in more subtle ways, particularly in regard to its spiritual message. The Brahma Kumaris have managed to assimilate the various native traditions, as well as other cultural ideas, of the countries that they have penetrated.[7] For example, the Christian notion of 'what you sow, you will reap' is linked with the notion of karma while Christian millenarianism is welded onto Lekhraj's apocalyptic vision. Similarly, western philosophical and psychological terminology such as 'ego', 'conditioning', 'blockages' as well as elements of New Age thought, environmentalism and, indeed, science have been turned to the Brahma Kumaris' end. However, having said this, the bulk of the courses and the terminology utilised therein still retains a distinctly Hindu feel, albeit tinged with western terminology, with, for example, the law of karma being compared to Newton's First Law of Physics. Again, this may be the result of native centre co-ordinators attempting to interpret the Brahma Kumaris' theodicy in terms that either they or their prospective members will understand. Although, as one centre co-ordinator told me, Dadi Janki and others in the Indian hierarchy have self-consciously adapted elements of the revealed knowledge in this way for greater understanding by non-Hindus.

Another fundamental development in the Brahma Kumaris' theodicy concerns the status of Lekhraj and the murlis. While alive, Lekhraj had claimed merely to be a soul chosen to be a medium for God, and had always, therefore, played down the notion of he himself being worshipped. However, the devotion that was focused on him after his death by members led to a development in the Brahma Kumaris' theodicy, specifically that he had gone to the angelic realm to continue to act as a medium for God, as *BapDada*. Thus, ironically, he became in many ways the focus of devotion. This extended to the murlis also. Among the confusion and emotion directed towards Lekhraj by the Brahma Kumaris following his death there was a great deal of confusion regarding authoritative access to divine messages. Within this confusion, there was an upsurge of visions and trance states amongst members in the various national centres. The threat posed by this potential dispersal of sacred authority was dealt with by the University hierarchy stipulating that divine messages would only be delivered through one particular member, the trance-medium Sister Gulzar, at specified periods at Mt. Abu. Thus, in the first murli delivered by Lekhraj after his death on the 21st of January 1969, he referred to the problem of members 'having too many visions and going into trance' and it:

> ...being a waste of time. This is why that should not happen. It shouldn't be that you are not able to verify the parts being played by the trance messengers at the centres. This is why you will receive directions through which ever trance messenger [the senior sisters], who are the instruments, appoint as instruments (Avaktya Murli, 21.1.69).

As a result, the University operates a dual system of murlis. Those murlis given by Lekhraj while alive were organised on a 5-year rotation and became known as *Sakar Murlis*. The murlis delivered through Sister Gulzar became known as *Avaktya* (unmanifested) *Murlis*. These represent 'live' communications from Lekhraj from the spirit world to the University and are read out at murli sessions around the world after they have been 'delivered' to her.

From World-Rejection to Ambivalence: Some Concluding Thoughts

In this chapter I have outlined a general shift in the Brahma Kumaris World Spiritual University's world orientation/response, from world-rejection to, what I would refer to as, world-ambivalence. This process has occurred through three historical stages of institutional reflexivity/malleability: in terms of its use of Hindu tradition in its early years, the assimilation of 'world traditions' during its internationalisation programme as well as the on-going re-interpretation of the theodicy by the University hierarchy and, as I will show in a subsequent chapter, by its membership. Within the final part of this chapter I intend to pull this argument out further and say more about the nature of this ambivalence.

From the above analysis, it is clear that the University has, whilst still retaining its distance somewhat, become more world accommodating (Howell and Nelson, 1998). Indeed, as Wallis notes this shift is the usual outcome for many originally world-rejecting movements. Another claim, based on the work of Bryan Wilson (1969, 1970) may be that the University has shifted from being a 'revolutionist' to either a 'reformist' or 'utopian' organisation.[8] Whilst I feel that both these claims are in part correct, I would add that neither fully captures the nature of this shift nor the University's current world orientation/response.

Turning first to the claim that the University has become world-accommodating, at first glance this would appear to be the case. It may indeed be visualised as a 'break-away' Hindu group (in the sense of breaking away from the surrounding community), taking and yet adapting elements of its native faith in order to return to a putative, long-lost 'pure' message. Similarly, within the University's teachings there is an emphasis on the rejection of the secular, outer life in favour of the inner, spiritual life as well as a clear millenarian message. However, despite this emphasis within the teachings on spiritual perfection, this has global change as its goal. Whereas for Wallis (1984, p. 35) 'the world-accommodating new religion draws a distinction between the spiritual and the worldly' and concentrates on the former, the Brahma Kumaris see both as fundamentally inter-linked. Indeed, even in the University's early days when there was a strong emphasis on individual development, one of the aims of this was preparation for the new social order. In this way, the social and the spiritual are intrinsically linked with the former seen as ideally informing the latter in, for example, the *Sharing our Values for a Better World* project.

Another possible objection could be that it is possible within Wallis' schema for a world-rejecting movement to 'address themselves to the influential' in an attempt to 'meet the pressing cosmic timetable more effectively' (ibid., p. 12). For example, Wallis cites the instances of the Moonies support of Nixon and other anti-Communist figures and their attempt to counsel prominent American politicians as evidence for the manner in which world-rejecting movements may become active politically and yet still claim an explicitly religious mission. However, in contrast to these groups, I would argue that the Brahma Kumaris' political involvement is more ambiguous. Although they may court the powerful, as we shall see in the next chapter, the Brahma Kumaris' whole theodicy is based on the belief that world change is predetermined, inevitable and thereby largely outside of the influence of humanity.

Similarly, the claim that it has become a reformist sect would also appear to have a degree of truth to it. Following Wilson's definition it would seem that it does study 'the world in order to involve itself in it by good deeds...[taking] unto itself the role of social conscience...[accepting] a place in the world without being of the world or touched by its impurity' (ibid., p. 269; see also Wilson, 1970, p. 40). The Brahma Kumaris have, indeed, opened themselves up to the world, offering free courses in their beliefs, sponsoring conferences and apparently campaigning hard for world peace via their UN work and even going so far as to run special courses in spiritual values for western scientists. However, at a deeper level there is a fundamental problem with the nature of the reform sought. The University's whole *Weltanschauung* or 'conscience' is based on its founder's visions of the end of this corrupt world and the emergence of a new age totally unlike the present. Thus, while it may act as a social conscience on one level, wanting to share its values for a better world, this 'better world' is in no way connected with this world, except perhaps in its nullification. Similarly, although the University may attempt to become more worldly, there is still the emphasis within its teachings on a strong dualism between, for example, the purity of the few (who will be saved) versus the spiritually impure (who will not). It is also for these and other reasons that I would argue against the University being seen as becoming more of a utopian sect. While, again, it does indeed withdraw from the world to a great degree while yet engaging in it with the goal of 'radical reconstruction based on religious principles', unlike in Wilson's typology, the Brahma Kumaris do have a 'clear conception of divinity' as well as having little or no interest in re-constructing *this world* as it stands on a communitarian basis (op. cit., pp. 40, 370).

It is for these reasons outlined above that I would argue that the University at present has very much a world-ambivalent orientation. By this I mean that it appears to entail two distinct and unresolved orientations toward the world. Primarily, as I have outlined in this chapter, the University's whole worldview is based on the visions of its founder, the central of these being the end of the world by apparent nuclear holocaust or environmental catastrophe. Moreover, as I will discuss in the next chapter, this is seen as essential, desirable and indeed pre-determined in the nature of things. The current, spiritually impure world has to be destroyed in order for the new age of spiritual purity to come about. However, on the other hand, to cite Whaling (1995, p. 15) 'there is the spectacle of a University which has the word "spiritual" written into its very name becoming increasingly involved in frenetic activity on behalf of the world that is deemed to be beyond redemption in its present form'. To take an example, the campaign to raise *The Million Minutes of Peace* in 1986 would seem a worthless, and perhaps even a cynical, gesture in the face of what is held to be the inevitable and indeed desirable destruction of the world by *ipso facto* un-peaceful means. In this way, I would summarise the University's world-ambivalence as an interaction of its original state of world-rejection with a new spirit of liberalism toward the outside world. For example, where western scientists were, and to some extent still are, referred to as the self-destructive Yadavas of Indian mythology, the University now actively courts them on the international stage as well as offering them special courses on spiritual values.

The root of this ambivalent situation I would argue is located in the very process that brought the University onto the world stage, its internationalisation programme. This saw it being disembedded from its Hindu locale and re-embedded into the global sphere. However, in many ways it still retained its attitude of millenarianism and world-rejection as crystallised in its theodicy. Nevertheless, I hold that this theodicy developed ostensibly as a reaction to the persecution from the outside world. Lekhraj's vision could have been interpreted as a call to the Brahma Kumaris to halt the first scenario (world destruction) and bring about the second (the new age) through active conversion and campaigning for world peace or as a prophetic vision of the second world war and the development of a post-war global community. However, it was interpreted, I would argue, as a Nietzschian 'slave' reaction to the hostility of the outer world, that the 'meek shall inherit the earth' (see Nietzsche, 1998). By this I am not attempting to rewrite the Brahma Kumaris' theodicy, but rather to, firstly, point to the material factors that contributed to its development (persecution) and, secondly, to argue that the disembedding of the University from these factors (the Hindu locale) through its internationalisation programme has resulted in its ambivalent world orientation. The University still retains its original (world-rejecting) theodicy, but possibly through the desire to increase membership or promote its message it has had to temper this with a degree of utopianism or reformism.

Thus, to compare this notion of world-ambivalence to the previously outlined concepts of world-accommodation or utopianism/reformism, I would draw out the following point. The Brahma Kumaris' world-ambivalence may be characterised as, on one hand, a millenarian attitude of world-rejection or revolutionism and on the other a combination of world-affirmation, reformism and utopianism. However, the former largely tempers these latter tendencies. Reform of the world will occur and utopia will arise/the ideal community will be formed, but this will be a utopia precisely because it is not the present corrupt world. World 'reform' will be centred on all humans, as, to recall the point made by Ulrich Beck, global nuclear and environmental destruction does not draw distinctions between the good and the bad, the pure and the impure. However, from this carnage utopia will emerge; a utopia of and for the spiritually pure alone.

In this chapter I have outlined the historical development of the Brahma Kumaris World Spiritual University, concentrating on developments within the University and how, I would argue, these were the result of its changing relationship with the outside world. This has centred on the argument that the University has gone through three distinct stages of growth. Within the first stage, stretching from its formation in 1937 to roughly 1950, the proto-University developed a highly malleable form of Hinduism characterised by a strong message of world-rejection largely as a reaction to external persecution. This was superseded, from the 1950s onwards by a reflexive assimilation of the various world traditions that it encountered through its internationalisation programme. However, the tension engendered through the inherent dissonance of this original message with the desire to promote itself on the world stage, particularly through its 'reformist' or 'utopian' schemes, has resulted in the University's world orientation now being best characterised by what I have referred to as world-ambivalence: world-rejection tempered somewhat by a spirit of liberalism. Finally, and linked to the last point, within the University there is an ongoing re-interpretation and re-application of the theodicy by all levels of membership.

Another example of the University's willingness to reflexively re-interpret its message, as well as its desire to promote their spiritually in a more instrumental, world-affirming manner, is its development of free four-week courses in 'positive thinking' and 'stress-free living'. Within the UK these are run both at the local and the national level and essentially offer a spiritually-based instrumentalism, with individuals been taught personal skills to combat stress or negative thoughts and feelings. Indeed, these are often utilised as a preliminary to courses in the more advanced theodicy in that they attract people to the centres as well as offering an introduction to the University's basic concepts and practices. This suggests the beginnings of a bifurcation within the University between the original, 'ascetic', world-rejecting theodicy and a more New Age, 'instrumental', world-affirming set of practices. It is the analysis of this division that I will turn to in the next chapter.

Notes

[1] Until almost the eleventh hour I had utilised the term 'theology' to describe the Brahma Kumaris' beliefs. However, I was aware that this could potentially raise objections from some scholars, particularly those alive to what they perceive as the dangers of 'Orientalism' in western discussions of Eastern Religion (see, for example, King, 1999). Nevertheless, whilst acknowledging that the term was not ideal, I reluctantly decided to use it for no other reason than for pragmatism and because western Brahma Kumaris members (who are the focus of my investigation) would – because of their backgrounds – consider their beliefs to comprise a theology. However, during the final stages of preparing this manuscript for publication I happened across Colin Campbell's discussion of the nature of theodicies and realised that this provided a more appropriate way of looking at the material.

Campbell (2001, p. 74) defines theodicies as 'those cultural systems that specifically serve to meet the universal human need for meaning at the highest level'. Whilst these are, in keeping with the origin of the term, often religious and deal with the fundamental question of good and evil, this is not necessarily so. Rather, he argues, the term can be usefully applied to a other 'comprehensive meaning systems':

> ...there seems to be no very good reason for restricting the usage of the term in this way since the need to have answers to the fundamental questions of existence would appear to be a cultural universal, as apparent among the non-religious as among the religious, while among the latter it is as apparent among non-theists as among theists. It is also important to recognise that theodical systems do not simply deal with issues of justice or morality – even though this may be their focus – but necessarily also deal with meaning puzzles more generally (Campbell, 2001, p. 75).

On this basis, Campbell distinguishes between three 'dimensions of meaningfulness' that theodicies are required to supply. First, theodicies provide *cognitive meaning* in the sense of giving 'a descriptive account of reality that human beings experience' (ibid.). Second, as well as providing cognitive meaning, theodicies are also concerned with *emotional meaning*; that is they indicate 'what general attitude or emotional tone individuals should take towards life' (ibid.). For example, should they feel awestruck, resigned, fearful or hopeful and joyous. Finally, theodicies are perhaps more than anything else concerned with *moral meaning*, with the questions of, for example, human pain and suffering, failure and disappointment.

[2] I will also present non-English words or phrases as they are presented within the Brahma Kumaris' literature.

[3] Chander (1983) offers the following translation of this: *om*, a sacred syllable representing the Absolute; *mandli*, 'circle' or 'association'.

[4] According to the University, the literal translation is *The Prajipita Brahma Kumari Divine University*. The word divine is the English equivalent to the Hindi term meaning 'Godly'. Thus, Chander (1983) speaks of the 'Godly University'. Female members are referred to as *Brahma Kumari* (daughters, maidens or princesses of Brahma) while male members are referred to as *Brahma Kumars* (sons of Brahma). Both are often shortened to Brahmins, Raja Yogis or BKs.

[5] According to Whaling (1995), women were given such senior posts for three reasons. Primarily, because there were a lot of gifted middle and upper-class women involved in the movement. Secondly, it was a reaction to what was perceived to be the unfair oppression of women in Sindh witnessed by Lekhraj as a businessman. Thirdly, it was an attempt to

redress the balance of past female oppression in what the University considered to be a transitional age into the post-apocalyptic age where both sexes would be equal.

[6] International expansion has also necessitated a number of organisational changes within the University above and beyond the need to co-ordinate centres in different time zones. Whereas the 'Indian Template' of the organisation was, and to some extent still is, characterised by members living exclusively in centres and female members abstaining from outside employment, Howell and Nelson (1997) note the growth of *bhavans* (non-centre co-residence of members) as well as female members being obliged (at least for financial reasons) to seek employment. Again, this may be seen as a further compromise to 'the world'.

[7] It is, however, possible that Lekhraj as a cosmopolitan businessman, friend of the Raj and particularly through his childhood learning of English, would already have been familiar with elements of Christianity and western philosophical ideas.

[8] In the case of the Brahma Kumaris I prefer to utilise the term world-rejecting *organisation* rather than world-rejecting *sect* for two main reasons as outlined by Dawson (1997). Primarily, there is the questionable validity of applying the term, based as it is on a Troeltschian church-sect division, to an religious organisation that has not developed from a 'church' in the western sense. As Wilson (1970) notes, due to the pluralistic and diffuse nature of Hinduism, sectarianism exists in a more limited sense than in the west. Thus, whereas in the west where sects are viewed *vis-à-vis* the church, the Hindu model is characterised by diverse traditions of worship co-existing. Equally, in many respects the term is historically and culturally relative, with it being possible to classify a particular organisation as a sect in one context, a church in another or a denomination in another. For example, accepting for the moment the 'church' metaphor of Hinduism, the Brahma Kumaris could be seen in India as a denomination or sect, a cult in its early (world-rejecting) period and possibly as a sect at the present time.

Chapter 4

The Ascetic and the Instrumental: Two Contemporary Renditions of Raja Yoga

In the previous chapter I argued that the Brahma Kumaris World Spiritual University had evolved from a world-rejecting to a world-ambivalent movement. The most recent stage of this development was, I proposed, the on-going re-interpretation of the University's message by those within its hierarchy as well as by centre co-ordinators and members themselves.

In this chapter I would like to further develop my analysis of the Brahma Kumaris' historical development. In particular I intend to develop the argument that I presented toward the end of the last chapter concerning a bifurcation within the University's teachings between a newer spiritually-based instrumentalism and the original, world-rejecting spiritual message. To this end I will present a discussion of these two aspects of the University's theodicy. This will involve drawing broadly on the typology of religious cults' orientation to the 'divine within' proposed by Bruce Campbell (1978). However, in contrast to Campbell, who argues that within a particular cult either illumination or instrumentalism will be predominant, I intend to argue that due to the Brahma Kumaris' world-ambivalence, both find their expression simultaneously.

In this way, I shall join Campbell in labelling as 'instrumental' that aspect of the Brahma Kumaris' teachings stressing 'inner experience...for its effects [and] its ability to transform the everyday personality so that it can better meet the demands made upon it' (ibid., p. 233). That which emphasises 'illumination', 'detachment from the personality and a search for direct inner personal experience of the divine within' (ibid.) and, in particular, world-rejection or renunciation and bodily discipline, I shall refer to following Weber (1965) as other-worldly asceticism or as 'the ascetic' for short.

This chapter will therefore be divided into two sections. Within the first part, *the ascetic*, I will develop the claim made by Howell and Nelson (1997) that there is a stark distinction drawn within the Brahma Kumaris between those inside the University and 'the people of the world'. Moreover, I will argue that stemming from the world-rejected/world-rejecting dialectic that distinguished its early years, the University's theodicy is characterised by a strong world-rejecting dualistic dynamic. In addition, I will situate this theodicy within Hinduism as well as, finally, noting its current assimilation of world traditions.

In sum, I will argue that the Brahma Kumaris' theodicy represents a development out of the Hindu cultural/religious experience hallmarked by a strong emphasis on the rejection of the external in both the literal and metaphorical sense and a form of what Weber would refer to as other-worldly asceticism. In contrast, in the second part, *the instrumental*, I will demonstrate the manner in which this theodicy has been re-interpreted by the University within recent years so as to produce a spiritually-based, world-affirming instrumentalism emphasising intra and interpersonal skills for life in the external world.

My sources for the analysis presented in the first part will be the University's own literature. Through my fieldwork I built up an archive of a variety of primary literature, such as leaflets, books, magazines, audio/video cassettes and teaching materials. Primarily leaflets obtained from both local and national centres provided a brief overview of the University as well as highlighting certain areas or events, e.g. lectures, open-days or courses. Generally speaking these events were concerned with the more instrumental aspect of the University's message. For example *Personal Effectiveness with Malcolm Piers Anthony, Free to be Me, Self Esteem: The Secret of Sustained Success* and *The Four Faces of Women* (a seminar on female empowerment). In contrast, books provided more in-depth information on a range of issues such as the University's history and, in particular, the more world-rejecting aspect of its theodicy. In addition, many works of 'spiritual insight' written by senior members have also been published by the University in which they describe their spiritual journeys. These are not an intrinsic part of the various courses run at the centres, however, and there is no 'recommended reading' list, but rather they either run parallel to the courses, providing more related insights and practices, or are intended to be read for pleasure and inspiration.

In terms of my understanding of the Brahma Kumaris' theodicy, three books proved to be particularly valuable, with each elaborating similar themes in an increasingly advanced way. Firstly, *Practical Meditation* (Brahma Kumaris World Spiritual University, 1995b) contains a condensed version of the first seven lessons in the 'Foundation Course in Raja Yoga' that I attended in January 1998. More advanced concepts covered in the 'Foundation Course' are also dealt with in *New Beginnings* and *Pathways to Higher Consciousness* by Ken O'Donnell (1995, 1996). Both books cover similar themes and give similar examples. However, the latter is written in a more technical style, often utilising Hindu terminology, and contains more advanced teachings. These themes are also covered to a lesser degree in *Meditations and Jewels of Knowledge* (Brahma Kumaris World Spiritual University, 1988), a pocket-sized introduction, and children's book entitled *The Voyagers* (Shubow, 1988).

The University also publishes a monthly newspaper, *Purity*, and a bi-annual magazine, *Retreat*, to both of which I had access to. *Purity* is published in India and distributed to centres and subscribers throughout the world and on the whole serves to keep members informed of events that the University has participated in or organised as well featuring articles relating to the Brahma Kumaris' theodicy; for example, 'Vegetarian Diet is Well Founded' (April 1998, p. 7), 'Modernity and Value Crisis: A Challenge for Society' (May 1998, p. 11), 'Remembering Mateshwari Jagadamba Saraswati: The Divine Mother' (June 1998, p. 5). Similarly, *Retreat*, to cite its subscription form 'is dedicated to those who seek to deepen their understanding and application of spiritual principles and values to their lives' and consists

> of around twelve articles [written almost exclusively by members] covering a wide variety of topics in the context of spirituality and spiritual growth including; science and spirituality, creativity and the arts, leadership and empowerment, psychology and spirituality, education and values, meditation and the mind, media and spiritual communication.

Audio/video cassettes produced by the University also served to supplement some of the information presented in print, as did the Brahma Kumaris' websites (www.bkwsu.com; www.rajayoga.com). Throughout the introductory courses, and indeed throughout all the meetings I attended, extensive use was made of these tapes in terms of guided meditation, music to accompany meditation or lectures by senior members on aspects of the theodicy. The co-ordinator of the centre where I conducted my participant observation was also good enough to allow me access to her own collection and to intercede with other centres to secure loans of informal recordings of guest speakers made at centres. Finally, again with the co-ordinator's help, I was able to draw on a variety of teaching materials utilised in the courses that were used to supplement my notes. This was particularly the case during my stay at the Global Retreat Centre where I had access to a well stocked study room containing a variety of such materials as well as a collection of murlis.

As can be imagined from the intended audience and subject matter of the books, the language employed, especially by O'Donnell, is highly eulogistic and at some points somewhat over-zealous. In order to capture this, and indeed to do justice to the texts, I intend as in the previous chapter, to let the texts 'speak for themselves' and quote directly from them as much as possible.

The source material for the second part is also presented in some of this literature (particularly the University's website), although my analysis will not be taken from this source. Rather, I will draw heavily on my own fieldwork conducted at several of the University's centres in the north of England between 1997 and 1998. The majority of my research involved intense overt participant observation at the Chesterfield Brahma Kumaris centre as well as, to a lesser degree, other centres within the UK. This began in November 1997 with my participation in several courses in meditation and spiritual values run by the Chesterfield centre. 'Classes' lasted for roughly ninety minutes on a one-to-one basis with the centre co-ordinator and generally followed the format of an introductory guided meditation to introduce the subject of the class, the class *per se* and then a concluding guided meditation reflecting on the subject covered.

On completion of these introductory courses in February 1998 I was invited to attend a regular Thursday evening (7-9 p.m.) meditation and discussion class at the centre along with others who had completed the courses. These meetings took place in a separate, slightly larger room than the introductory classes which contained a variety of posters representing various aspects of Brahma Kumaris' theodicy as well as a large framed picture of Lekhraj. As with the introductory courses, these featured two meditations; an introductory meditation lasting roughly thirty minutes and a concluding one lasting under ten. This was followed by an informal chat over spicy cakes or buns (referred to as *Toli*) baked by the centre co-ordinator that day. Similarly, meditation was again always accompanied by specially recorded meditation music and focused on central aspects of the theodicy such as 'I am a soul'.

Aside from these regular meetings I also took part in some social evenings run between centres. These included a number of video evenings where videos of lectures by senior members of the University were shown, a one day 'Spiritual Retreat' in Leeds, a Christmas party, a special weekend programme in early January 1998 to mark the anniversary of Lekhraj's death, a number of lectures by prominent members and a summer party. Finally towards the end of my fieldwork I was invited by Maureen Goodman, the University's programme co-ordinator in the UK, to spend three days and then a weekend at the Global Retreat Centre in Oxford.

1. The Ascetic

Raja Yoga

Yoga, in particular what is referred to as *Raja Yoga*, is the central element of the Brahma Kumaris' theodicy. Indeed, the phrase Raja Yogi and Brahmin are interchangeable to refer to a member of the University. This should, however, not be confused with the *Brahman* caste, nor should the Raja Yoga promulgated by the Brahma Kumaris be confused with the Raja Yoga discussed by Patanjali in the *Yoga Sutras* (1st century CE). *Yoga*, deriving from the Sanskrit word *yug* (union or link), refers to a form of meditation involving mental as well as physical discipline (see Smart, 1995). *Raja* is Sanskrit for sovereign or king; the term *Raja Yoga* therefore has two meanings. Firstly, it is 'Sovereign Yoga' ('The King of all Yogas' or the 'Royal Yoga'); the yoga through which the individual becomes the master – or sovereign – of themselves. Secondly, it is 'Supreme Yoga' or 'Union with the Supreme'; the yoga which develops a relationship with the Supreme Being.[1]

On this basis it is possible to differentiate somewhat arbitrarily between Raja Yoga the technique and Raja Yoga the theodical system, although in practice both are intrinsically linked. The technique of Raja Yoga is achieved, I was told, through a remarkably simple technique although my own experiences were somewhat disappointing. Yogis sit either on the floor or in a chair with their eyes open and either direct the meditation themselves or, in centre classes, by following a guided commentary provided by either another experienced yogi or audio tapes. The meditation begins by 'relaxing the muscles of the body and mind', tensing and relaxing the muscles of the feet, followed by the calves, thighs, torso, arms, hands and face and finally one's thoughts. After a brief pause in the commentary, one's thoughts are pointed in a certain direction. For example:

> I now withdraw my attention, away from my physical organs...my open eyes are rested...my body sits there...
> I focus my thought energy on myself, I-self...I now feel light as the burden of physical thought diminishes...I am thinking, remembering, observing myself. I am this eternal point of light energy...this life energy that powers the body...I am non-material light...eternal soul...thinking, deciding...acting...observing...remembering...I the soul do action through the body...I the soul observe the result of my actions...I am the rider, my body is the chariot...
> I concentrate my thoughts now on this one aspect...that I am a concentrated spark of life-energy...radiating light...
> As my thoughts concentrate I fill with power...I become light...floating...and I find deep peace within (Brahma Kumaris World Spiritual University, 1988, p. 12).

Often this is presented in the literature and courses as an instrumental process. For example, the author(s) of *Practical Meditation* outlines eight practical spiritual 'powers' which may be developed and deployed in daily life, such as tolerance, courage, co-operation, accommodation, (positive) discrimination, judgement, and the power to pack up and withdraw from stressful situations (Brahma Kumaris World Spiritual University, 1995b). In this way, Raja Yoga can be, as we shall see in part two, quite utilitarian. It can be, and often is, used for world-affirming purposes such as improving interpersonal relationships, career success or personal esteem. However, strictly speaking the meditation is intrinsically bound up in the University's world-rejecting theodicy. This is expressed in Raja Yoga as the distinction between *being* (the experience of yoga or peace *per se*) and *knowing*, *becoming* and *giving* (the meditation as a way of life and spiritual goal). In this way, the Raja Yoga technique should be envisaged as an intrinsic part of the Raja Yoga theodical system as the method whereby the belief (*knowing*) is engendered and experienced (*becoming*).

The central idea that is produced through the meditation is the division between the physical and the metaphysical. At the core of Raja Yoga there is a strong symbolic and practical division between the body which is seen to represent all that is false, transient and material and, most importantly, mortal and the soul which is seen to represent all that is true, unlimited, spiritual and, most importantly, immortal. This is linked to the soul's awareness of its own existence and identity. Following on from the distinction between the body and soul, there are two forms of binary opposed and mutually-exclusive forms of consciousness discussed within Raja Yoga: *body consciousness* and *soul consciousness*.

Body consciousness is the soul's identification of itself with its transient (external) physical body as perceived by the physical senses. In this state the soul is said to exist in a state of what Babb (1982) terms 'spiritual amnesia'. It is ignorant of its 'true identity' as a soul and instead identifies with 'false' physical attributes such as gender, race, nationality and religion. Body-consciousness thereby represents to Raja Yogis all that is negative in the external, physical world. It is 'the underlying cause of the poor health of our individual and collective world...[and] the basis of sexual, racial, social and religious prejudice' as well as being the reason why 'I have remained imprisoned by certain habits and characteristics' (O'Donnell, 1996, pp. 41, 49). In radical contrast, within soul-consciousness, the soul is said to identify with its 'true' remembered nature as a soul and as a result sees the body or its role as merely the outward manifestation of itself.

This realisation of *Om Shanti*, 'I, the soul, exist in a state of peace' (see O'Donnell, 1995, p. 6), is achieved through the Raja Yoga meditation technique and is its chief *raison d'être*. Senior BK Dadi Janki sums it up; 'the truth is not: I am a body and I have a soul; but rather I am a soul and this is my body. The body is *mine*' (Stillerman, 1998, p. 85, emphasis added in original). The yoga facilitates within individuals an awareness of this fundamental qualitative distinction between their psychology, their 'true self', and their physical form; between 'a living, spiritual, eternal being' and 'my temporal physical costume' (op. cit., p. 14). Often this is described through the analogy of a motor car and its driver; just as the driver is obviously not the car, although (s)he may be identified as the driver of a certain car (role), the soul plays a variety of changing roles with each one being a facet of, rather than actually being, the core self.

In order to achieve its ends via the physical body, the soul has three faculties, the *mind*, the *intellect* and the *sanskars*, comparable in many ways to Freud's tripartite division of personality. The mind is the faculty through which one imagines, thinks and creates ideas. These form the basis of one's emotions, desires and sensations. The intellect is the awareness and understanding of the thoughts. It assesses the value of the thoughts presented in the mind, discriminating between and judging various thoughts and ideas. Finally, sanskars are the unconscious impressions left on the soul by the actions we have performed as well as our temperament, personality traits, habits and emotional tendencies. An individual's state of consciousness is therefore the result of how these three faculties interact. For example, various subconscious impressions emerge from the sanskars, manifesting themselves as thoughts, desires or emotions in the mind. These are then 'processed' by the intellect which decides whether to allow the thoughts to be expressed by the physical body. The results of the action, or non-action, collected via the sense organs then leaves an impression on the soul, either creating, reinforcing or cancelling an existing sanskar. Where an action is performed repeatedly, a 'deep' sanskar, or habit, is formed, which has the most likelihood of re-emerging into consciousness in the future. The intellect, or 'Higher Self' as it is sometimes presented in the courses, is therefore of fundamental importance in a manner akin to the Freudian notion of the Super-Ego 'censor'. It determines whether a sanskar is formed by either action or non-action. Meditation aims therefore to strengthen the intellect or 'fill the intellect with power' so that it may direct all thoughts and actions toward this awareness of soul-consciousness; seeing and experiencing oneself as a soul. Thus, in a self-fulfilling way, by telling oneself that one is a soul, and attempting to experience the world in this way, one begins to develop this awareness of soul consciousness. This then serves as a way of further interpreting oneself and the world.

Stemming from the belief in the non-physical, immortal nature of the individual is the belief in both reincarnation and different planes of existence above and beyond the physical plane. Beyond this plane, visible only to those who have developed soul consciousness, Raja Yogis claim that there are other, more important planes including the home of all souls and the Supreme Soul. In the teachings this is typically presented as a circle enclosed by a larger circle which is itself enclosed by an infinitely larger circle, these circles representing the *physical*, *subtle* and *incorporeal* realms respectively.

The subtle realm represents an intermediate region between the physical and incorporeal realm. It is here where experienced Raja Yogis claim to journey to experience visions regarding world history and their place within it as well as being the place where Lekhraj and Shiva as BapDada jointly communicate directly to the University through the Avaktya murlis discussed in the previous chapter. Further beyond the subtle regions is the incorporeal region which is 'remembered' by Christians as Heaven, by Hindus as Shantidham or Paramdham and by Buddhists as Nirvana. Within Raja Yoga it is called the 'Soul World' or the 'Home of Souls' and is characterised by 'light', 'silence', 'peace', 'liberation', 'stillness' and 'complete purity' and is experienced as 'golden-red, divine light' (op. cit., p. 33). It is here that the souls exist 'totally untainted by matter...as a starlike point of light' until they have to 'play their part' within the world drama on the physical plane (op. cit., 1996, p. 47).

This descent into the material world is determined by a strict chronological order based on the quality of the soul's sanskars, with pure souls (soul-conscious Raja Yogis) going first and impure (body-conscious) souls going last. At the apex of this descent, the Supreme Soul does not descend into the material world. Rather, He remains in the soul world 'perfectly stable, constant and unchanging while the rest of the universe and the souls go through constant change' (op. cit., p. 61). In Raja Yoga the Supreme Soul is called Shiva Baba, or 'Benevolent Father', in reference to the aspect of God popular in the University's birth place of Sindh (Babb, 1984, 1986). However, the Brahma Kumaris' image of Shiva is radically different from that of Indian mythology. Whereas, in the latter He is seen to swing regularly between extremes of asceticism and eroticism, for the Brahma Kumaris, He is purely an ascetic deity, the erotic aspect of his character being seen as a *later* body-consciousness addition to the original mythology which the Brahma Kumaris have rediscovered/remembered (see, for example, O'Flaherty, 1973; Babb, 1984, 1986; Kinsley, 1993). Similarly, in contrast to the usual symbolic representation of Shiva as a phallic *linga*, within Raja Yoga He is seen to possess an asexual form similar to the human soul, albeit in its most perfect form. However, whereas humans forget their original qualities of peace, 'He remains eternally peaceful, blissful and powerful...the unlimited ocean of virtues' (Brahma Kumaris World Spiritual University, 1995b, p. 44), and is therefore recognised as the Supreme Soul. One is able to communicate with Shiva Baba through meditation where one experiences His qualities of peace and love. The Raja Yoga technique is therefore, in its fullest form, the communication with the Supreme Soul. It is the Yoga whereby the soul achieves union (yoga) with God and becomes a channel for His love into the world by detaching oneself from the 'negative, wasteful and mundane thinking' of the external world, creating pure or elevated thoughts about one's original nature (a soul) and one's original home (the soul world) and then finally visualising oneself as a 'point of light energy in front of God in His radiant form'.

In this way, the Supreme Soul is envisaged as both asexual and existing outside the physical universe of time and space and cause and effect and therefore having no influence on nature or human lives. Rather, the physical, chemical and biological laws of nature are seen as automatic, operating within the law of *Karma*. Raja Yogis believe that karma is eternal and that the soul's purpose in taking a body and descending to the world stage is to perform and experience it. Although the souls descend from the soul world pure, through the process of many rebirths, they now perform only negative (body consciousness) *Vikarma* rather than (soul conscious) *Sukarma*. Similarly, as it is impossible to settle all karmic accounts in one life, the soul has to take on another body to continue the process. This past karma determines the social condition, moment, place and gender of the body and family of birth. For example, a rich individual who squandered their money in one life might be reborn as an extremely poor person. However, unlike in many conceptions of karma, within Raja Yoga the human soul never transmigrates into the body of a non-human animal.[2] Rather, the human soul has to work within human karma for eternity.

Everything therefore that happens in the individual's life, for good or bad, is a result of acts that (s)he has performed either in this or a previous life; one reaps the sorrow or joy that one has sown. Similarly, the manner in which individuals react to this determines future karma. One is therefore portrayed as constantly being affected by one's past and creating one's future. Rather than feeling helpless in the face of eternal karma, Raja Yogis believe that one should 'transform sorrow into learning' through meditation and, by understanding the law of karma, make a better future for oneself. For example, past negativity is seen to have led to 'karmic debts' with others which need to be 'settled'. By performing pure actions one may 'pay off' these debts and 'be freed from the bondages of karma'. This involves purifying the thoughts through meditation and by filling the intellect with power and drawing on the qualities of the Supreme Soul so that negative thoughts do not emerge and lead to negative actions. With the intellect strong, correct decisions and actions follow which purify the sanskars and in turn lead to positive karma.

As with the notions of karma and Shiva, the Brahma Kumaris' conception of time as a cycle draws heavily on and yet radically alters existing ideas. Within the Vedanta tradition the cycle (*kalpa*) is said to represent a Day of Brahma and last for 4,320,000,000 years, subdivided into four ages (*yugas*) of progressive decline (Kinsley, 1993).[3] Conversely, the Brahma Kumaris' conception of the kalpa spans a mere 5,000 years in which a particular soul may be born up to 84 times with this being determined by the innate potential of the soul. The more pure (soul conscious) souls will take the maximum number of births per cycle (84) while others may take just one and spend the rest of the 5,000 year cycle in the soul world. In this way, every soul experiences both 'liberation' in the soul world and 'bondage' on the physical plane and passes through pure (*sato*), middling (*rajo*) and impure (*tamo*) stages searching for the spiritual knowledge it has lost. This search is governed again by the soul's innate capacity. For example, the 'well' souls (Raja Yogis) will search harder than the 'glass' souls who in turn will search harder than the body-conscious 'thimble souls'. At the end of the cycle or 'world drama' the souls return to the soul world and are perfected so as to begin the cycle again, with the 'well' souls descending first, followed by the 'glass' and 'thimble' souls (see O'Donnell, 1995, pp. 100, 151-2). But what is the 'world drama'?

> The drama is the story of human souls, their rise and fall, victory and defeat, happiness and suffering, knowledge and ignorance, liberation and bondage...of good and evil forces and of the different stages through which the souls pass in five different epochs. It is a story of how the souls mistakenly identify themselves with their perishable bodies and how this leads to a decline in all levels of human activity... until souls turn again to God and restore their true identities and regain their former spiritual heights. Decline, consequences of the law of cause and effect, the emergence of vices, the increase in worship, the advent of pure souls as the founders of pure religions, the emergence of many religions, the growth of fanaticism and confusion, war and disease, and finally the liberation of souls from their self-created bondages; these are the salient features of the drama (ibid., p. 75).

Thus we have the basis of a 'drama' in four 'acts' stemming from prehistory to the present and beyond, about the 'fall' of humanity from a state of perfection (soul-consciousness) on both the personal and global level in the Golden Age to one of degradation (body-consciousness) and ultimately destruction in the Iron Age before the souls return to perfection to begin again *ad infinitum*.

The prehistoric Golden Age (*Sat Yuga* or 'Age of Truth'), as its name suggests was the period of perfection or 'heaven on earth'. However, unlike the prehistory of current understanding complete with dinosaurs or proto-humans, the Brahma Kumaris claim that 'our ancestors were neither monkeys nor cave dwellers but human beings who had a deep and natural understanding of the world they inhabited' (ibid., p. 83). It is a world that draws heavily on the symbolism of Lekhraj's early life as a jeweller and friend of the monarchy.

In this age a small number of (pure, Raja Yogi) souls exist in *Bharat* (India) in a perfect system based on spiritual hierarchy of divine values. Each member will be ascribed the role befitting their natural qualities, with some being subjects and others being rulers; 'there is no sorrow, but there is a difference between wealthy and less wealthy people...There will be differences, but no one will have sorrow' (Brahma Kumaris World Spiritual University, 1996, p. 44). Similarly,

> The king and the people are equal. Even though there are different types of status, all live as a family. No one will say that this one is a servant. There will be positions and there will be work, but there will not be the feeling of service being a servant (ibid., pp. 42-3).

The monarchy during the Golden Age is referred to as 'Sun Dynasty' and lasts for eight generations, the first emperor and empress being Lekhraj and Radhe, incarnated as the Hindu deities Narayan and Lakshmi respectively. This is the perfect human state, a system 'held together like a perfect, crystal lattice [where] everything is at its highest stage of purity and beauty [and] concepts such as value, profit and loss, misery, property, sorrow and death do not exist' (ibid., p. 83). This society knows no shortages, ill health nor famine and so trade and exchange is carried our purely for the purposes of distribution. It is:

> the peak of human civilisation in every field of human endeavour; teaching, music, government, drama, linguistics, painting and science...[where]...only the best materials are used in the construction of perfect architecture, the best that nature can provide: gold, diamonds, rubies, etc...[and] Art, dance and music are at their most expressive (op. cit., p. 84).

As all souls exist in a vision of universal brotherhood and live by the law of love, there is no need for law or law courts. Moreover, there is no need for political or religious philosophies as the monarchy 'treat their subjects as their own mothers and fathers would'. There is also no need for 'ministers or advisors because of [the monarch's] inherent wisdom and divinity'. Although 'there are meetings to organise and programmes to attend, there is no concept of the word "problem" nor the word "advice"' (op. cit., p. 85). There is therefore no imposition of order or authoritarianism but a 'vision of brotherly love'; a society in tune with each other and so there is no challenging of the status quo. Indeed, 'the very idea of "challenging" does not exist...[as] natural law is at work' (op. cit., p. 86).

The Silver Age (*Treta Yuga* or 'Three Quarters age') begins with the changing of dynasties, the end of the Sun Dynasty of Lakshmi and Narayan and the beginning of the twelve generation rule of the Moon Dynasty of Rama and Sita. During this period there is still hardly any sorrow or negativity although there is slightly more than in the previous Age because of the increasing numbers of souls descending from the soul world. This necessitates the expansion and division of the kingdom into principalities as well as meaning that resources begin to be spread more thinly. However, more importantly, those souls being born are progressively less pure. Over the generations, these souls forget their 'true nature' and gradually begin to be 'tempted' by 'the world of the senses and sensual desires'. This descent into body-consciousness eventually reaches such a point that the souls become one with the material world. This is marked particularly by souls beginning to procreate physically rather than continuing to procreate, as they had in the Golden Age, through yogic intercourse. Indeed, Lekhraj himself, in the guise of King Vikramaditya, helps in this process by commissioning the carving of erotic temple art (Babb, 1986). This situation, Raja Yogis claim is represented in the Biblical Fall, the myth of the sinking of Atlantis or the creation of 'hell on earth'.

The Copper Age (*Dwapur Yuga* or 'Age of Duality') marks the beginning of both recorded history and 'the search to gain back the lost paradise...though it is truly "lost"' (op. cit., p. 90). The population that once existed in the paradise kingdom become scattered over the globe, although (fortunately for a Indian-based movement) 'the majority still remain in India' (op. cit., p. 92). Some of the population are said to have become isolated and degenerate into what are seen as 'primitive' societies while others move from India to Egypt, Sumeria and Babylon still possessing their advanced technology, presumably building the Sphinx and Pyramids. However, these too eventually begin to degenerate and either somehow lose or forget how to use their advanced Golden Age technology. However, deep within themselves, the souls remember vague memories of their former state and begin to create religions and philosophical systems to rationalise what has occurred. During this age, the major world religions are founded in an attempt to regain this knowledge. However, rather than uniting peoples, these merely serve to increasingly divide individuals and cultures. New, progressively more impure, souls descend from the soul world and take their places within conflicting ideologies and faiths in different cultures.

During the Iron Age (*Kali Yuga* or 'Age of Death'), 'the search for something higher is becoming desperate, as impurity and decadence become extreme [as] human beings by this time are totally chained to the vices, creating unlimited sorrow and unrest' (O'Donnell, 1995, p. 93). Moral, ethical and spiritual values continue to decline as more and more impure souls continue to descend from the soul world. Chaos and anarchy begin to grow and the souls 'are continually being incited on the basis of language, religion and political belief...against themselves, others and nature'. Religion is supplanted by science, which replaces spiritual values with 'gross materialism' and most importantly provides 'the weapons and equipment...which can bring about the physical transformation [mass destruction] of the world'. In the final moments of the Iron Age, 'souls are liberated from their bodies and return to the soul world. The river of history has run its full course' (ibid.).

During these final 'moments' of the Iron Age, the Confluence Age (*Sangam Yuga* or 'Age of Illumination') begins in order to prepare the lucky few ('well') souls for the new Golden Age. This is hallmarked on the physical plane by Shiva Baba's descent into the body of Dada Lekhraj and the founding of the Brahma Kumaris (who will establish the New Age) and on the spiritual plane by the appearance of the subtle region, discussed previously, that only exists during this age. It is here that these souls 'can enter into such a powerful and detached state of meditation that its rays reach back to the physical plane, adding fuel to the flames of destruction of all that is old and impure'. It is also here where the Raja Yogi may have an 'incorporeal meeting with Shiva Baba...through the angelic form of Brahma [Lekhraj]' (ibid., p. 125).

This history is also expressed within Raja Yoga through the notion of the *World Tree* that represents the beginning, growth, decay and, ultimately, rebirth of all civilisation. Using this image, Shiva Baba is the essence of the tree, the seed from which the tree grows. From this seed comes the foundation of the tree, the true spiritual knowledge that has been rediscovered by the Brahma Kumaris. The trunk of the tree is formed during the Golden and Silver Ages. The unity of the souls, with 'one religion, one culture, one language and one system of government' (ibid., p. 111), being reflected in the single, strong trunk. During the Copper Age, the solid trunk begins to branch out into numerous religions, philosophies and ideologies. Finally, during the Iron Age, each soul (leaf) hangs helplessly onto a particular twig (philosophy, ideology or religion), distant from the solid trunk and the seed.

However, at the point of the tree's optimum growth during the Confluence Age Shiva Baba comes into being in order to 'plant a new tree'. This represents the meeting of the old age and the new; the destruction of the Iron Age and the creation of a new heaven on earth – the Golden Age. This is achieved by Shiva Baba coming:

> to reactivate the 'root-souls', those very souls who had participated in the creation of the tree at the end of the previous cycle and who had later taken birth during the Golden and Silver Ages...[by]... reminding them who they are, and through them His message spreads to all souls of all religions (op. cit., p. 117).

To this end, He adopts a physical body (Dada Lekhraj) in order to transmit the knowledge and give the human souls a spiritual rebirth. In this way, the Brahma Kumaris are the pure 'root souls' who are 're-activated' in order to perform the task of (re)creating the new spiritual age. This knowledge then goes on to form the basis for the spiritual knowledge of the next cycle *ad infinitum*. Thus, the Brahma Kumaris claim that rather than developing out of Hinduism or any other of the world's religions or philosophical systems it is in fact their basis. The meaning behind the tree is that far from different religions being paths to the same source, they are in fact paths *away* from the source, Shiva Baba. In contrast, the teachings of Raja Yoga are seen to represent the remembering of the truth of the cycle or the world tree. It is the true path from which all faiths have deviated.

The Brahma Kumaris and Hinduism

In the above exposition, I have presented Raja Yoga as it was presented in the literature and taught to me in the 'Foundation Course in Raja Yoga' in early 1998. Like a tower of wooden blocks, it is possible to see how each belief rests on the foundation of a previous belief or beliefs. For example, the belief that one's 'true self' is a non-physical point of light provides a basis for the idea of reincarnation which in turn provides a basis for the belief in cyclic time. However, looking at these beliefs one may argue that they in turn rest on another set of 'wooden blocks', those of the Hindu religious experience – specifically the Brahmana or Vedanta tradition.

What I intend to convey through this is the manner in which the Brahma Kumaris, like other Hindu 'reform' movements of the post-colonial era, drew on a Hindu metaphor – for example references to the Bhagavad Gita, Shiva, and the kalpa – and Hindu practice – most evidently yoga and dietary requirements – and radically reinterpreted them into a new theodical model that is then projected backwards into the past (see King, 1999). Kranenborg (1999) in his article *Brahma Kumaris: A New Religion?* develops this idea, arguing that rather than representing a new religion *per se* the Brahma Kumaris clearly belong to a trajectory stemming from the Hindu tradition. Having said this, however, he does acknowledge that the University's emphasis on gender, and its increasing use of a psychological and New Age metaphor does not stem from this source nor does its use of channelling. For example, Raja Yoga, itself a reference to the Yoga Sutra of Patanjali, utilises notions of karma, the physical world as maya, a model of time as cyclic (kalpa) as well as referring to the Supreme Being as Shiva, the first monarchy as Lakshmi and Narayan and situating the Golden Age kingdom in Bharat.

However, in many respects, particularly in the case of Shiva, the Brahma Kumaris' rendition is radically different. As I argued above, whereas in Indian mythology Shiva is characterised as both erotic and ascetic and is represented as a phallic linga, the Brahma Kumaris reject the erotic, phallic aspect and emphasise the ascetic. Similarly, karma and reincarnation are reinterpreted so as to deny the possibility of humans being reborn as animals to repay karmic debts. For example, one Raja Yogi told me that she believed that disabled individuals, who were unable to express their emotions to others and instead merely received love, were the souls of those who in a previous life were unable to receive, cherish or understand such emotions while, as McGovern (1996) notes, in some cases the Holocaust is seen to be a result of Jewish 'bad karma'. Moreover, celibacy and renunciation of the secular life have clear precedents within Indian culture, as evidenced by Sanyasi monks or by the custom for higher caste males in their latter years to withdraw from work and family and live a spiritual life (Kinsley, 1993). However, whereas these are traditionally male domains, within Raja Yoga they are open to all (Babb, 1984, 1986).

Nevertheless, the most significant re-interpretation of Brahmana cosmology concerns the kalpa, which the Brahma Kumaris have severely truncated from 4,320,000,000 to a mere 5,000 years. As Babb notes, what Lekhraj appears to have done with the kalpa is accept the standard dating for the *Mahabharata* war and the beginning of Kali Yuga (3102 BCE) and then simply placed all of recorded history into the period between then and now. This then serves to re-invest the cycle with psychological meaning. Whereas in the standard kalpa the 'very large numbers express a disposition toward the world, devaluing history by miniaturising events in relation to almost unimaginably spacious vistas of time', the Brahma Kumaris' view of the kalpa as a mere 5,000 years signifies that 'the time ahead is much shorter than you think' (Babb, 1986, p. 124; see also Babb, 1982; Kinsley, 1993, p. 90). Similarly, the present is re-invested with an urgent meaning, with limited time being left for the individual soul to both reach spiritual purity and to endure worldly persecution and sufferings. In this way, the urgency of the Brahma Kumaris' kalpa both justifies the necessity of their (early) world-rejection (to prepare in the limited time for the new Golden Age) as well as relativising external persecution which is seen as ending shortly with the destruction of the world and the beginning of a new cycle. Indeed, within this new (Golden) age the souls who remembered their true nature, the Brahma Kumaris, will live a regal existence and be the very deities that their persecutors worship.

This may be seen as just one example of the manner in which Raja Yoga manifests clear world-rejecting tendencies. Another, more fundamental division, as I have argued, concerns the qualitative distinction that is emphasised between the inner and the outer world and between body and soul. Within Raja Yoga, the inner life is seen to represent all that is true, eternal and good while the outer is seen to represent all that is false, transient and evil. This may be represented in tabular form – table 4.1.

Table 4.1 Comparison of the view of the 'internal' and 'external' world presented within Raja Yoga

Characteristic	Inner/Soul	Outer/Body
Nature	Eternal True Knowledge/Remembrance	Transient Maya Ignorance/forgetting
Consciousness	Soul Consciousness	Body Consciousness
Knowledge of God	Personal contact with true nature of God (Shiva Baba)	False (e.g. linga) or no contact with God
Karma	Sukarma: Ability to deal with karmic accounts	Vikarma: Inability to deal with karmic accounts
World Drama	Knowledge of Cycle and one's part within it	False or no understanding of Cycle
Type of Soul	'Well' soul. First to descend from Soul World	'Thimble' soul. Last to descend from Soul World
Descent into Physical Plane during	Golden Age	Iron Age
Strength of Intellect	Strong	Weak
Perception	Spiritual 'third eye'	Sensory

This is by no means an exhaustive list but I hope that it serves to emphasise the strong qualitative distinction that is drawn within Raja Yoga between the inner and the outer 'worlds'. For example, whereas the internal realm is characterised by knowledge of one's true self and personal contact with the true God (Shiva Baba), the external realm (maya) only leads to a false or inaccurate understanding of both the self and God. Similarly, whereas the inner represents the knowledge of true spirituality, the outer represents its ignorance or degraded form.

This distinction may be further emphasised with reference to the lifestyle recommended to Raja Yogis, or, as it is known within the University, 'the Four Pillars of Raja Yoga': 'sattvic diet', celibacy, regular study and practice of Raja Yoga and 'good company'. For example, the eating of meat or food that has not 'been prepared by someone in the loving remembrance of God and who is following a path of purity [a Raja Yogi]' is seen as 'definite hindrances to meditation' in that it corrupts both body and soul (O'Donnell, 1995, p. 166). The Raja Yogi therefore adheres to a sattvic diet of vegetarianism. Similarly, 'sex-lust' is seen as a barrier to soul consciousness by encouraging body-conscious desires and processes. As O'Donnell succinctly puts it, 'It is a "soul-trap"...the nectar of God communion and the negative influence of "sex-lust" do not mix' (ibid., p. 168). Therefore, the Raja Yogi is enjoined to live a celibate lifestyle and keep 'good company' with Raja Yogis as opposed to the bad company of body-conscious outsiders. Indeed, according to O'Donnell again, as aspirants progress in their yoga, they will naturally find themselves in the company of like-minded people and less and less so in the company of those body-conscious souls leading 'artificial lives'. Finally, to underpin all this, the Raja Yogi should study and practice Raja Yoga regularly.

To apply the work of Mary Douglas (1995a, 1995b), I would argue that these practices as well as the previously discussed distinction between the inner and outer world, serves to represent in symbolic form the Brahma Kumaris' relationship to the outside world during their early, world-rejecting years as well as providing a set of guidelines for delineating themselves from 'polluting' others. Within Raja Yoga the physical body represents symbolically the social body, its 'inner' world representing the Brahma Kumaris and the external representing the 'outside world'. Moreover, control of the body through yogic practice is directly related to strong social control within the group itself. To paraphrase the title of one of Douglas' books on this phenomenon, the 'internal' represents all that is characterised by *purity* while the 'outer' is characterised by *danger*. Indeed, the ideal Brahma Kumaris lifestyle detailed above may be seen as a method for controlling and dealing with (dangerous) events or persons that threaten the group's purity (see Douglas, 1995a, pp. 40-1). For example, vegetarianism, celibacy, 'good company' and regular study delineate the pure (insiders) from the dangerous (outsiders), while simultaneously strengthening the pure's vision of themselves *vis-à-vis* the outside world. By following the recommended lifestyle a symbolic (bodily) boundary is thereby drawn between the inner and outer world while simultaneously the outside danger is controlled to some degree.

Indeed, considering this division, it is somewhat ironic that currently the University is actively courting the very outsiders that its theodicy was designed to protect itself from. What is even more noteworthy is the manner in which it has re-interpreted its message in order to attract new (*ipso facto* outsider) membership by appealing to their instrumental, worldly lifestyles through a New Age metaphor of 'self spirituality'. The theodicy that developed as a reaction to the instrumentalism of the outer world is now being promulgated and utilised in a heavily-diluted fashion to attract outsiders by appealing to their materialistic concerns.

2. The Instrumental

In the first part of this chapter I argued that Raja Yoga may best be conceptualised as a form of Hinduism characterised by a strong emphasis on the qualitative distinction between the inner and outer world both physically and metaphysically. I went on to relate this to the social conditions in which it developed and argued that it represented symbolically the Brahma Kumaris' reaction to the persecution of the outside world as well as offering a set of techniques to both control and minimise this danger and to delineate the 'elect' from the 'forsaken'.

Relating this more explicitly to the analysis presented in the previous chapter, two points may be made. Firstly, the University has assimilated elements of the various world traditions and philosophies which it has encountered through its internationalisation. Secondly, stemming from this, in doing so it has developed more of a world ambivalent stance. These two strands are manifested in the

University's attempt to attract membership and promote its message on the international stage by offering spiritually-based introductory courses in instrumental, worldly issues such as 'stress management' and 'positive thinking'. It would be a gross over-simplification, however, to suggest that the Brahma Kumaris have rejected their original message and simply become world-affirming. Rather, as I discussed in the previous chapter, the situation is more subtle. The development of these instrumental courses represents another example of the Brahma Kumaris' world-ambivalence and another level of its re-interpretation of its message to suit a larger audience that would potentially be put off by its original world-rejecting message.

In this way, the courses serve to introduce the basic concepts of Raja Yoga and a spiritually-based life to individuals while simultaneously satisfying their instrumental desires. Put crudely, it may be seen as an attempt to get individuals through the door of the centres by offering them courses in inter and intra-personal skills, with the hope that there will be a form of 'interpretative drift' and that they will stay on to learn about the University's spiritual message (Luhrmann, 1996). However, as I shall discuss below, this would appear to be at odds with the University's original message of spiritual exclusivity as well as their view of radical and imminent world 'transformation'.

Positive Thinking and Stress-Free Living

In many ways the positive thinking and stress-free living courses may be best envisaged as preliminary introductions to Raja Yoga in which any overtly spiritual language is replaced by a more psychological language and in which spiritual goals are represented as instrumental ones. Both courses begin with the assertion that negativity and stress are not ideal states and that the ideal state 'which everyone is looking for' is positivity and stress-free living respectively. The courses then offer both a method to overcome this (the Raja Yoga meditation technique) backed by a philosophy that humans are inherently stress-free/positive but have forgotten this because of the dehumanisation of the modern (external) world. The key that is presented to achieve this goal is the knowledge of one's 'true nature' and a lifestyle based on this knowledge. This 'true nature' is however replaced with a more western, psychological metaphor: 'soul' becomes 'self' while 'purity' becomes 'stress-free' or 'positive'. Similarly, the previously introduced notion of sanskars are replaced with 'sub-conscious' while the super-ego like intellect is replaced by the quasi-spiritual 'Higher-Self'. In all other respects, however, the basic message is still the same; negativity/stress is caused by basing one's self image on the external world of circumstances, people or past experience (body-consciousness). In contrast, positivity/stress-free living is based on a self-image stemming from one's internal world of love, peace and strength (soul-consciousness). In order to develop this latter image, it is necessary to awaken the Higher-Self (intellect) so that negative thoughts may be subjected to scrutiny (*vis-à-vis* one's true nature) before they are manifested as behaviour.

This is said to lead to freedom ('the ability to express what I want when I want') and choice ('free from external resources, relying on inner resources of peace, love strength') rather than being the captive of acquired reactions that lead to 'dependency, lack of self-respect, more influence, lack of clarity, mistakes, waste of time and energy, stress [and] too many choices'. It also results in, recalling the law of karma, positive returns to the sender, with positive intention leading to positive responses, the giving of love leading to the receiving of love, the giving of respect leading to the receiving of respect and a sense of self-confidence leading to the confidence of others.

A number of experiential exercises were presented during the sessions for individuals to practice at home and then discuss at the next session. The first, stemming from the belief that we can create our thoughts, was to transform negative thoughts into positive thoughts by listening to internal influence through the process of *SOS*:

Stand Back
Observe
Steer

This involves initially standing back from a situation, 'I pause and put things in perspective', observing 'my thoughts and remembering I have a choice over what I think' and finally, 'gently beginning to create the type of [positive] thoughts I wish to think – free from external influence, negative thoughts about myself, other people and situations'. The next exercise, to create a positive image was based on three steps. Firstly, *Stand Back from Problems* and accept that 'problems don't last forever. Tomorrow holds a solution' which may be perceived by standing back from the situation and clearing the mind. Secondly, *Dis-identity from Possessions* by accepting the distance between one's role and 'true' self. Thirdly, See *Something Positive in Everyone* as a 'positive attitude creates positive reactions and spreads positivity'. Finally, through meditation one may 'learn to keep in touch with myself – *my true self*', leading to the emergence of inner qualities of contentment, peace, love and compassion during meditation; 'I think my true qualities and experience them:- Peace, Love, Power, Joy, Silence. Slowly I build a new personality exactly as I want to be...no fear, confidence, lightness, wisdom and happiness.'[4]

In the final session these techniques were placed in the larger context of '*Eight Ways to Help us Manage our Lives*':

> *Being Conscious*: taking the time to reflect on the day as well as listening to the self;
> *Observation*: becoming aware of how thoughts are created and how external influences affect us for the worse;
> *Detachment*: standing back from situations;
> *Recovery*: not blaming the self but accepting that 'it's ok to fail' and being more forgiving of the self;
> *Understanding Time*: making space for inner silence and peace;
> *Managing Myself*: not allowing others to rule one's life;
> *Rebuilding Self-Respect*: only when I have respect for myself can I truly care for others';
> *Meditating Every Day*: in order to 'stop being a human-*doing* and become a human-*being*'.[5]

Thus, as with the original 'ascetic' teachings the emphasis is on introspection as a basis for individual growth and an understanding of one's true inner nature as a basis for change.

Conclusion: Spiritual Teachings, Instrumental Concerns?

What I hope to have demonstrated in this chapter is the bifurcation within the Brahma Kumaris World Spiritual University between the original, world-rejecting (ascetic) theodicy and a more recent quasi-spiritual, world-affirming re-interpretation. Thus, the instrumental courses provide both an experiential and philosophical basis to the original, world-rejecting theodicy, albeit with any overtly spiritual ideas such as soul, purity, karma being replaced with more psychological *cum* New Age terminology such as 'self' and 'higher self'. This then, ideally, serves as a way of getting individuals thinking in a certain way by introducing spiritual ideas in the guise of instrumental concerns and issues. For example, to return to the 'wooden blocks' metaphor utilised previously, the idea that one is an inherently stress-free/positive self, whose negativity is brought about through identification with the pressures of life and whose 'true nature' may be brought about through 'awakening the higher self' draws on and leads logically onto the basic assumptions of Raja Yoga. In this way, a basic set of comparisons may be drawn up – table 4.2.

Table 4.2 Comparison between terminology presented in 'ascetic' and 'instrumental' renditions of Raja Yoga

'The Ascetic'	'The Instrumental'
Soul	Self
Intellect, Sanskars	Higher Self, Sub-consciousness
Purity	Inherent positivity, stress-free nature of self
Karma	Returns of positive for positive, negative for negative
Soul Consciousness	Awareness of 'true nature' of inner world
Body Consciousness	Identification with negativity/stress of external world

To return to the analysis presented in the previous chapter, this re-interpretation may be seen as both an example of the University's current world-ambivalence and also as a result of their internationalisation programme. In other words, this bifurcation of Raja Yoga between world-rejecting and world-affirming elements, or rather the utilisation of an originally world-rejecting theodicy for world-affirming purposes, expresses on a central level the University's current world-ambivalence. It would appear from this that the University accepts, and indeed promulgates, two largely mutually exclusive elements within its teachings. On the one hand there is the emphasis on a strict demarcation from the corrupt outside world and the preparation by the few for their life as deities in the Golden Age, while on the other there is the application of these values towards instrumental, world-affirming purposes for the many. Other levels of potential contradiction within the University's current world orientation may further be pointed out in relation to the notion of cyclic time. For example, as discussed in the previous chapter, there is the image of the University campaigning on the world stage for global love, peace and understanding while simultaneously holding the view that the end of the world is pre-determined and, more importantly, close. It logically stems from the nature of the cycle that global human affairs are naturally pre-determined within the law of karma with previous events in the cycle determining the future. Indeed, the future, in terms of the end of one cycle and the beginning of another, brings the individual back to his/her current situation in the present cycle. In this way, despite the emphasis within the literature on global and indeed personal change, such things are seen as a naturally pre-determined part of the cycle with human choice being seen as similarly pre-determined. To quote Dadi Janki, 'both pre-destination and free will work together. If there isn't a proper understanding of both these concepts and how they work together, difficult situations will slow you down or even stop you' and again

> the interesting thing about the concept of destiny is that, as well as being in your hands to create, it is also pre-determined. It is important to understand how these two concepts – usually thought to be contradictory – in fact work together, for our own exclusive benefit (Stillerman, pp. 113-14).

Similarly, the internationalisation programme has required the University to attempt to broaden its appeal by offering such instrumental courses while assimilating elements of western philosophy, religion and culture into its framework. As Babb (1986) notes, this is often the University's policy in India with, for example, the assimilation of Hindu festivals – such as *Diwali* – into its own calendar. Similarly, within the West, the University is able to assimilate elements of particular religious and spiritual systems of thought. For example, the world denial of Gnosticism and Neo-Platonism are seen as stemming from the pure seed of Raja Yoga, as are Christian notions of 'reaping what you sow'.

Moreover, scientific theories are also often utilised to provide symbolic representations or evidence for a particular view. This is again somewhat ironic in that the Brahma Kumaris' view of history as only 5,000 years *ipso facto* sets them against the scientific, geological and historical orthodoxy. This irony is perhaps best emphasised by the fact that one of the buildings within the grounds of the Global Retreat Centre in Oxford is utilised by Oxford University to house palaeontological finds, specifically dinosaur bones. Nevertheless, scientific theories are often brought to bear in relation to elements of Raja Yoga, such as comparing Newton's first law to karma or theories of atomic physics to the study of the soul, as well as various attempts to 'scientifically prove' that humanity is indeed less old than conventionally held. For example, chapter headings in Jagdish Chander's book *The Eternal World Drama* include *Is Evolution Theory Universally Accepted? Views of Some Prominent Scientists Against It* (chapter 7), *Were Apes the Ancestors of Man or Now Man has Become an Ape* (chapter 10), *How Old is Our Globe? Great Controversy Among Scientists. Constant Revision of their Estimates* (chapter 12 & 13) (Chander, 1998a; see also Chander, 1988b). Again, this is justified on the basis that these are corrupted fragments of the basic, underlying 'truths' rediscovered by the Brahma Kumaris.

The Brahma Kumaris: Institutional and Personal Reflexivity

In this and the previous chapter I have concentrated on the historical development of the Brahma Kumaris World Spiritual University and its message. This has focused particularly on a discernible shift from an orientation of world-rejection, manifested in a theodicy characterised by the rejection of the outer life, to a more world-ambivalent orientation, in which the original theodicy interacts with a recently developed world-affirming spiritually-based instrumentalism. This latter (instrumental) form I have argued, develops out of the former (ascetic) and may be seen as offering an introduction to the former for those who may be put off by overt spirituality through appealing to their instrumental, worldly lives and their personal empowerment. I have also pointed out other possible points of ambivalence between this and the original message, focusing particularly on issues of pre-determination and choice as well as the viability of personal development within a framework of an immediate and radical apocalypse.

This analysis has been informed by typologies of New Religious Movements emphasising their status *vis-à-vis* 'the world'; e.g. 'deviant responses to the world' (Wilson), 'orientation to the world' (Wallis). However, this criterion has been criticised by Dawson (1997) on the basis of its implicit Troeltschian emphasis on the tension between sect and Church, representing protest and dominant structures respectively. In contrast he proposes the utilisation of the Weberian criterion of mode of membership and subsequent form of social organisation. Relating this back to the three methods of investigating reflexive traditions proposed by Mellor, Dawson would appear to be proposing the analysis of 'personal reflexivity' (i.e. the interaction of the individual member and normative structures) as utilised by Howell and Nelson (1997, 1998) rather than the analysis of 'inter-tradition' or organisational development (i.e. the sect-church-sect shift) or an 'intra-tradition' analysis emphasising the relationship of the organisation to 'the world' (*à la* Wallis and Wilson). However, as I have shown, in the case of the Brahma Kumaris, changing modes of membership were the result of a shift in world orientation and response. Similarly, while analysis of membership may reveal, for example, differing levels of commitment, this arguably only makes sense when related back to the University's international development and shift in world orientation/response. In this way, following on from the previous two chapters' concern with institutional and theodical developments within the University (intra/inter-traditional reflexivity), I propose now to turn to the analysis of 'personal reflexivity', specifically – in the light of Dawson's comments – the analysis of the relationship(s) between individual members and the University's normative structures.

Notes

[1] This definition is based on that presented within the Brahma Kumaris' literature, see for example O'Donnell (1995, p. 4).
[2] See Walter and Waterhouse (1999) and Walter (2001) for a discussion of different historical and cross-cultural views of reincarnation.
[3] Basham (1967, pp. 323-4), however, in his discussion of the kalpa doubles this figure to 311,040,000 million years by incorporating the 'Night of Brahma' also. In addition, he has each kalpa divided into fourteen manavantaras of 306,720,000 years. Each of these manavantaras contains seventy-one Mahāyugas, each of which is divided into four yugas: [Krita], Tretā, Dvāpara and Kali (4,800, 3,600, 2,400 and 1,200 'years of the gods' respectively).
[4] Another exercise directed toward this end consisted of :

> (1) Begin your day by creating positive thoughts about yourself (2) During the day try to be aware of your thoughts and words – especially positive ones! (3) Every night review your day and remember when you had negative thoughts about someone or any situation - keep a notebook if it helps.

[5] All these examples are taken from my fieldnotes.

Chapter 5

Users, Drifters and Searchers: A Typology of Brahma Kumaris Membership Patterns

As we saw in the previous chapter, the question 'Who am I?', and its answer ('*Om Shanti*, I am a peaceful soul'), is of paramount importance to the Brahma Kumaris, providing the ontological basis for both everyday life and metaphysical speculation. Going further, one may argue that the goal of Raja Yoga is the (re)definition and (re)construction of the individual's identity on the basis of its 'true', forgotten characteristics. To this end, it provides knowledge and a set of metaphysical tools to affect this change from stress, negativity and body-consciousness to 'stress-free living', positivity and soul-consciousness.

Within this chapter I intend to explore three inter-related questions pertaining to individuals' use of Raja Yoga in the ongoing reconstruction and redefining of their identity.[1] Firstly, what are the socio-demographic backgrounds of the people who attend the University's events? Howell and Nelson (1997) have already addressed themselves to the socio-demographic makeup of the Brahma Kumaris, although their analysis focuses exclusively both on Australian patterns and on full-time members at the expense of those less-committed. In contrast my own analysis draws on responses from a range of individuals within the UK representing the whole scope of membership, from those who attend infrequently and do not follow the teachings to any extent through to senior members. In this way, whilst making no strong claims to being representative, I hope to provide a sketch of the general membership patterns that I encountered through my participant observation.[2] Secondly, why are such individuals attracted to groups like the Brahma Kumaris, what are their motivations? Finally – and arguably most importantly – what are the consequences of membership on these individuals' life narratives? To this end, after discussing broadly the University's socio-demographic composition, I will propose a fourfold typology of ideal membership types based on my interviews and discussions with members. Stemming from the analysis presented in the previous chapter, this will focus on a distinction between those drawn for instrumental reasons, who I will refer to as 'Instrumental Users' and 'Eclectic Users', and those who, for a variety of reasons, are drawn for more spiritual ones, who I will refer to as 'Spiritual Searchers'. I will also discuss individuals, who I will refer to as 'Interpretative Drifters', who were initially drawn to the University for instrumental reasons but now continue to attend its events for more spiritual ones. Finally, I will discuss how these membership styles relate to the thesis that I have been developing in the preceding chapters.

Before doing so, however, it would be pertinent to briefly describe the different ways in which individuals may first encounter the University. Amongst those I spoke to the most popular method of introduction was friends recommending the courses in 'stress-free living', positive thinking or self-esteem to each other. This was particularly the case at the Chesterfield centre, where a number of those who attend its events have known 'Pam', the centre co-ordinator, through her work in schools or through her past involvement with a local church. For example, one interviewee recalled how her first contact with the University:

> was something that was passed on to me. The letter of introduction from Pam was sent to a minister from church and she passed it onto me. She said 'you go and find out what it's all about and tell me'.

Likewise, another told me:

> well, I know Pam from work, and...since she'd retired from work I didn't realise what she was doing. And then she came to work and gave a talk one night because we'd got an OFSTED inspection and I think she thought that she could come and give us a talk to give us a bit of a boost and bit of confidence [through] positive thinking.

This was often linked with the method whereby I first encountered the University, the 'Stress-free Living and Positive Thinking Courses in Chesterfield' leaflet on display in the foyer of the town library. Often, tracing back through the friends cited above, one finds that an 'original friend' had discovered the University in this way.

The University's active self-promotion through lectures, fairs and open-days was another popular method of introduction. As part of my fieldwork I attended two of these events. The first was a well attended lecture on positive thinking (*Self Esteem – The Secret of Sustained Success*) given by senior sister Maureen Goodman at a local library to advertise a soon-to-begin course in positive thinking. Aside from Goodman's lecture on stress-free living and self-esteem, the event consisted of songs, a guided meditation and questions from the audience. After the event, attendees were also given small gifts of 'Virtue Reality' dice,[3] containing small, home-made cakes. Similarly, in late June 1998 I attended a similar open-day run by the Global Retreat Centre in Oxford (*Through the Looking Glass – A Magical Adventure of Self-Discovery*) that aimed to attract local residents into attending positive thinking classes. At this event, guests were able to attend lectures and meditation classes and also wander around the Retreat Centre and its grounds. In the evening there was music and songs and the members living in the Centre performed a Raja-Yoga-influenced adaptation of several scenes from Lewis Carroll's *Through the Looking Glass*. As Babb (1986, p. 94) has noted, such events have been a prominent marketing tool of the University since at least the early 1960s. Drawing on his fieldwork in India, he notes how the Brahma Kumaris 'are inveterate sponsors of exhibitions, often associated with Hindu festivals, to which they give wide publicity in newspaper advertisements'. At these exhibitions individuals are shown large pictorial representations of, for example, Lekhraj,

Shiva, the World Drama or the Golden Age, 'encouraged to purchase literature, and urged to visit one of the movement's many local centres' (op. cit.). Another prominent feature of such events, evidenced by the attendance of *Bee Gee* Robin Gibb and Uri Geller at the Oxford event, is the conspicuous presence of public figures, particularly those involved in business or politics, as guests of honour. These figures are typically photographed with senior members of the University, their photographs appearing in its official newspaper *Purity*. For example, of the 412 pictures published in the twelve 1997 editions of *Purity*, 60% featured members of the University with senior politicians or other social or economic figures; usually presenting a gift, talking with them or sharing a podium at a conference or event. Indeed, 92% of the covers of *Purity* from this year featured such photographs, with the inside-facing page featuring a similar amount (the remaining 8% featured, for example, images of Lekhraj, Mt. Abu or Om Radhe).

The Socio-Demographics of Membership

Turning next to the University's socio-demographic composition, four main observations may be made.

First, the University's membership is predominantly female; the number of female respondents to my questionnaire being almost three times higher than males (73%/27%). This was the case in all the centres that I sampled,[4] and would support my experience of females greatly outnumbering males at all the events organised by the University that I attended during my fieldwork.

Second, as well as there being a gender imbalance, the University's membership is also imbalanced significantly in relation to age. Membership is almost exclusively dominated by the older – mid-life onwards – age cohorts. The number of members sampled who were over forty-five years of age, for example, was almost twice the number of those under forty-five.[5] Indeed the number of those in the 45-54 year age cohort was only slightly higher (1%) than both the 25-34 and the 35-44 cohorts combined. The University's youth membership is virtually non-existent. None of those, for example, that I sampled were aged below twenty-five years of age and my own experience was of meeting only a handful of full-time members of a similar age to myself (mid twenties).[6] Those young people present at centres, usually at social events, attended as part of a family unit with parents who are involved and often appeared to be indifferent to the University's teachings. For example, at a lecture I attended by Dadi Janki, one young person sat wearing headphones passing the latest football results on to his friends. Similarly, at a summer party I overheard young teenagers discussing which local pubs would serve them alcohol underage, while their parents were at the other end of the garden discussing a recent murli. Having said this, some young people (usually students) do participate in the instrumental courses, usually during stressful exam periods. This is capitalised upon to some extent by the University giving presentations and lectures at universities. For example, towards the end of my fieldwork the University organised an event at Sheffield Hallam University – *How to*

Increase Mind Power: A Powerful Mind is a Free Mind – that aimed to 'explore how we can fuel our minds with positive energy through meditation'.

Third, the sample was also dominated by members of non-manual socio-economic groups. Those classified as A, B, or C1 comprised 58% of the sample, whilst those classified as C2, D, or E made up 23%. The remaining 19% comprised students (4%) and those who responded with 'housewife' (15%). This did, however, vary between centres with, for example, the Sheffield centre comprising of 100% C1 and above members, Chesterfield and Leeds having 83% and 64% respectively whilst the centres in Bradford and Hounslow had below 50% (42% and 38% respectively). These centres did however feature a large number of unclassifiable responses, particularly those who responded as 'housewife' when asked about their occupation.

Fourth, moving away from general socio-demographical issues, individual members' length of involvement with the University would not seem to suggest a high degree of long-term involvement. For example, while just under a third of those I sampled had been involved for over a decade, the majority (42%) had only been involved for under five years. Whilst I did find evidence of some degree of longitudinal commitment – although, as we shall see later, this may be sporadic and not necessarily evidence of serious commitment – just over two-thirds of the sample had been involved with the University for less than ten years. This is an interesting point considering the length of the University's involvement within the UK (thirty or so years). Indeed, aside from those involved with the University for a decade or more, the majority of those I sampled had only been involved for between one and two years. This, however, may be explained to some extent by organisational factors such as the growth in the number of centres over the last decade, the University's increased prominence internationally and perhaps most importantly the previously discussed New Age-ification of the original 'ascetic' message which arguably broadens the University's appeal.

In sum, were the reader to walk into a typical Brahma Kumaris event in the UK and sit down, the probability would be that the person sat next to them would be a professional woman in her forties or fifties who would have been involved with the University for under five years, most likely for around two years. By contrast, it would be, statistically speaking, highly improbable that one's neighbour would be a young, working class male or, for that matter, highly unlikely that they would be a male at all.[7] If, however, according to Howell and Nelson (1997), the reader were to attend a similar gathering in Australia the only difference that would be that it would be more likely for their neighbour to be in their mid-thirties. In all other demographical respects, the picture would be very similar. Indeed, these patterns would appear to be cross-cultural, or at least be similar in both India, Australia and the UK. Babb (1984), for example, noted during his ethnography at the University's New Delhi centre how, aside from the gender and age imbalance, the majority of those present were drawn from middle and upper class Government service families.

'Negotiating' *Om Shanti*

The fact that membership of a spiritual organisation or even interest in spiritual matters being dominated by females, particularly middle-class and middle aged females, is in itself not particularly noteworthy. Indeed, one might go so far as to suggest that statistically speaking it would be expected that this group, rather than young, working class, males, would be over-represented within such activities.[8] This is not to say, however, that those who attend the University's events are motivated exclusively by explicitly spiritual or salvational considerations. One of the salient observations of my interviews and discussions was the differing levels of influence that the University's normative structures had on individuals' everyday life. Whereas my participant observation of meetings seemed to suggest, in Foucauldian terms, a situation of individuals being disciplined through yoga, dietary restrictions and the control of social interactions, interviews with those attending the University's events often revealed a completely different picture (see Foucault, 1991, part 3). The picture that emerged was one of individuals participating in the activities for different reasons and with differing levels of seriousness without their having to demonstrate commitment to the University in any form. Nobody, for example, was chastised for their sporadic attendance at meetings, their apparent ignorance of sometimes even the University's most basic tenets (such as the name of its founder) or for not following the recommended lifestyle. There was, in other words, often a high degree of individual malleability, or 'negotiation' between the individual and the University at the level of the centre around issues of commitment, motivation and interest. In this chapter I intend to outline an ideal-typology of the different 'membership styles' based on three main dimensions.

Firstly, an initial broad distinction may be made between those individuals whose involvement with the University stems from a desire for self-improvement and those whose goals are more philosophical or spiritual; that is, to draw again on Campbell's (1978) terminology, between those motivated by 'instrumental' factors and those seeking 'illumination'. Secondly, linked to the above, individuals may be placed on a continuum on the basis of their self-conception, ranging from those possessing a 'material self-conception' to those possessing more of a 'spiritual self-conception'. Finally, drawing on the work of Richard Jenkins (1996), a distinction may be made based on the nature of individuals' social identity.

Jenkins rejects both the view that personal identity and social identity are different and Giddens' thesis that only in late modernity does the former become a focus of reflexivity. Rather, he argues, both personal and social identity 'can be understood as similar (if not exactly the same) in important respects...each is routinely related to – or, better perhaps, entangled with – the other' (Jenkins, 1996, p. 19). Indeed, Jenkins argues, '*both* are intrinsically social' (ibid.), the result of an ongoing process of negotiation; 'it is the systematic establishment and signification between individuals, between collectives, and between individuals and collectives, of the relationships of similarity [that which is *collectively shared*] and difference [that which is *individually unique*]' (ibid., p. 4). Thus, whilst individuals are individually unique and variable, selfhood is thoroughly socially-constructed through, primarily, the process of socialisation and then, on an ongoing basis, through human interactions.

Individual and collective social identities are therefore the result of what he terms an internal-external dialectic of identification, the ongoing synthesis of internal self definition and the external definitions of oneself provided by others. For example, individual identity is formed through the interaction of how we see ourselves ('I am the king of France') and how others see us ('no, you are insane or have delusions of grandeur'). Likewise, collectives may be either internally defined in terms of group identification (e.g. 'we are members of the new religion, *X*') as well as through external social classifications (e.g. 'applying a typology, these people are members of a "sect"'). In both cases, identity is based upon that which makes us to some extent unique and that which, whether we know it or not, we share with others. For example, in defining who 'I' am, an individual necessarily draws upon that which (s)he feels set him or herself apart from others or that which makes them, relatively speaking, unique (their ability on a musical instrument or personal style of playing the said instrument) and that which (s)he shares with others (gender, occupation, nationality and so on). Similarly, in relation to group identities:

> [l]ogically, *in*clusion entails *ex*clusion, if only by default. To define the criteria for membership of any set of objects is, at the same time, also to create a boundary, everything beyond which does not belong...one of the things that *we* have in common is our difference from *others* (op. cit., p. 80).

Nevertheless, like individual identities, collective identities, especially when they are structured within organisations or institutions, are also based upon differences. Thus, whilst all Catholics will share to some extent a similar Catholic identity that will distinguish them from, for example, Protestants or Jews, at a fundamental level amongst all Catholics there is an internal differentiation between those who are ordained to say Mass and those who are not. Similarly, amongst those who possess this sub-identity of priesthood, there is further internal differentiation ranging from the Pope on the one hand through to a novice priest in a small village on the other. In this way, when in the proceeding analysis I distinguish between individual identity and collective identity, I will be seeking to distinguish between those social identities defined by individuals predominantly on the basis of what (s)he perceives to be unique about him- or herself and those, in varying degrees, which are defined predominantly on the basis of a shared identity as a soul-conscious, Raja Yogi and committed member of the University. This is not, of course, to claim that all Raja Yogis are the same or have roughly the same sense of identity, but rather to highlight that despite the obvious individual differences in status, knowledge, experience and so on between a senior Dadi at Mt. Abu and a committed member at a small centre in the UK, both will share a common identity – summed up in the statement *Om Shanti* – that will distinguish them in both an objective and subjective sense from (body conscious) outsiders.

On this basis, then, for the remainder of this chapter, I intend to explore the interaction of personal reflexivity and the University's normative structures by outlining four ideal membership types – *instrumental users, eclectic users, spiritual searchers* and *interpretative drifters* – in relation to the three key inter-linked issues outlined above: goal of involvement, self-conception and nature of social identity. In sum, I will be attempting to ascertain, firstly, why and to what extent individuals choose to place themselves within the University's normative structures and, secondly, the influence of these structures on their ongoing (re)construction of identity.

A Typology of Brahma Kumaris Membership Patterns

Instrumental Users

Instrumental users are initially drawn to the University through what they perceive as the benefits to their life of following a stress-free or positive-thinking life style. Although this is not universally the case, such individuals have typically recently experienced either minor psychological or medical problems or a loss within their personal life, or they generally feel that they are agitated or suffering from stress. For example, 'Janet'[9] became involved with the University in early 1997 after being diagnosed with a serious illness:

> ...they told me not long after that I wasn't very well...And when they told me that, the doctor said 'but you've got to be positive', so I thought 'I need positive thinking. I need Pam' (laughs). So I rang Pam up and that's how I came in the January and I've sort of been popping down since. That's why I started coming.

Similarly, 'David', was attracted by what he referred to as the 'solitary, peaceful, calm way of life':

> I felt at that time there was a lot of anger in my life and I was seeking out peace and calmness really...I feel I want more calmness in my life. I feel there's too much stress in my life (laughs) and so it's a way of unwinding.

Likewise, when instrumental users are asked what they feel they have achieved or, further, what their aim in continuing attending is, they are again likely to respond in predominantly instrumental terms. For example, for 'Betty', as with 'Janet', inner peace and calmness are methods to overcome the stress of her illness:

> *Is there any particular goal that you are aiming for in your practice?*
> To be a better participant in everything...to achieve inner peace.
> *Why would you say that's your goal at the moment?*
> Well, what I've got is very stressful and I feel that if I can calm down and be more peaceful it might help.

'Janet' too emphasised the calming, relaxing benefits of the meditation:

> *Do you think that you have changed in any way since becoming involved with the Brahma Kumaris?*
> A bit calmer and more relaxed, I think.
> *Why do you say that?*
> I listen to my tapes at night before I go to bed and it helps me to relax and helps me to unwind at the end of the day. You feel calmer. You think about what you've done in the day. It brings it all together rather than rushing and tearing from one day to the next, it ends the day off quite nicely.

To instrumental users, then, the Raja Yoga technique represents a means to a particular end rather than being a spiritual end in itself. When asked, they will describe the benefits of Raja Yoga in terms of how it has helped them to become calmer, more relaxed or able to deal with a particular situation or malady more effectively. Sometimes this may even, as in the above example of 'Betty', be expressed in quasi-spiritual or therapeutic terminology, such as 'achieving inner peace' or 'becoming centred'. Indeed, instrumental users may even state that since they have begun meditating they have, on the surface at least, taken up aspects of the University's recommended lifestyle, particularly vegetarianism. However, when questioned further on this, instrumental reasons emerge. 'Mark', for example, during his interview described how he had become a vegetarian since attending meditation classes. However:

> it was more because the doctor said that I had to cut down on my cholesterol (laughs). So I have cut down on meat but the trigger was the doctor rather than the spiritual.

Stemming from their utilisation of Raja Yoga as a tool to empower their life rather than to transcend it (Heelas, 1996e), instrumental users' involvement with the University is often infrequent, usually occurring only when they are able to put time aside and feel that they would benefit from either the meditation or the peaceful environment of the centre. When asked, for example, they will emphasise the benefits of the peaceful or quiet atmosphere within the centre or the friendliness of those present, rather than overtly spiritual reasons, as a factor for their continued involvement:

> I find that just coming and sitting sometimes quietly in [the group meditation room] is really all I want really and it's just nice to sit and be quiet after a busy day at work. I benefit from that...I think the sitting together in a small group that you get to know, I think you do benefit from that; knowing that there's one or two others sitting and enjoying the peace and quiet.

For instrumental users the University's normative structures are somewhat down-played. Instrumental users that I spoke to, although having often been involved with the University for a number of years, were often vague when asked about the normative, spiritual side of the practice. One, for example, referred to the murli as 'Merlin', another referred to Lekhraj as 'Buddha' and yet another to him as 'their [the Brahma Kumaris'] guru'. Another described how the 'spiritual side' of the University's message was 'tricky' for her because of her Christian upbringing.

This apparent vagueness, especially when considered in relation to the strict 'rules and regulations' recommended by the University, was also expressed by 'David':

> It seems that the Brahma Kumaris organisation does not have such a big textbook of rules and regulations which is partly the attraction of it to me. I suppose there must be some textbook of rules and regulations...I know one or two, I guess. I don't think really any rules and regulations of the hierarchy of the organisation really affect my life.

This situation is made all the more noteworthy when it is considered that these individuals have often been attending courses, meditation evenings and discussion groups at a centre for a couple of years. All those I spoke to had, for example, taken the *Foundation Course in Raja Yoga* and attended, albeit erratically, murli classes and evening meditation sessions. Some had also purchased or borrowed tapes and literature from centres. One cannot, therefore, claim that they had not been exposed in some way or another to the University's 'spiritual side'. Part of the answer to this issue lies, I would argue, in instrumental users' attitude to the meditation. As the meditation is being given for free, they feel that they should show respect to the 'giver' by politely listening to murlis, for example, even though they may be of little or no interest to them or by giving something in return – usually, the effort of participating in group discussions. This view was expressed concisely by 'Betty':

> *So how do you approach the beliefs?*
> Well I don't really take as much notice to that side. I suppose I ought to really. If you're coming you ought to take part in it all.

In this way, instrumental users manifest clear characteristics of epistemological individualism (Wallis, 1974). They accept only those aspects of Raja Yoga, specifically the meditation technique and the idealised idea of a stress-free or positive lifestyle, that they feel will benefit their life in the here-and-now. As a result, the spiritual, normative aspect of Raja Yoga is down-played or treated with indifference:

> So, I tend to go for the practical ways it can affect my life as far as seeking out peace and calmness rather than any reason of feeling that I'm in contact with God. I find that a bit off-putting when there's someone talking about God. So the language of 'Baba' or 'Shiva Baba' and that aspect of it is not one I feel enthusiastic about.

Eclectic Users

Many of the characteristics of the instrumental users detailed above, are also to be found amongst those who I refer to as eclectic users. Eclectic users also place a strong emphasis on utilising the meditation practice for practical benefits. Indeed, when asked what their reasons are for attending the University's events, there is little to distinguish between both types:

> My reasons [for taking the meditation course] were that it sounded interesting and something that I could use in my life.
> *In what way use in your life?*
> To be a calmer person, to think more positively about myself, to enhance self-esteem and positive thinking.

However, whereas instrumental users employ a predominantly pragmatic approach to the meditation by stating, for example, 'I find that it relieves the pain caused by *X*', eclectic users link the instrumental with what they consider to the spiritual, this being typically expressed through the notion of 'self development' or, to use Heelas' (1996e) term, self spirituality. In other words, for eclectic users, self development – the development of the 'higher self' – takes on the status of a spiritual quest. For example, after discussing the benefits of attending the 'stress-free living' and self esteem courses one interviewee told me how she felt that it had 'brought [her] closer to God', adding 'I think I'm a unique person and that's what I want to explore'. Similarly another told me that the University's 'idea of looking after yourself and therefore being a better person to other people seems to fit in very nicely with the other things I'm involved with'. In contrast, then, to instrumental users' somewhat sporadic use of the meditation technique, eclectic users consider themselves to be 'on the spiritual path' to 'empowerment', 'being more centred' or simply being a 'better person'.

Like instrumental users, eclectic users also remain uncommitted to the University and, indeed, to the other techniques or groups they utilise in their spiritual quest. However, whereas, to develop Stark and Bainbridge's (1979, 1985) terminology, instrumental users remain as 'clients', eclectic users are best characterised as a form of 'audience' on the basis of both their lack of commitment to the University and the manner in which they are 'constitutional nibblers'; '"interested" in all new ideas in the general area of the eccentric and the mystical' (ibid., p. 28). Eclectic users may therefore be best pictured as eclectic instrumental users, characterised by, to use a phrase borrowed from one that I spoke to, an attitude of 'dipping into things'; picking and choosing from a variety of spiritual consumables on the basis of 'what feels right' or 'makes sense' to them.

For them 'the spiritual path' involves what one of my interviewees referred to as a 'toolbox' approach to spirituality, with Raja Yoga (as a whole or broken down) representing one 'tool' (amongst possibly many) for self development or empowerment. To quote 'Margaret' fully:

> I go to [a spiritual centre in Sheffield]...What it is a chance to meet together, *beyond any creed or doctrine*, and so there's people there who have studied Buddhism and people like me who are *dipping in to things*... people can bring tapes, people read from books, people write their own essays. And it can be about aspects of spiritual practice. People have done it on nutrition, people have done it on self-esteem....I also do peace-dancing which is different from circle dancing. You do it in a circle but it's much more centred on taking sacred phrases from faiths from the entire planet and you dance to these phrases. Again, I find that very meditative because you just say them over and over again but a lot of the music is beautiful and a lot of the steps are simple. The other thing I like about it is that you can sing along with it as well – that's what you do, you sing along with it – and I've always enjoyed singing, which is something the BKs aren't really hot on (emphasis added).

Similarly, another who I spoke to told me how Raja Yoga *'fits in with my belief system'* and how, although she did not accept most of what she was told, 'that isn't a problem as the Brahma Kumaris *don't make you believe anything and they're quite happy to accept you right where you are*' (emphasis added). This is particularly the case with the meditation which is again favoured above and beyond the belief system *per se*. One of my interviewees, for example, described it as 'one of the most useful meditations...a really practical way of calming down and being more centred' but added that during the meditation course:

> [the centre co-ordinator] got onto the Golden Age and the going round and I thought 'no, this isn't for me' and I nearly didn't come back. Then I had a chat with [her] about it and said 'Even if I don't swallow it all, I like the meditation and I like the other things that you're saying. Is that OK?' and she said 'Yes, that's fine'.

Eclectic users, then, like instrumental users, exhibit clear characteristics of epistemological individualism; they determine what 'truths' to accept and in what degrees, they determine how committed they will be to any particular 'truth' or organisation and, most importantly, they will fit the Brahma Kumaris into their belief system rather than fitting themselves into it.

Interpretative Drifters

In some cases individuals who initially attended the University's events for instrumental reasons gradually become more and more oriented towards the more spiritual aspect of Raja Yoga. This membership type I refer to, drawing on the work of Tanya Luhrmann (1994), as interpretative drifters. Through participating in an initial course in, for example, stress-free living, interpretative drifters begin to develop the basis of the University's *Weltanschauung*. This is then further developed and gradually more and more confirmed in the more advanced courses and through practicing the meditation technique more seriously. However, 'rather than realising that their intellectual habits have changed they feel that they have discovered that the ideas [behind the belief] are true' (ibid., p. 124).

Like instrumental users, interpretative drifters will describe how they initially attended one of the University's events – typically an event focusing on 'stress-free living', self-esteem or positive thinking – for specifically instrumental reasons such as the need to unwind or 'de-stress' themselves. To take the example of 'Christine', a full-time Raja Yogi:

> When I came along to learn meditation I had a vague idea that it might have something to do with God (laughs) but for me the idea of God was just some kind of source of energy. That would be about it. I was very unsure about the whole thing and I didn't want to get entangled up in anything religious, what I would see as religious belief; blind faith or that type of thing...And I would say that over the five years up until now that it really has been a *process* of liking what I heard initially, thinking 'well, yeah, that sounds really good, but I'm not sure personally whether that's true' (laughs) and then through meditation and also through continuing to study the ideas and discuss them and think about them then over time *those initial ideas that were put forward gradually, gradually have become confirmed through different experiences either in meditation or daily life* and so that whole aspect of relationship with God, or Baba, that has become *an unfolding thing* which is really beautiful. And so, five years ago I would never have imagined that I'd quite happily talk about God or just feel that there would be this being that I would be able to experience love for and love from on a daily level (emphasis added).

Similarly;

> I suppose it's in someway *awoken the spiritual*...in some ways the spiritual was dormant and what the Brahma Kumaris [are] saying is putting a few of the bits into context that were never satisfactorily answered when I was at school and when we did religious knowledge at school (emphasis added).

It is this gradual confirmation of initial experiences or 'awakening of the spiritual' that distinguishes interpretative drifters from the previous membership types in terms of their orientation to the 'divine within'. Instrumental users are typically not interested in the spiritual or in becoming spiritual. Rather their aim is more pragmatic and therapeutic; their attention is directed to finding a practical means to cope better with a particular ailment or issue in their lives. Likewise, for eclectic users, self development is equated with the spiritual path. In contrast, interpretative drifters, whilst they did not initially attend for spiritual reasons, typically find, to cite one, that after attending events for a period of time 'all these other [spiritual] things come up and you start to think about them'. In comparison to the other membership types so far outlined the interpretative drifter may perhaps therefore be best envisaged as representing a transitional stage between an orientation to the 'divine within' based on instrumentalism and one seeking 'illumination' (Campbell, 1978). As a result, amongst interpretative drifters a continuum may be sketched ranging from those for whom the instrumental orientation is dominant, albeit coloured by their 'awakened spirituality', through to those for whom the spiritual orientation has come to the fore.

Turning first to 'newly awakened' interpretative drifters, they will still be attending events for instrumental factors but, in contrast to instrumental users *per se*, they will be beginning to explain any improvements in their life in relation to their 'spiritual awakening'. For example, changes – both good or bad – in interpersonal relationships will be related to succeeding or failing to seeing individuals as souls whilst setbacks will be cited as an example of karmic accounts. Likewise, they will feel that various events on both the personal and global level add credence to the Brahma Kumaris' *Weltanschauung*. In sum, they become like a specialist in any subject; they begin to learn 'a new way of paying attention to, making sense of and commenting upon their world' in which

> there are new ways to define evidence which offer grounds to the expert that the non-specialist cannot see, and ways to order events so that the specialist sees coherence where the non-specialist sees only chaos; there is a body of specialist knowledge which gives discrimination and depth to the specialist's interpretations (Luhrmann, 1994, p. 124).

However, at this early stage in the process of drift – or conversion – they may still be encountering difficulties with religious concepts that either lie outside of the religious tradition (typically Christianity) in which they were brought up or which contradict conventional scientific wisdom. For example, 'Joanne' described how she felt that she had a 'cut-off point' because of her cultural 'programming':

> You're always brought up with the idea that time is linear, you've only got one life and Darwin, that sort of thing. There's much more than five thousand years of civilisation behind. And I don't feel there's enough things to make me change those inherent beliefs that I've grown up with.

As a result, whilst they have little or no problem accepting the claims 'you are a soul', 'there is a God' or 'the fruits of good and bad actions will be reaped', they do encounter difficulties in relation to Eastern spiritual concepts:

> I think some of the ideas I think I try to apply. I think a lot of the affirmations and values are very relevant...somehow they seem more relevant to today's world and today's life. Whether I believe it all, I don't know. I perceive that there is a life after death – in the sense of I can relate in my own mind to the concept of souls in some other existence. I can relate to that. And I can relate to the idea of rebirth. I can't necessarily relate to the cycle – the Golden Age, the Silver Age and all that. A lot of what Pam says I can sort of relate to it in my own terms, which is probably why I still come along. If I was finding I couldn't relate to any of it, put any of it into any meaning for myself, I would have probably have got bored by now...I suppose I'm not entirely convinced. We watched the video last week, I'm not convinced that [Dadi Gulzar] goes into a trance. I suppose that in some ways is alien to me, but I don't really know why.

Similarly:

> I'm not completely sure about the succession of lives and time being circular rather than linear. I try and grapple with it but it won't completely settle. Is it really Baba talking through that person in India? That's another area I find 'well it could be, but I'm not completely convinced of it'.

In contrast, 'fully awakened' interpretative drifters will claim to have discovered their 'true' spiritual path above and beyond any instrumental goals. In this connection, the following was perhaps the most common scenario that I found in my discussions with committed Raja Yogis. They described a similar narrative of how they had once been atheists or agnostics and how they had only been attracted to the University because of its courses on stress and positive thinking. Indeed, many claimed that they had been positively put-off by the course's spiritual overtones, almost to the point of ceasing to attend. However, around this time they claim that they had either a profound experience during meditation or a 'moment of clarity' in which 'everything clicked into place' and they realised what they claim to be the great spiritual truth embodied within Raja Yoga. In other words, to return to Luhrmann (1994, p. 340), through practising the yoga, attending classes and meditation sessions and even speaking to centre co-ordinators, interpretative drifters become 'progressively more skilled at seeing new patterns in events, seeing new sorts of events as significant, paying attention to new patterns'. Armed with these new perceptions, their sense of identity and perception of the world is reformulated; the world appears as Kali Yuga poised at the brink of 'transformation'; evidence is found to suggest the nature of some of their previous lives; and, most importantly, they gain an awareness of themselves as a soul who has remembered their true identity in contrast to those 'body-conscious' souls who remain in ignorance.

Spiritual Searchers

In radical contrast to the orientation of both instrumental and eclectic users, one finds those who I refer to as 'spiritual searchers' for whom Raja Yoga serves as a method for transcendence. Like eclectic users, spiritual searchers consider themselves to be on 'the spiritual path', however, what is significant about spiritual searchers is that their involvement with the University grew directly out of a 'spiritual crisis' or sense of disenchantment with conventional religiosity. Terry Lovat, for example, in his discussion of the University's Australian membership notes how they are predominantly former Christians or at least people who have been brought up within a Christian environment. As he sees it, such individuals' movement into the University 'has followed upon a lengthy search for a spirituality and values system that offers a meaning no longer (or perhaps never) found in the religion of their upbringing' (Lovat, 1997, p. 110). In some instances, for example, their involvement may stem from their rejection of what they perceive to be the negative attitude of organised religion. This was the case with 'Wendy' who was drawn to what she felt was, in contrast to the Christian faith, the University's positive message:

> Within the church...it tends to make you negative inasmuch as you're always feeling guilty – you've done this wrong, you've done that wrong, you're not worthwhile – whereas with the Brahma Kumaris it's totally different. You're told that you are worthwhile and this [the Church's way] is the wrong way of looking at things.

Alternatively, (s)he may be attempting to find answers to the questions that they believe are either ignored, glossed over or not satisfactorily answered by their existing faith. This view was expressed in some depth by 'Annette':

> Brahmin faith makes more sense than Christian faith, really. It's the same God to me and Jesus is part of that faith but it doesn't just end there, it's an extension. I don't know if you've found that, but lots and lots of questions that I used to sit in church and think from books that I'd read and deeper thinking...you don't get any sermons on souls and as Christians you're supposed to have a soul somewhere but they don't seem to do a sermon on souls and I wanted to know deeper things about Heaven and the afterlife and things like that. It seems just a bit fuzzy in church somehow. You're just there for the here and now, you're not there for what's been before and what's coming afterwards, whereas I find that with the Brahmin faith you know what happened before, you know all about Heaven and who God really is.

Interestingly, Lovat also cites a similar response from his interviewees:

> ...for me, questions such as 'Who am I?', 'What is my life all about?', 'What will happen to me when I die?' were not answered satisfactorily within Catholicism (op. cit., p. 111).

In this way, spiritual searchers will claim that Raja Yoga not only answers these questions but also provides a technique that allows them direct, largely unmediated contact with this spirituality. As Lovat (op. cit., p. 112) puts it, '[t]he major attraction [of Raja Yoga] and its sustaining power for these people [is] in the simple but firm harmony between God and self that is implied and effected by the BK creed and the practice of Raja Yoga'. Thus, in contrast to Christianity's perceived 'fuzziness', with Raja Yoga they feel that not only are they told what a soul actually is but also, perhaps more importantly, taught a technique that both engenders their self-perception as a soul and also facilitates union (literally *yoga*) with God.

As would perhaps be expected, since spiritual searchers believe that they have discovered their true spiritual path, they typically become more involved with the University, attend more events and practice yoga more frequently than those for whom it represents one particular lifestyle sector or 'spiritual consumable'. Following their preliminary involvement with the University, spiritual searchers describe how they had to re-evaluate their existing faith in the light of the new spiritual message. As a result some cross over totally while others attempt to, while favouring the new, straddle between both. Such views were expressed by 'Annette' and 'Pam' respectively:

> I think now I consider myself more a Brahmin and then a Christian, but I've not left the Christian faith.

> And at that point I had to re-assess my involvement with Christianity and I had to say 'yes, for me this is God speaking and this is what I want to follow'...But as far as *I* am concerned, my life is the Brahma Kumaris now and not Christianity.

Concentrating on the latter example, this essentially marks a move from one spiritual tradition, or one set of normative structures, to another. On the more practical level this may be manifested as a move from attending Church services to attending murli classes or from practising Christian devotion and prayer to practising yoga and following a sattvic diet. Moreover, as noted previously, this may often involve them reinterpreting their previous faith in light of the new. Membership is seen as 'answering Baba's call'; the result of being the reincarnation of one of the University's original members and having their sanskars reactivated when they come across Raja Yoga again. Likewise, the 'fuzziness' of their previous faith is rationalised as a result of it being the historical distortion of the original, previously long lost, truth of Raja Yoga. One full-time Raja Yogi, for example, described to me how she was now able to understand and correctly interpret parts of the Bible that before, as a Christian, she either did not understand or which she felt didn't make any sense. Similarly, as with 'fully awakened' spiritual searchers, one finds spiritual searchers merging their personal goals and identity with those of the University. Their personal goal becomes, for example, spiritual perfection, becoming a 'Golden Age' soul or one of the 16,108 'wives' of Krishna. To quote fully the response of a centre co-ordinator when asked what her aims in continuing to practice Raja Yoga were:

> To become perfect [laughs]. Because Raja Yoga is complete union with myself and union with God. We've got mind, intellect and sanskars and all three run off in the same way and it's learning to unify and bring the three into line so I have complete inner peace and I'm not shaken by anything. Because obviously, as time goes on – and Baba's warning at this time when we were in Madhuban – that there are going to be many, many upheavals of nature. Some quite devastating things are going to occur. Now, to be able to be stable in my mind, to enable me to remain stable in whatever happens, to be strong and to keep close to my union with God and fulfil the aim, because all the time the murli is giving us an aim for the Golden Age. Now it isn't just for me it's for the world, because one thing I say to myself in the morning – and I have to admit there are some mornings I might like to stay in bed when four o'clock comes – but I say 'this is the Confluence Age and I'm not only doing it for myself, I'm doing it for the world' because a certain number *have* to get their thoughts right in order that world transformation will take place and it will be obvious towards the end that those who are taking part in the Brahma Kumaris and giving their time will be needed because they will be the ones who can give peace and harmony to everyone else in a world that will seem like utter chaos at the end. So, yes, my goal is to bring harmony to myself and world transformation, so we will have our new age, our Golden Age.

Instrumental *Lifestyles* v. the Spiritual *Life*

There are of course individual variations within these broad membership types. What I hope to have conveyed, however, is the general characteristics of each and the manner in which they suggest that there are different levels of involvement within the University – see figure 5.1.

Figure 5.1 Different membership types in relation to their goal, self-conception and the nature of their social identity

		Goal			
		Instrumental	**Philosophical**		
Identity	**Individual**	*Instrumental Users*		**Material**	**Self-Conception**
		Eclectic Users	*Interpretative Drifters*	**Spiritual**	
	Collective		*Spiritual Searchers*		

Looking at each of these in turn, as the term suggests, instrumental users are defined predominantly by their instrumental attitude to the 'divine within'. Instrumental users' goal is, as I have described above, to alleviate the symptoms of physical ailments or to find a successful means of coping with stress or self-esteem issues. Stemming from this, their self-conception is more materialistic. They express no interest in the 'spiritual side' of Raja Yoga and, indeed, many are often ignorant of the University's basic beliefs despite even, in some cases, their long involvement with it. Finally, as instrumental users characteristically remain in a 'client'-like relationship to the University, their sense of social identity is defined more on the basis of their perceived individuality than with reference to the University's collective identity. In other words, Raja Yoga is utilised to help the existing personality to cope better in the world instead of as a basis to recreate or rediscover a new (soul conscious) personality.

This is equally the case with eclectic users although, as I have noted, there are important differences between the two membership types. Primarily, whilst both are motivated by a desire for self-improvement, eclectic users differ from instrumental users by expressing this goal in more spiritual or philosophical terms. For them, relieving stress, becoming more centred or building self-esteem are not ends in themselves, but rather steps on a long term process of self-development or, put in spiritual terms, developing their 'Higher-Self'. Similarly, whilst eclectic users' sense of social identity is again highly unlikely to be influenced by the University's collective identity, unlike with instrumental users, this is not the result of ignorance or a lack of interest. Rather, it stems from their epistemologically individualistic attitude to the various traditions that they draw on, combine and utilise in their spiritual quest. Having said this, however, Raja Yoga is more likely to play a role in eclectic user's sense of social identity, or 'spiritual path', than in that of the instrumental user's, albeit in combination with other ideas. For example, (s)he may accept the Brahma Kumaris' conception of the soul but may prefer to express it through the metaphor of Celtic spirituality or by colouring it with a belief in reincarnation through different levels of existence. As a result, it is likely that with eclectic users the meditation technique (being) will become further decontextualised, divorced from the meditation knowledge (knowing) and aim (becoming), and cross-fertilised with other spiritualities or therapies.

The social identity of spiritual searchers and 'fully awakened' interpretative drifters, in contrast, is more likely to be influenced by Raja Yoga. For these membership types, Raja Yoga takes on the status of an external voice of authority, providing not only a salvational system but also the basis of a spiritual life narrative. As a result, through the process of conversion, biography is reinterpreted in the light of Raja Yoga. (S)he remembers his/her true, forgotten identity as a soul and consequently false, body conscious, identities are discarded. Similarly, as I said previously, there is a merging of personal goals and self-identity with those of the University. This may be effectively illustrated with two examples from my fieldwork. On a long car journey with one Raja Yogi, our conversation turned to cars, specifically the particular model of car that, resources permitting, I would like to buy. She replied that she too was considering buying a new car although on reflection it would not be worthwhile doing so as she would only get a limited amount of use out of it before the world was destroyed. Likewise during my stay at the previously mentioned Global Retreat Centre in Oxford, I was discussing the University's purchase of a digital multi-track recorder with a member. After he had outlined the benefits of digital *vis-à-vis* analogue recording, he paused briefly and added 'Yes, you can tell the Golden Age is coming just by the quality of music technology nowadays'.

In sum, a distinction may be drawn between those seeking to improve their *lifestyle* and those, in varying degrees, seeking the spiritual *life*. Broadly this distinguishes between those individuals for whom Raja Yoga serves as a lifestyle sector or, at the most, part of their reflexive biography, and those for whom it serves as the basis of biography. The practical consequence of this is that the University's membership may be visualised as a large number of uncommitted (world-affirming) instrumental and eclectic users surrounding a small nucleus of committed (world-rejecting) members (see Babb 1986, pp. 131-2; Howell and Nelson, 1997, pp. 8-9). For example, taking the example of the Chesterfield centre, although at the time of my fieldwork around three hundred individuals had passed through its doors in one context or other over the last decade, the semi-committed membership (who attend on average five times per year) numbered less than ten while the only fully-committed member was the centre co-ordinator.[10] Likewise, if one accepts the University's official membership figure (450,000), my fieldwork would suggest that only around 10,000 of these would be fully committed, the rest being casual members or simply those who have attended one of the University's events.[11] This figure, I would support Skultans (1993) in arguing, is an exaggeration and serves more of an ideological purpose as according to one interpretation of Lekhraj's eschatology the total number of members at the end will be 450,000.

Linking this back to the world-rejection/ambivalence and theodical bifurcation arguments presented in chapters three and four respectively, the following point may be drawn out. Through its internationalisation programme – and particularly in recent years with the introduction of courses addressing 'stress', 'negativity', 'empowerment' and so on – the University has sought to increase its membership, or at least the profile of its message, by appealing to the 'expressive revolution' (Parsons, 1978). Repackaging itself as an 'identity expert' (Bauman, 1998) or one of the contemporary world's many 'experts of subjectivity' (Rose, 1996), it may be seen to have self-consciously addressed itself to both the New Age and therapeutic/human potential 'cultic milieu' (Campbell, 1972). In doing so it has produced a form of 'BK-*lite*'; Raja Yoga with all the overtly world-rejecting aspects filtered out. The organisation that once referred to membership as 'death-in-life' now offers 'success in life' or 'empowerment in life'. Similarly soul consciousness becomes another aspect of self-spirituality (Heelas, 1996e) while, as I will explore in the next chapter, Lekhraj's apocalyptic fantasies are repackaged as 'world transformation' or as 'the New Age'.

Notes

[1] An earlier version of this chapter entitled *Reflexive Traditions: New Religious Movements and the 'Negotiation' of Identity* was presented to the BSA Sociology of Religion Study Group Annual Conference, Durham, 9th April 1998 (Walliss, 1998; see also Walliss, 2000b, pp. 53-61; Walliss, 2001, pp. 91-2). I am indebted to Wayne Spencer for his many helpful comments on this chapter.

[2] Short questionnaires were sent to five centres within the UK; Bradford, Chesterfield, Hounslow, Leeds and Sheffield. Questions focused on general demographical issues, e.g. gender, age and occupation, in addition to the respondent's length of membership and whether they are a full-time committed member. The 74 responses received form the basis for subsequent analysis.

Interestingly, Howell and Nelson's (1998, pp. 6-7) attempts at a similar study had to be abandoned because the University's hierarchy in the UK and America did not wish to have the questionnaire distributed amongst the centres. For my own part, I also encountered some difficulties in getting my questionnaire distributed. Initially, I was told by a centre co-ordinator that a senior sister had refused me permission although when I spoke to this person she denied this and gave permission on the condition that an extra question was added to ascertain whether the respondent was a regular student or not. However, this was largely unnecessary as the questionnaires I received back had, with few exceptions been distributed at morning classes which are as a rule only attended by regular students. Hence, no comparison of the socio-demographics of regular and non-regular attendees is possible.

[3] These are small dice made of card, brightly covered with the kind of images found within the Brahma Kumaris literature. On each of the faces one finds a virtue such as 'Positivity: I am positive and attract positivity from others'. It is intended that individuals should roll the dice and let the virtue on the upward face be their affirmation for the day.

[4] Bradford (76/24%); Leeds (86/14%); Sheffield (55/45%); Chesterfield (75/25%); Hounslow (69/31%).

[5] The over 45/under 45 ratio was 64%/36%.

[6] A different picture to this is presented by Howell and Nelson (1997) in their discussion of the University's Australian membership patterns. For example, in comparison with my sample they found a greater number of younger members (under twenty-five years of age) and, as a result, reported a younger mean age: 36.5 years (Australia) to 48.5 years (UK). In all other respects, however, our findings are almost identical; i.e. a prevalence of professionals, a membership drop-off point at ten years as well as a female/male gender imbalance.

[7] By way of comparison, the total percentage of females within this age range and SEG *alone* is only slightly lower than the percentage of *all* the males in the sample combined (27%/24%).

[8] I do not intend to present a full review of the literature pertaining to the relationship between age and gender and religiosity/spirituality here. Rather, in summary I would simply say that a great deal of the literature produced on this subject would suggest that females would appear to be more superstitious or religious – specifically Christian – and more likely be church attendees than males and that religious self-image and involvement increases with age, as does superstition generally. For recent discussions of the literature see, for example, Wolfe (1993), Davie (1994), Walter and Davie (1997) or Rose (1998) on, amongst other things, the relationship between age and gender and interest/participation in New Age activities.

[9] All the interviewees cited in the chapter will, of course, be referred to by pseudonyms.

[10] This was not the case, however, in other centres, most notably the Leeds and Sheffield centres, where there appeared to be a high degree of commitment.

[11] Chryssides (1999, p. 366) also gives the figure of 'over 450,000' for the total Brahma Kumaris membership world-wide. However, he also gives the figures for 'regular students' (committed members) outside India (5,715) and within Britain (1,200). Whilst I cannot verify whether there are around 440,000 Raja Yogis in India, my fieldwork would suggest that the UK figure is reasonably accurate.

Chapter 6
Manifesting Ambivalence: The Pursuit of the Millennium

Over the course of the previous three chapters I have drawn on Mellor's (1993) notion of a 'reflexive tradition' to examine the Brahma Kumaris World Spiritual University. Using this as a hermeneutic tool I have focused on three main empirical sites.

First, drawing on the work of Wilson (1969, 1970) and Wallis (1984), I argued that the University's orientation or response to the world has developed – or perhaps mutated – historically from one of (revolutionist) world-rejection to what I termed 'world-ambivalence'. This development, I argued, was related ostensibly to the University's changing relationship with the outside world; from a situation of mutual antagonism in its early years to, more recently, its wider acceptance by the outside world from the 1970s onwards. The ambivalent orientation displayed towards the world may be seen to be manifested in numerous ways within the institutional life of the University. For example, as I noted, over the last two decades, the University has taken a prominent role in United Nations activities, such as the *Visions of a Better World* project, while simultaneously holding and promoting a theodicy that has as its basis the belief in a radical, predetermined, desirable and *ipso facto* unpeaceful eschatology. Similarly, on another, related, level there is the phenomenon of what I have referred to as a theodical bifurcation between this original (ascetic) theodicy and a newer (instrumental) world-affirming message couched in the terminology of the Human Potential and New Age movements. On the one hand there is the emphasis on strict delineation from the corrupt outside world and the preparation of the few for a Golden-Aged paradise ('Death in Life') and on the other the application of these practices towards instrumental goals for the many (empowerment for life).

Following on from this, in the previous chapter I drew on the work of, amongst others, Richard Jenkins (1996) to examine the different membership patterns found within the University and, in particular, the role that Raja Yoga plays in the social identity of those who attend its events. In doing so I distinguished broadly between four main 'ideal type' membership patterns on the basis of their respective goal of involvement, their self-conception and, finally, the nature of their social identity. At the more detraditional, reflexive end of the spectrum I located instrumental and eclectic users, both of whom utilise Raja Yoga (or elements of it) for pragmatic or world-affirming purposes. Thus, as I noted in the previous chapter, instrumental users will describe their reasons for becoming and staying involved with the University in terms of how the meditation has helped them to, for example, cope with the symptoms of a physical ailment or deal with stress or low self-esteem more effectively. Moreover, again when asked they will claim to be either ignorant of, or uninterested in, the University's spiritual message. In contrast, eclectic users explicitly describe their goals of involvement and their self-conception in more philosophical or spiritual terms. For them, relieving stress, becoming more centred or building self-esteem are not ends in themselves, but rather steps on a long term process of self-development or, as they would put it, developing their 'Higher-Self'. As this involves them drawing on and recombining the 'Truths' found within a number of spiritual paths, eclectic users will typically remain detached from any one group or spiritual ideology. As one put it, they will fit Raja Yoga, or at least some aspect of it, into their own personal belief system rather than fitting themselves into it.

At the more normative end of the spectrum I located spiritual searchers and, to some extent, 'fully awakened' interpretative drifters. For these individuals, Raja Yoga serves as an external voice of authority, providing not only a salvational system but also a spiritual life narrative. Consequently, their membership patterns are inclined to be more serious and committed than the two types previously outlined. Moreover, stemming from their belief to have found both a salvational system and to have 'rediscovered' their 'true identity', their locus of authority tends to be epistemologically authoritarian, albeit mediated by their 'soul consciousness'.

In this way, it may be seen that within the University, mode of membership (personal reflexivity) and institutional organisation (intra/inter-tradition reflexivity) are intrinsically linked and have evolved through three stages; early, transitional and contemporary.

Within the early, and to some extent the transitional, period (1936-50s), world-rejection was manifested both through the 'ascetic' theodicy and the detached, fully involved membership patterns with both serving to delineate the inner world from the outer world or members from non-members. However, during the transitional period (1950s-90s), this distinction began to be weakened by two key factors. Firstly, active proselytisation and the associated acceptance of outsiders into the University. This had, of course, happened before to some extent but never in such an organised way and never in terms of large, international numbers. Secondly, through the University's international work and, on an individual level, the phenomenon of Raja Yogis undertaking paid work outside centres, it has begun the process of becoming re-embedded into the world that it originally rejected and sought to transcend (see Howell and Nelson, 1997, 1998). Again, as will be discussed later, great play is made within the University of the view that it is possible to do so whilst still remaining spiritually detached from the world; being a 'detached observer' or a 'carefree emperor in elevated consciousness' as it is known. However, this does not avoid the fact that on the surface at least, to quote Whaling (1995, p. 15) again, 'there is the spectacle of a University which has the word "spiritual" written into its very name becoming increasingly involved in frenetic activity on behalf of the world that is deemed to be beyond redemption in its present form'.

Finally, within the contemporary period (1990s to present), world-ambivalence is manifested within the University both at the institutional level, in terms of its world-orientation and theodical bifurcation, and also at the level of membership, in terms of the divergent modes of membership. Changing membership patterns are therefore symptomatic of the erosion of the original division between inner and outer (members and non-members) and *vice versa*. Similarly, theodical bifurcation may be seen as both a result and an ongoing factor in both this erosion and the changing membership patterns. In this way, one may argue that at present the University is locked into an ongoing process of increasing secularisation from within. In the final section of this chapter I intend to say more about this phenomenon and offer possible future scenarios for its development. However, for the moment, in the following section I would like to examine the interplay of these three issues with reference to a single concrete example, the University's millenarianism.

Manifesting Ambivalence

Millenarianism lies at the very heart of Raja Yoga and continues to provide a whole *raison d'être* for the University. As will be recalled from chapter three, Lekhraj's spiritual calling centred around his reported visions of imminent world destruction and the subsequent earthly paradise that would be enjoyed by a few lucky souls. However, it was only during the period of the University's outside persecution that it developed as an intrinsic part of its theodicy as, I would argue, a form of Nietzschian 'imaginary vengeance' against that outside world (see Nietzsche, 1998; First Treatise). Thompson (1996, p. 14) has also noted how millenarianism is 'the consolation of the persecuted'; a 'genre born out of crisis, designed to stiffen the resolve of an embattled community by dangling in front of it the vision of a sudden and permanent release from its captivity'. It is with this in mind that I have argued that the manner in which the original millenarianism has developed historically closely mirrors the University's changing relationship with the 'outside' world – from one of mutual rejection to one of ambivalence – and that it continues to provide a fundamental site of reflexivity at both the institutional level and amongst the University's membership.

Institutional Reflexivity

Firstly, within the University there are the institutional strategies through which the theodical bifurcation, levels of membership and, by extension, the different 'millenniums' are managed and negotiated. This is achieved through two main, related techniques; the literal and metaphorical spatialisation of members and the reflexive deployment of metaphor.

Use of spatialisation The first technique involves the differentiation and organisational separation of those instrumental, world-affirming activities that are open to all (i.e. the eclectic and instrumental users) and those world-rejecting activities that are reserved for committed members only (Howell and Nelson, 1998; see also Skultans, 1993, p. 58). In other words, to draw on Goffman (1969; see also Jenkins, 1996, pp. 71-2), the University – through the differentiation of activities in regard to types of membership – effectively separate its world-rejecting, 'backstage' self-identity and its public, 'frontstage' world-affirming identity or image.

Examples of this phenomenon have been mentioned in previous chapters and include the distinction between courses in 'stess-free living' and positive thinking and the 'official' theodicy, the University's emphasis on its UN affiliations and its use of heavily publicised lectures and events involving prominent public figures despite its views regarding the inherent corruptness of such organisations and individuals. However, the prime example of this phenomenon focuses around certain restrictions on access to the University's Mt. Abu. headquarters. Although all those who attend the University's events, and indeed, non-members, are theoretically able, if they wish, to visit Mt. Abu during most of the year, this is not the case during the 'murli season'; the period when it is claimed that the disembodied Lekhraj communicates 'live' to the University through Dadi Gulzar. This of course is only to be expected due to the murli's often frequent references to the corruptness of the outside world, the forthcoming destruction and the future paradise and, indeed, the nature of their communication. For example, the content of one Avaktya Murli that was read out at the Chesterfield centre recommended that members should enjoy the silence within the centres while they could because pretty soon

> when there's a little 'knock' of destruction people will come queuing at [the centre's] door and you'll have to say you've no time. But just at the present time people are saying 'we have no time to come' and when they do you'll have to say 'it's too late'.

Attendance during this period is strictly by 'invitation only'; open only to those members who have been following the strict purity rules outlined in chapter four for half a year and who have been successfully 'vetted' by their home centres (Howell and Nelson, 1998). As a symbol of their pilgrimage (s)he is given a status-conferring ring inscribed a representation of Shiva Baba, to be worn on the wedding finger. Thus, in many ways the Mt. Abu 'pilgrimage' serves, as with the Raja Yoga lifestyle generally, to differentiate; to distinguish between committed members and outsiders/non-members and also to strengthen the former's view of themselves *vis-à-vis* the latter. By this I mean that an individual may access the University's web page, attend public lectures, the various courses and workshops, murli classes (and to some extent the morning classes) without having to publicly demonstrate their faith. However, in order to progress to the next stage – the visit to Mt. Abu – they have to not only do so through following the recommended lifestyle but also, more importantly, be seen to be doing so by the University.

Use of metaphor This is intrinsically linked with the second technique; the reflexive deployment of different metaphors or 'readings' of Raja Yoga to different audiences. Again, this has been discussed previously in terms of a distinction between the original 'ascetic' theodicy and a newer spiritually-based instrumental one. In practical terms this involves the utilisation and negotiation of different metaphors at the different events and in the different types of literature in relation to its intended (core or periphery) audience.

At the (backstage) core of the University among fully involved 'surrendered' members, at events such as morning classes and spiritual retreats such as the one I attended in June 1998

> ...the tradition is lived [and expressed] *without apology, translation or dilution*; one is there not in the first instance to relieve stress or to equip oneself to provide better business leadership but to be with God as taught and manifest through a particular Indian teacher (ibid., no pagination, emphasis added).

It is here that the original, world-rejecting rendition of Raja Yoga is manifested and perpetuated and where members often engage in the 'interpretative overload' characteristic of millenarian groups historically where events are seized upon as a sign of the end (see, for example, Cohn, 1993; Thompson, 1996). This, of course, involves the standard phenomena that would be expected – such as floods, international hostilities, global warming and so on – but also, interestingly, draws on a range of seemingly mundane 'signs' that, it is claimed, speak directly to Raja Yogis only. For example, during my stay at the Global Retreat Centre, I observed members discussing – possibly in an ironic way – numerological re-readings of Australian football and cricket as well as re-interpretations of the latent content of Lewis Carroll's *oeuvre*. Likewise, the symbolism of the move from analogue to digital recording technology, recycling and the invention of film is often cited as evidence that Shiva Baba is preparing human consciousness for the idea that history is cyclic, predetermined and involves a fair amount of corporeal 'recycling'.

In radical contrast at events geared towards those on the periphery or outside of the University the terminology of the New Age is deployed and the University is keen to market itself at *Mind, Body and Spirit* fairs and the like. This, as was noted in chapter four, essentially marks a substitution of terms; destruction becomes 'transformation' or 'new age', soul becomes 'self' or 'higher self' while soul-consciousness becomes, among other things, 'empowerment', 'becoming centred' or 'wholeness'. Indeed, often the material presented can be read in either way, depending on how the phrases or terms are interpreted. To give an example from the Sheffield centre's Spring 1998 newsletter:

> We live in the most exciting of times – ever. The *old ways of thinking and being are breaking down*. The world is going through great social, political, economic, moral, technological, environmental and climatic changes. Even time seems to be speeding up as we approach the new millennium.
>
> We are entering uncharted waters, drifting without a compass. As the global tide of change threatens to engulf us, *new ways of thinking and being are opening up. The old, rational, mechanistic approach to life is giving way to a more creative, holistic, intuitive and spiritual approach, which goes beyond organised religion and might even be replacing it.* There is a huge open-mindedness that is reflected in the huge sales of

> spiritual books. Never have so many books been available on such a wide range of spiritual subjects from past life therapy and reincarnation to meditation, angels, conversations with God and everything in between.
> *Human beings are turning 'within' to explore the last frontier, i.e. the forgotten world of the soul and of God* and the need to re-establish the connection that has been lost over time. Here can be found the source of peace, love and happiness, which will see us through these difficult times; *here we will find the answers to all the social and moral dilemmas that we now face; here we can rediscover our values and our sense of purpose and so transform ourselves and the world* (emphasis added).

The above example can, therefore, be read in two senses. On one level it can be read as an example of the standard narrative found in much New Age literature; that the 'Old Age' dominated by science, rationality and so on is ending and the New Age is dawning; human beings are discovering their 'Higher Self', and in doing so bringing about world transformation. However, on another level it can equally be read in a millenarian sense; the (old) world is breaking down – 'the world is going through great social, political, moral, technological, environmental and climatic changes' – and humans must turn within (become soul-conscious) in order to 'transform [themselves] and the world'. Indeed, 'even time seems to be speeding up as we approach the new millennium'. To give an other example, towards the end of 1999 I was sent a newsletter entitled *Aspire to Change* from the Chesterfield Brahma Kumaris centre in which the reader was told that

> we are heading towards the Millennium and lots of things will be happening, some we know about and some we don't know about [sic], so in order to have a really good time we thought it would be a good idea to spend some time in contemplation and reflection for ourselves.

We were also invited to a 'Victory Celebration' on the first of January 2000.

However, often the shift in metaphor is much more subtle than this, with certain views being either understated – if stated at all – or expressed in a deliberately vague manner. In the booklet *When We Change...The World Changes*, for example, Lekhraj is described merely as 'a man of vision...[who] saw that the world was going through a time of traumatic and intense change, yet ultimately reaching a much better state of affairs' (Brahma Kumaris World Spiritual University, n.d.). Similarly, on the University's official website his apocalyptic fantasies, whilst still retaining the use of the theatrical metaphor, are presented in the vaguest of terms as a period of darkness through which 'we can see the glimmer of light of the new dawn' at which souls will 'dance their way gradually off the stage united in the vision of a golden morning'.[1] Likewise amongst the University's publications one may clearly distinguish between those aimed at the periphery and those aimed at committed, core members on the basis of what is omitted and the manner in which the remaining material is presented. Within the former category, in books such as *Practical Meditation* (Brahma Kumaris World Spiritual University, 1995b), the instrumental aspects of the meditation are emphasised and the millenarian element is omitted whilst within books such as the aforementioned *Visions of the Future* (Brahma Kumaris World Spiritual University, 1996) the situation is reversed. This situation is, however, perhaps best exemplified by Ken O'Donnell who simultaneously decries the 'artificial lives' of non-Raja Yogis and celebrates the forthcoming destruction in *New Beginnings* (O'Donnell, 1995) whilst presenting very much an optimistic message of self spirituality in *Pathways to Higher Consciousness* (O'Donnell, 1996). Indeed, throughout both the only similarity or guiding thread is the emphasis placed upon human potential and the experience of practising meditation.

Utilising these techniques, the University has been able to manage its world-ambivalence fairly successfully. However, in some cases the University's increasingly Westernised, world-affirming sphere has caused discontentment amongst many of the more culturally conservative Indian members (Howell and Nelson, 1998). In recent issues of *Purity*, for example, a number of members have written to the editorial board to respond to the high number of 'outsider'/Raja Yogi photographs featured within its pages; for example, 'Why do you meet and publicise the photos of your meetings with politicians most of whom are corrupt and unscrupulous?' (August, 1997, p. 10) and 'Why does *Purity* publish photos of bigshots only?' (January, 1998, p. 10). In their defence, however, the editorial board (Jan 1998) have argued that there is no incongruence between their public- and their self-image. Such meetings and photographs, they claim, are needed as the 'character and conduct [of such individuals] bears on and affects the lives of common people'. Indeed, they are essential in order 'to bring spiritual awakening to all levels of society' (ibid.). In a more detailed earlier answer in the August 1997 edition, they also stated that their meetings with such persons are intended to change 'even in a small way, the mindset of people in politics into altruistic, noble and virtuous [individuals]' and are therefore 'in no way aimed at seeking or giving publicity but [are] intended to spread and strengthen the awareness and acceptance of universal values among politicians as well as [the] general public' (ibid.).

In many ways, however, this may be seen as an other level of the University's current world ambivalence in that according to the murlis, such famous or successful individuals are only so because they are specifically iron aged souls who experience their (materialistic) golden age during the iron age rather than during the (spiritual) Golden Age. Nevertheless, for some individuals – in particular a schismatic group who refer to themselves as the *Advance Party* – the incongruence is real, and more importantly, seen as symptomatic of what they allege to be the corruption and worldliness of the University hierarchy generally.

The Advance Party

In many ways the 'Advance Party' (*Adhyatmik Ishwariya Vishva Vidyalaya* or AIVV)[2] may be envisaged as the Protestant reformers to the Brahma Kumaris' mediaeval Catholic Church. A constant theme reiterated through their website (www.shivbaba.org) is what they claim to be the increasing incongruence between the University's actions or public identity and what it professes to believe. In particular, the Advance Party are exceptionally hostile to both the University's willingness to promote itself through a New Age metaphor and its UN involvement. Both of these phenomena, they claim, represent if not the rejection then at least a disservice to the University's Lekhraj-era world-rejection. For example, the Indian Advance Party member who refers to himself only as 'ShivBaba21' in 'An Open Letter to All BKs' comments on how he became disaffected with the University – the 'five star Raja Yogis' – after becoming 'alarmed and surprised' at the 'declining divinity [of] the whole Brahmin family, with the Knowledge being pushed in the background and [the] upsurge of materialistic interests in the forefront'.[3] Likewise, at another part of the website it is claimed that, following Lekhraj's death in 1969:

> There was a visible change in the attitude of the sisters of various centers and wealthy students were given preference over the not-so-wealthy ones. The power-crazy Brahmins slowly became commercial as money started pouring in by ignorant students, who are still taken for a ride in the name of God. In fact the whole organisation has now become a true Ravan Rajya where pomp and show and grandeur are given preference over true Godly knowledge. **How long can this last? Certainly it has to end.**[4]

However, at a deeper level the Advance Party's critique is aimed at the Brahma Kumaris' theodicy, in particular the manner in which they allege it has been misunderstood and misrepresented. In many ways this is connected with the previous point in that the Advance Party claim if the Brahma Kumaris had the 'true' knowledge, they would not have embarked on the process of New Age-ification and so on in the first place. Therefore, somewhat ironically, in a manner identical to the proto-Brahma Kumaris' attitude towards their native Hinduism, the struggle between the two groups is hallmarked by a conflict over exclusive access to divine revelation and validity of theodical interpretation or accurate 'remembrance'; this struggle being expressed in particular in relation to the millennium.

In the first instance, whilst accepting the importance of Lekhraj, the Advance Party claim that he was only one 'chariot' or earthly manifestation of God. Indeed, the Advance Party claim that it was Lekhraj's business partner, Sevak Ram, rather than he himself who was 'the corporeal medium of Shiva'. According to the Advance Party's website, Ram not only explained Lekhraj's divine visions to him but also played a key role in the formation of Om Mandali alongside Lekhraj and a person named Geeta Mata.[5] However, the website goes on, within a very short period Ram left 'because of differences' with Lekhraj and died in 1942.[6] From 1942 until 1969, Shiva continued to speak to the world through Lekhraj. When, in 1969 Lekhraj also died, the Advance Party claim that Shiva 'entered HIS permanent chariot to continue HIS unfinished task', that person being one Virendra Dev Dixit.[7] The Advance Party therefore reject the University's claim that Shiva and Lekhraj jointly communicate to it as Bapdada through the trance medium Sister Gulzar. Rather, they argue that it is impossible for this to happen as, according to the murli, Shiva cannot 'mount a virgin'. Rather, they claim that He is in fact manifesting Himself through Dixit from their headquarters.[8]

Secondly, like the Brahma Kumaris, the Advance Party, also employ the metaphor of 'amnesia' and 'remembrance' to describe the relationship of the two groups to the murlis. In particular, through close readings of the texts and with the benefit of divine interpretative authority, they claim that the Brahma Kumaris have only superficially understood the 'Basic Knowledge' message presented within them. The Advance Party, in contrast, claim to have been given the 'Advance[d] knowledge' by Shiva through Dixit. These 'correct' interpretations are then presented in often painstaking detail on the Advance Party's website:

> AV 31.5.77. 'The Greatest blessing of the Confluence Age is that Brahmins can meet the Supreme Soul in person on this earth' (where is that person through whom you can meet the Supreme Soul? After 1969 is it through Dadi Gulzar? Or Somebody else playing the role of Prajapita incognito? Please think).[9]

> God Shiva will be revealed through the person who becomes the '**Lord of the weak and poor**' (it is written in the Bible that Blessed are the weak and the poor shall inherit the earth). Dada Lekhraj is the Lord of the BKs who are at present the richest and most powerful spiritual organisation in this world [sic].[10]

In addition, they accuse the University hierarchy of actively censoring or altering murlis that could potentially undermine their privileged position or which 'don't suit their philosophy'. The 'Special instruments' (senior members) are, they allege 'constantly revising Murlis' to the extent that, for example, a passage from a 1969 murli referring to Shiva being unable to 'mount a virgin' was altered in the 1990 revised edition before being removed completely in the 1993 revision:

> Example (15/10/69 page 2): 'Should I enter the body of a pure virgin? But there is no rule. After all Father, how can He mount a virgin.' Revised (7/11/90): 'Should I enter the body of a pure virgin? Sitting here Father explains.....' Then finally in the published UK edition (march 1993) of the English 'Avyakt Bapdada 1969' the whole murli of that date was expunged.

These revisions are then rationalised as being the result of practical necessity; '[t]he old murlis of 10-12 pages [being] impractical for reading in the morning classes, where everybody is rushing for time'.[11] If, however, the Advance Party claim, a member challenges these revisions or asks 'why the Murli points are being [cut] out, he is told to mind his business'. Moreover, 'if a student is listening to Advance Knowledge then he is spied upon and not allowed to talk to his fellow Brahmins and he is considered a rebel. Later if he persists then he is told not to attend the classes in the centre'.[12]

This latter point was borne out to some extent by the email and telephone exchanges I had with Advance Party members and my own experiences trying to gather information on them from the Brahma Kumaris. One female Advance Party member described with some sadness how she was no longer welcome at her local centre whilst 'ShivBaba21' confided to me in his first email that 'I have to tell you quite openly that Adv. Godly knowledge is not accepted by Mt. Abu. In fact Mt. Abu is quite hostile to it. Hence you may encounter resistance if you try to spread it among the BKs'.[13] Likewise, whilst following up rumours of the group's existence I met with a wall of silence from within the University and, indeed, received a highly irate phone call from one member who told me that whatever she and the University did know they weren't prepared to tell me. Moreover, the University would 'block [me] every step of the way if [I] persist[ed] along this line of investigation'. Finally, however, after much negotiation and many unreturned telephone calls I was finally given the Advance Party's URL on the understanding that it was my karmic accounts that were at stake and that I should act with that knowledge in mind.

Such reactions were and are, of course, to be expected for the simple fact that the University's membership are the target audience for the Advance Party's message. The University is therefore understandably keen to restrict its member's knowledge and access to the group so as to prevent any further defections by disaffected members. For example, one of the first things that 'ShivBaba21' wrote in his response to my initial email was a question about whether I was a 'regular student' of Raja Yoga and, if so, how many times had I visited Mt. Abu. In other words, was I a committed member? Following this email, I began to receive long telephone calls – often around two hours long – during which an Advance Party member would attempt to convert me to their cause. The telephone calls stopped, however, when I told them that I was neither a committed Raja Yogi nor a potential convert to the Advance Party.

The Advance Party would therefore appear to consist mainly of disaffected ex-members of the University who found that at one point or another the gaps in the Raja Yoga system, or at least the University's rendition of it, caused them to feel spiritually dissatisfied. For example, in his 'Open Letter to all B.K's' posted on the Advance Party website, 'Shivbaba21' describes how in the early 1990s his 'intoxication with [the] Godly knowledge started to decline...on churning the knowledge more unanswered questions started cropping up' and how after joining the Advance Party

> there was a miracle change in me and I was on cloud nine. I was completely rejuvenated and got a new lease of life. Suddenly life appeared to be more meaningful than ever before and past, present and future knowledge became clear.[14]

Indeed, Dixit himself only became aware of his role as the corporeal medium of Ram/Shiva after he became disenchanted with University. As it is described on the website, in 1969 'Dixit got the Godly knowledge propounded by [the University]', although he found that 'he had many doubts about the knowledge which could neither be cleared by B.K. Sarala, the Zonal Incharge nor the senior brothers and sisters at Mt. Abu'. As a result, between 1969 and 1976 he studied both the Sakar and Avaktya murlis in depth and eventually concluded that although Raja Yoga was '100% true it [was] not complete'. In particular, he came to believe that not only had Lekhraj been 'guided by someone else during the early years of the establishment of the institution', but also that Shiva would be incarnated on earth 'till its transformation'. Later, after 'years of labour, introspection and churning' he felt confident enough to reveal these insights to the senior members of the University. Most of those that he approached, however, 'rejected his ideas [,] calling it a result of insanity', although a 'few brothers of sisters...did understand the importance of the knowledge clarified by Baba Dixit and realized that it was not his personal perception but was a unique clarification of [the murlis]...as revealed by **Supreme Soul Himself**. 'Debarred' from the University shortly after this, Dixit 'toured the country in general and Capital Delhi in particular', before settling in his native village of Kampil in Uttar Pradesh, Northern India from 1982 onwards in order to promulgate his spiritual insights.

In this way, aside from their critique of the University and its current world-ambivalence, the Advance Party may be also seen to provide an example of another level or interpretation of the original millenarianism. As with the original rendition, this represents a form of protest against an alleged spiritual decline within a dominant tradition, couched in the terms of that tradition. For example, the Advance Party draw on the notion of the kalpa to make a comparison between the decline of the world from its Golden Aged purity and the University's alleged increasing corruptness

> Just as the physical world starts on a righteous note in the beginning of Golden Age and become[s] unrighteous at the end of the Iron Age and is destroyed by nuclear war and natural calamities; so also the subtle world of BKs is initially righteous to begin with in 1937 but gradually becomes unrighteous toward the end in 2000 when Shankar destroyed the unrighteous Brahmins who are not following the Godly code of conduct and **gives inheritance of paradise to righteous Brahmins in this very life.**[15]

In both examples, then, the stated aim is to move beyond the corrupted manifest content and return to some putative uncorrupted core of the tradition by claiming exclusive access to divine authority as manifested through a particular 'corporeal medium'. Both also predict and comfort themselves with descriptions of a divine 'imaginary vengeance' that will be meted out to those corrupt 'outsiders' but which 'insiders' will be immune to.

Another issue that is raised by the Advance Party which is side-stepped by the Brahma Kumaris involves the former group specifying a date for the apocalypse. According to the 'timetable' published on their website, between 2004 and 2008, Dev Dixit will be revealed as '**Prajapita (Father of Humanity)**...[the] **World Emperor** or **Shri Narayan** [who] will control the world through **108** souls' firstly to 'the Brahmin family and then to the outside world'. Following this revelation, the Brahma Kumaris and the Advance Party will merge forming 225,000 couples. These couples 'known as **Angels** or **Farishtas**...will <u>not leave</u> their bodies during [the] destruction [of the world, but will]...become [the Golden Age] ancestors of the entire human civilisation of six billion souls'.[16] Between 2006 and 2008, the website goes on, the whole world will experience '[p]aradise on this earth before destruction', rather than afterwards as it is 'erroneously thought by most BK's'.[17] After the destruction, between 2008 and 2036, the 225,000 'couples will undergo divine transformation of their bodies' and will 'give birth to 225,000 twin children (one son, one daughter) making the total of 900,000 souls at the beginning of the Golden Age'. Finally, in 2036 – exactly one hundred years since the beginning of the Confluence Age – the Golden Age will begin with the coronation of 'Prince

Krishna', who will adopt the title 'Shri Narayan – from his Father – World Emperor **RAM**'.[18]

This level of clarity effectively renders the Advance Party's eschatology liable to the problems that have historically beset millenarian groups who provide a specific date for the apocalypse and who have to then rationalise the non-event afterwards to themselves and the outside world. The work of Festinger *et al.* (1964) is especially pertinent in this respect. In *When Prophecy Fails* he and his colleagues investigated a UFO cult that predicted the end of the world and the manner in which they reacted to the clear disconfirmation. Rather than abandoning their belief as folly, they instead began for the first time to proselytise and to claim that through a miracle the world had been saved. As will be discussed in the final section of this chapter, this phenomenon could suggest a plausible reason for several crucial events in the University's recent history. However, for the moment in the next section I intend to apply Festinger's thesis to the University's membership in order to analyse the manner in which the millennium is 'negotiated'.

Personal Reflexivity: Coping with Dissonance

For Festinger *et al.*, cognitive dissonance refers to a relationship between two beliefs, opinions or emotions held by a particular individual:

> Two opinions or beliefs, or items of knowledge are *dissonant* with each other if they do not fit together – that is, if they are inconsistent, or if, considering only the particular two items, one does not follow from the other (ibid., 1964, p. 25).

Festinger argues that this tension leads to psychological discomfort and attempts by the individual to reduce or eliminate the dissonance through one or all of three techniques; attempting to change one or more of the dissonant beliefs; acquiring new information or evidence to increase the consonance between the two elements; and/or forgetting or reducing the importance of the dissonance. For example, a smoker might deny the link between smoking and cancer, actively seek out scientific literature that denies such a link and/or avoid discussions with oncologists (Luhrmann, 1994). More specifically, he argues that in order for such techniques to emerge and be effective in millenarian groups after prophecy disconfirmation five conditions must be met:

1. individuals must have conviction in the prophecy and;
2. they must have made some commitment to the prophecy and the group;
3. the prophecy must be amenable to disconfirmation and;
4. such disconfirmation must explicitly occur, and;
5. social support must be available to the individual subsequent to the disconfirmation (ibid., pp. 4, 216).

However, looking at these conditions, what becomes immediately apparent is that the Brahma Kumaris example does not adequately fit into the schema. As outlined in the previous chapter, the University's membership is not homogenous, but rather encompasses a variety of membership types, differing in their orientation to the normative structures, commitment to the University and extent to which Raja Yoga impinges upon and influences their sense of social-identity. Thus, whereas a spiritual searcher or a fully-awakened interpretative drifter is highly likely to be committed to Lekhraj's prophecies this is not so for those on the periphery. For example, as noted in the previous chapter, those instrumental or eclectic users that I spoke to were often either oblivious or indifferent ('that's not really something that effects me') to this aspect of Raja Yoga, viewing it often as distinct from, if not alien to, their own interests or lifestyle. In contrast, those on the core of the movement are not only committed to the eschatology – through regular attendance and following the recommended lifestyle – but also experience themselves and the world through this 'remembrance'. To cite Sister Manda (1994, no pagination; emphasis added), 'I have to *feel* it, I have to *accept* it. It has to be *my vision*, in *my thoughts*, in *my words*, in *my attitude*. I have to *live that experience*'. Moreover, whilst, as we shall see later, the University were once explicit in setting a date for the destruction of the world, more recently – following its disconfirmation – they have, like the Jehovah's Witnesses (see Zygmunt, 2000) largely abandoned date-setting, preferring instead to speak of the destruction being 'close' or 'near at hand'.

For these reasons, Festinger's thesis can not be applied satisfactorily to the Brahma Kumaris case. However, this is not the case with the Advance Party who not only specify an exact date but also, due to its sectarian nature, are characterised by a much more homogenous – or at least less heterogeneous – membership. Tanya Luhrmann's (1994) analysis of ritual magician's attempts at negotiating the dissonance engendered by practising magic in the context of a modern, scientific culture is, however, much more applicable. As she ironically puts it, 'it is one thing to read your horoscope, it is another thing to have your boss stand naked in his living room and invoke Hermes for a more efficient secretary' (ibid., pp. 292-3). Following Luhrmann, two major areas of potential dissonance may be noted within the University. Firstly, there is the possible (inter-traditional) dissonance between what is claimed in Raja Yoga and what is held by the scientific, geological, archaeological and historical orthodoxy. For example, whilst the Brahma Kumaris accept a kind of linear time (in that *a* leads to *b*) they also, by believing in a predetermined cycle, believe strongly that *b* leads to *a*. This would mean, to take some absurd examples, that not only is the director James Cameron allegedly to blame for the *Titanic* disaster in 1912 by making a film of the sinking in the late 1990s but also that the Stonehenge monument was built as a historical memory of Black Sabbath's early 1980s stage set. In my own experience I have had a Raja Yogi confirm to me through the notion of 'memorials' or historical memories the possibility that not only did *Star Wars* influence cross-cultural hero myths but also that Conrad's *Heart of Darkness* (1902) was influenced by Stanley Kubrick's *Apocalypse Now* (1979). Similarly, the belief that human history is only 5,000 years old, as Whaling (1995) notes puts the Brahma Kumaris on a crash-course with most, if not all, scientific, historical and geological opinion. Secondly, there is the (intra-tradition) dissonance engendered by the individual elements of Raja Yoga or the University's world-ambivalence. How, for example, do members explain the University's dealings with the UN or attempts to attract members through New Age-ification in the light of the world-rejecting revealed wisdom?

Use of Spatialisation II: The Metaphor of Consciousness

In order to deal with such dissonance, Raja Yogis utilise the metaphor of 'consciousness'. This echoes the institutional use of spatialisation and involves – in a manner akin to the distinction made by the magicians studied by Luhrmann between different levels or planes of existence – the distinction between soul-conscious and body-conscious knowledge. This then serves not only to insulate members from any criticism from the outside world but also, perhaps more importantly, to rationalise why such criticism occurs. Again, in a manner akin to the Luhrmann's magicians, Raja Yogis then employ an (often inconsistent) patchwork of different explanations of the relationship between the two types of consciousness to different people at different times, although in general terms this involves three different attitudes towards the two levels. First, the dogmatic assertion that soul-consciousness is true and that body-consciousness is, by definition, false ('Realist'). Second, the claim that soul consciousness is true but cannot be understood or explained adequately in body-conscious terms ('Two-Worlds'). Third, the claim that all knowledge is relative and therefore ultimately a matter of personal faith or opinion ('Relativist').

Realist Amongst themselves, at the backstage area of the University, Raja Yogis generally employ a dogmatic distinction between the two types of consciousness in terms of their absolute truth or falsehood. In other words, they accept the dissonance between what they believe and what others outside the University believe and use it to argue that one is inherently true and the other, by definition, false. Thus, on the one hand there is the false, body-conscious (e.g. scientific, historical, archaeological) knowledge of the outside world and on the other there is the University's revealed true soul-conscious knowledge. This then allows them to argue that what appears to be falsehood to those in body-consciousness is actually the Truth and *vice versa*, although only Raja Yogis are aware of this. Indeed, some Raja Yogis told me that of course examples such as those given above appear extreme or indeed ludicrous to those outside the University, such as myself, but that is exactly because non-Raja Yogis are unable to view the world objectively through soul-consciousness. This links particularly with interpretative drifters' and spiritual searchers' retrospective account of their conversion. One of my interviewees, for example, referred to his conversion as a transition from 'living in falsehood' to 'living in truth – or call it awareness or soul consciousness…' Similarly, during one of the evening meditation classes that I attended during my fieldwork, a murli dating from the 1930s was read out in which Lekhraj's message to members was that they should be clear that anyone who claimed anything *contra* what he said were *ipso facto* 'liars'.

In other cases, Raja Yogis will self-consciously adopt a position of 'epistemological authoritarianism' (Wallis, 1974) and explain what they claim to be the validity of their beliefs by making reference to Shiva as the ultimate arbiter of Truth. For example:

> The very fact that we are transforming the self, *Baba is telling us how* to do this, so the fact that we don't have a date in a way doesn't matter because *Baba tells us that* through this transforming as we're transforming ourselves there's great happiness. Actually this is the happiest time of the whole cycle for us because there's contentment and peace, all these things that the knowledge brings us (emphasis added).

In this example, the key aspect of the explanation is that God ('Baba') serves as a voice of authority, explaining not only how to transform the self but why a date is not necessary as personal transformation will ultimately lead to global 'transformation'. More importantly, by citing His ultimate epistemological authority, what would appear to be dissonant to the outside world – predetermined millenarianism without a date – 'in a way doesn't matter' and is thus able to be downplayed. This is also shown here:

> Every religion has *some truth in it...But God tells us that each has the facet of the diamond, Baba says he is the complete diamond.* He is the truth and in all religions that is how he is spoken of; the truth, the light, the way. So he is that complete diamond. And each religion takes a part, without a facet it wouldn't be complete. So this is where it shows how necessary each religion is...(emphasis added).

This is part of a lengthy answer to the question of how the University could claim that Raja Yoga is the precursor to and influence of world religions that historically predate it by often a few thousand years. Again 'Baba' is cited as the source of ultimate authority although this member goes further utilising a metaphor borrowed from jewellery – a common theme in the University – to refer to other religions as mere 'facets' of the 'complete [spiritual] diamond' of Raja Yoga. A similar position is adopted by other members who draw on the metaphor of the world tree discussed in chapter four, to argue that all spiritual traditions are branches of the root tradition of Raja Yoga. In doing so, (s)he is not rejecting the validity of the other traditions *per se*, but rather arguing that their validity is inherently due to them being facets of the Raja Yoga 'compete diamond' or one of the many 'branches' on its 'trunk'.

Two worlds The second, much more common, type of explanation is deployed mainly in members' front-stage dealings with the outside world and represents a more *laissez-faire* and relativist approach to the relationship between the two levels of consciousness. As in the previous example, soul-consciousness is presented as objectively true, although justifications for this claim are largely made without direct reference to the self-authority of the tradition, i.e. 'Baba says…'. Rather, (s)he will attempt to explain the nature of Raja Yoga in experiential terms and/or with reference to scientific rationalism or other forms of culturally accepted academic discourse.

In many respects, within Raja Yoga the experiential dimension (*being*) gained through yogic meditation is valued more than what is often seen to be mere intellectual *knowing*. Indeed, some members I spoke to expressed the view that intellectual knowledge was not only incapable of grasping Raja Yoga but also possibly a barrier to it as it often imposed body-conscious categories onto it. Rather, they stated, it could only be understood fully through the experience gained through meditation. This view was expressed, for example, by long-term Raja Yogi Charles Hogg, who spoke in a recorded lecture of how 'knowledge plus experience of the knowledge brings so much power to the soul' and how

> the easiest thing is to know all this knowledge, it's so easy, and to repeat it to others, but actually experience the knowledge...Baba was saying every single point of knowledge has an associated experience...it's changing a form of knowledge into my own experience (Hogg, n.d., no pagination).

It is this experience that Raja Yogis will attempt to communicate to outsiders in order to both explain their beliefs and also, if necessary, to argue that what appears to be dissonant in intellectual or body-conscious terms is not actually the case. In other words, such members will be simultaneously epistemological individualists and epistemological universalists; holding the view that they access truth via their experience and that this truth is of a universal order (Heelas, 1998b). Good examples of this may be found in the spiritual autobiographies published by the University. Within these, Raja Yogis will attempt to communicate their meditation experiences, of, for example, being in the soul world, in order to either inspire others, as in the case of Dadi Janki's books, or to act as guides for the listener's or reader's meditation. For example, Ken O'Donnell in *Pathways to Higher Consciousness* describes many such experiences through prose and verse, such as being a soul, knowing God and this on soul consciousness:

> *Personal Experience*
> *I used to think that everything was unreal or an illusion but, after going into it deeply, I realised that the drama of life, the stage of the world, the actors and the roles are real enough. I concluded that my vision of things, and therefore my deductions, can be illusionary or not. The basic illusion, 'I am this body', was a thread running through my existence. Upon this illusion all other thoughts, decisions and actions were strung* (O'Donnell, 1996, p. 40, italics in original).

Nevertheless, Raja Yogis are aware that to outsiders such experiences could appear to be the result of, for example, an over-active imagination, and so will often attempt to explain their experiences or justify aspects of Raja Yoga with reference to forms of academic discourse. In particular, in frontstage discussions with outsiders, Raja Yogis will cite scientific or psychological evidence for the physical and emotional benefits of vegetarianism, positive thinking and meditation. Similarly, as in the New Age more generally, certain writers such as Blake, Huxley, Jung and Maslow are 'name-dropped' to support claims regarding self-development and human potential. Indeed, in one piece of literature both Woody Allen and Friedrich Nietzsche were cited as believers in cyclic time and reincarnation, the former due to a one-liner, the latter due to his notion of 'eternal recurrence'.[19]

Similarly, in the backstage area, scientific explanations are also often deployed where they are congruent with the revealed wisdom and rejected where not with, for example, members citing arguments against the validity of radiocarbon dating, geology and evolutionary theory to criticise amongst other things both the linear model of time, the existence of dinosaurs and the accepted length of human civilisation. For example, senior member Jagdish Chander has written two lengthy books where he simultaneously attacks scientific evidence contrary to Raja Yoga declaring it invalid and body-conscious while citing other scientific evidence to support the revealed wisdom (see Chander, 1988a; 1988b; see also O'Donnell, 1995, pp. 81-2 on evolutionary theory). Likewise, Neville Hodgkinson a former scientific correspondent for an English national newspaper, in discussion with me at the Global Retreat Centre, questioned the existence of dinosaurs on the basis of the lack of bones that been found while another Raja Yogi cited contemporary physics to argue that dinosaurs exist in a parallel time/space dimension and that because of a warp hole or somesuch their bones end up in this dimension buried underground.

Such views are also expressed in latent form in the University's newspaper, *Purity* in the *Gleanings from the Press* and *Mr Wise* columns. In the first, examples of 'Golden Age technology' (such as the CD player, cloning, the helicopter and 'intelligent' machines) and world events such as population statistics, global warming predictions and stories of corrupt public figures are presented to support the revealed wisdom although no direct reference is made to the fact. Likewise, the *Mr Wise* column applies a form of *non sequitur*-prone Socratic debate to argue against certain aspects of scientific orthodoxy. As in the example below, the end result is always that *Mr Wise* 'cannot say' and eventually has to admit that the questioner 'is right':

> Mr Wise?
> *Yes.*
> There will be no end?
> *If there was no beginning.*
> Shall we call this space-time continuum the ultimate history and geography of the universe?
> *I cannot say.*
> And Mr Wise?
> *Yes.*
> What then is death and destruction?
> *Souls are immortal and Matter is indestructible, they only change form.*
> Which is necessary for the drama of life to go on?
> *I cannot say.*
> Lastly.
> *Yes?*
> New Becomes old?
> *Quite. And old becomes new, or gets renewed, to be more accurate*
> Because the cosmic drama is eternal and so, cyclic?
> *You are right* (*Purity*, May 1998, p. 12).

This, then, represents an ambivalent orientation towards the two types of consciousness; simultaneously believing in their relative truth and falsehood and yet citing the latter where necessary to support various claims. In this way, it echoes the common New Age approach to scientific discourse noted in chapter two wherein science is at once 'villain' and source of authority. Moreover, it also represents a middle position in regard to the relationship between the two types of consciousness between the realist position discussed previously and a position of relativism.

Relativism Finally, on some occasions what would appear to be a statement of relativism is also deployed to either deflect certain questions or to end a debate that is going round in circles. This involves two key strategies; arguing that both types of consciousness are incommensurable and therefore a matter of faith and, as at the institutional level, the use of metaphor. Both are perhaps best illustrated by drawing on my experiences of questions, my own included, that were raised during some of the evening murli classes that I intended.

In the first instance a question was raised regarding the validity of the view of history presented within Raja Yoga. Firstly an experiential explanation was given such as that discussed above. The questioner then challenged this by arguing that an individual suffering from schizophrenia has experiences that they consider real and asked how could she, the Raja Yogi, not be sure that they too were not suffering from delusions. In response to this she made vague reference to a piece of scientific research questioning the reliability of radio-carbon dating and stated that much research from a variety of disciplines questions both the linear model of time and also the orthodox view of human history. 'Yes', the questioner went on 'but scientists never agree and they change their minds all the time. If you look hard enough then you can find evidence to support any belief you want'. At this point the Raja Yogi subtly signalled that she wished to return to reading the murli by stating 'well, ultimately it comes down to faith and it's not really up to me to try and convince you one way or another'.

The second example comes from one of the final evening classes that I attended, at which the core content of the murli was the destruction of the world. During one part of this an eclectic user asked 'so, you're an end-of-the world cult then?', to which the centre co-ordinator replied, 'no, we believe in world *transformation*'. In response, the questioner asked 'well, surely the "transformation" that you're talking about is destruction? The population is going to shrink almost instantly down to a couple of thousand, whole areas of the world are going to be flooded, nuclear bombs are going to be going off'. 'Well', replied the co-ordinator, '*it depends how you look at it*. We like to see it as transformation – which is what it is – but I suppose in body-consciousness it could look different' (emphasis added).

In both these examples, little or no emphasis is placed on the inherent truth of one position *vis-à-vis* the inherent falsehood of another. Rather, in the first example, such a distinction is seemingly abandoned in favour of a radical perspectivism where truth exists solely within the eye of the beholder. Likewise, in the second example, what Raja Yogis hold to be the inherent truth of Lekhraj's revealed eschatology dissolves into nihilistic language games; is a nuclear holocaust 'destruction' or 'transformation'? Indeed, ultimately, does it matter which metaphor is used?

Conclusion: From World-Ambivalence to...?

In this chapter I have discussed the type of negotiations made use of by the University and its membership in managing its millenarianism and current world-ambivalence. This argument may be summarised as follows.

The University's current world-ambivalence is characterised by the dynamic coexistence within the same organisation of, firstly, disparate levels of membership differing in their commitment to the organisation and the degree to which the University's normative structures impinge on their daily lives; secondly, different and largely antithetical theodical renditions (ascetic and instrumental); and, thirdly, by extension different 'millenniums': one world-affirming and couched in the terminology of human potential and the New Age, the other exclusivistic and world-rejecting. This ambivalence is managed by the University delineating, in Goffman's (1969) sense, its frontstage from its backstage – its public and its private identity – and, on this basis, presenting different metaphors or types of events when dealing with the different 'areas'. Likewise, amongst members one finds the utilisation of a patchwork of explanations and justifications of the relationship between the University's worldview (and its sometimes disparate elements) and that of the 'outside' world – ranging on a continuum from realism to relativism, these again, being deployed in different (frontstage or backstage) contexts and with different audiences.

Developing these ideas and turning from the present to the future I would argue that any future evolution of the University will develop out of this dynamic interaction between frontstage and backstage and world-affirmation and world-rejection.

On this basis three scenarios suggest themselves. Firstly, the University may for one reason or another slide into world-affirmation through, for example, a theodical shift from the literal to the metaphorical millennium. This would involve an increased emphasis on New Age-ification and the world-affirming, individualistic 'millennium' of self-development and human potential and an associated decline in importance of the original world-rejecting theodicy. Lekhraj, for example, would, as in the leaflet described above become simply a 'man of vision' who showed the need for self-development in spite of, or perhaps because of, his material success. Likewise, the University's original mythology would, in a manner akin to Jungian psychology, be (re)presented as an analogue of the life-course with, again, Lekhraj's own life perhaps been held up as an example of such a process of individuation. At the other extreme, the University could reject its world-affirming aspect as meaningless and body-conscious, completely contradictory to its original message, and return to its original world-rejection. This would involve, for example, a demand for total, all-or-nothing-commitment from its members and, as one finds with the Advance Party, a dogmatic restatement of the literal millennium. Similarly, public lectures – where they occurred – would be concerned not with human potential or self-management but with rather communicating the revealed wisdom on its own terms to the outside world.

Neither of these two scenarios, however, I would argue are likely to occur. Complete world-affirmation, for example, is unlikely due to the backstage, world-rejecting theodical 'baggage' that the University carries and which it cannot conceivably reject without renouncing much of its own identity and status. Indeed, such a shift is in fact largely unnecessary because of the previously discussed distinction between frontstage and backstage. Not only is the University to all intents and purposes, and – most importantly – in appearances a world-affirming group to the outside world, but also through the frontstage/backstage distinction it is able to effectively reconcile world-affirmation with world-rejection. The reversion to world-rejection is also unlikely for these reasons also. Through its UN connections, community work and self-publicity, the University has invested too much of its reputation and credibility in the 'outside' world to merely reject it at this stage. Likewise, as I noted above, at both the institutional and individual level emphasis is placed on the belief that it is possible, and indeed necessary, to straddle between both worlds, to be both 'in' and yet not involved with or attached to the world. Moreover, through the institutional use of spatialisation and metaphor the University is able to effectively satisfy its world-rejecting sphere through, for example, the Mt. Abu 'pilgrimage' and morning classes, while in another space and through another metaphor attend to its world-affirming sphere. Having said this, however, this shift is highly likely to occur within groups, such as the Advance Party, who will break away from the University, rejecting what they allege to be its increasing worldliness and who will claim instead to be returning to some putative original, uncorrupted message.

A more likely scenario is that the present situation will continue with the University and its membership developing more and more sophisticated methods to negotiate between frontstage and backstage and also between the 'inner' (in the sense of the University and its membership) and the outside world. In particular I would argue that the prime site at and through which this will occur will continue to be the millennium, around issues such as whether it should be seen as literal or metaphorical, predetermined or malleable. Indeed, again drawing on the work of Festinger *et al.* (1964), it could be argued that the millennium – in particular its failure to appear as predicted – is in fact the driving force behind many of the changes in the University that I have discussed in the preceding pages.

Looking closely at the University's history, one finds an interesting correlation between significant dates for the University (derived from Raja Yoga) and its increasing proselytising and internationalisation. In particular, one may note as significant the period of the University's non-proselytising (1937-1950), the 100 year anniversary of Lekhraj's birth (1876-1976; see also Babb, 1986, p. 117) and the Golden Anniversary of the University's inception (1937-1987). In other words, one cannot, for example, argue as the Advance Party do that the University's proselytising is a direct result of Lekhraj's death and thereby the result of a lack of guidance as the process had begun much earlier. Rather, it could be plausibly argued, following Festinger *et al.*'s thesis, that it may have resulted from the fact that 'world transformation' did not occur in 1950, thirteen years after the formation of Om Mandali.

As will be recalled from chapter three, a central aspect of Lekhraj's sermons to the group was that they were the historical 'memory' of the Pandavas who were exiled for thirteen years but then returned from the wilderness. Likewise, one could note the University's increasing proselytising during the last two decades and its attempts at recruiting membership through New Age-ification is significant in relation to the two anniversaries mentioned above. For example, according to the Advance Party website, before his death Lekhraj gave 1976 as the date for the end of the present cycle. Moreover, he continued to espouse this view in the Avaktya Murlis for another five years following his death. On the twenty-fifth of October 1969, for example, he stated that '[t]he final destruction of the whole world takes place within 6 years. Those who tell it to be 7 years have their position reduced'. Similarly, on the fourth of February 1974 he confirmed this; '[f]rom 10 years (of the declaration), only 2 years are left. Soon Kaliyug has come to an end. The drama is certain'.[20] Indeed, according to the Advance Party website, Lekhraj went so far as to produce a declaration notifying the Indian government and 'other dignitaries…of the coming destruction of the world and the establishment of heaven'.[21] If this is correct, one could therefore perhaps speculate, following Festinger's hypothesis, that this disconfirmation may have played a crucial role in the growth of the University's proselytising from this period onwards.

Indeed, going further one could draw on subsequent reformulations of Festinger *et al.*'s 'failed prophecy' thesis to illuminate the possible 'human, all to human' factors behind the Advance Party's schism in the late 1970s. In a recent review of the literature on failed prophecy, Lorne Dawson (1999) concludes that proselytising is only one possible reaction to failed prophecy. Instead, he argues that aside from attempts to proselytise, such groups will typically make attempts at what he terms 'rationalization' and 'reaffirmation'. The strategy of reaffirmation, Dawson argues, is employed by all the groups discussed in the literature post-disconfirmation, and involves them turning inward and engaging in a process of group (re)building. For example, Schmalz (2000, p. 240) noted that following their 1975 disconfirmation, the Jehovah's Witnesses engaged in a 'five year period of denial and purge' in which members of the governing body blamed the rank-and-file membership, expelled 30,000 Witnesses in one year alone (1978) and, more generally, made even greater insistence on doctrinal orthodoxy. Likewise, in their study of the Institute of Applied Metaphysics (IAM), Palmer and Finn (2000) observed how disconfirmation can be utilised by some groups as a form of 'collective rite':

> In such cases, the rite of apocalypse, ostensibly aimed at destroying the old order of planet Earth, actually functions to bring about a new order within the cult or sect. When examined within the framework of the charismatic career of the leader-founder, or the group's changing relationship with its host society, the 'acting out' of Endtime often

> appears to function as a collective rite of passage into a new group identity (ibid., pp. 229-30).

Following, or sometimes bound up with, any attempt at reaffirmation there are likely to be attempts at rationalisation. Indeed, for J. Gordon Melton (2000, p. 149) rationalisation is 'not just another option, but the common mode of adaptation of millennial groups following the failure of a prophecy'. In particular, he argues that following prophetic failure, groups consistently engage in what he terms a process of 'spiritualization'. Here 'the prophesised event is reinterpreted in such a way that what was supposed to have been a visible, verifiable occurrence is seen to have been in reality an invisible, spiritual occurrence'. In other words, 'the event occurred as predicted, only on a spiritual level' (ibid.). Similarly, as with the Jehovah's Witness example discussed above, an attempt may be made to level the blame for the failure on the outside world or even on the members themselves. In some cases, the failure of the prophecy may be attributed to a human error, such as a miscalculation or a misunderstanding of the prophecy. Finally, a leader may attempt to frame the failure in positive terms as a 'test of faith' which the group, by undergoing the necessary trials, have successfully 'passed'.

For both Dawson (1999) and Melton (2000), then, rationalisation and reaffirmation are the key strategies utilised by millenarian groups following prophetic failure. Indeed, Melton (ibid., p. 155) goes so far as to state that Festinger *et al.*'s (1964) claim that groups will attempt to reduce dissonance through proselytising 'has found no confirmation in subsequent studies' and should therefore be best seen as an 'idiosyncrasy' of the group in question. Dawson, whilst not going so far, also concludes that only a very small number of the studies on such groups report that prophetic failure led to proselytising.

Leaving to one side the question raised previously of whether the Brahma Kumaris could perhaps be seen as an example of this latter phenomenon, if we accept the Advance Party's account of the 1976 prophetic failure two points may be drawn out. The first is that, it is clear that several attempts at the various forms of rationalisation were made by the University. In the first instance, the Advance Party claim that when

> the destruction did not materialize...many Brahmins left the [University] because their hopes were dashed. Those who stayed had their faith reduced by half. They [had] sacrificed their lives in this godly institution, left their families and invested all their wealth in this cause. How [could] they go and where [could] they go? They [had] no choice but to stay because they were dependent on the institution for their bread and butter.[22]

Next, they claim that any mention of the prophecy was removed from the murlis, becoming **'hidden from those who came after 1976'**, and members 'were told that this was a test of faith'.[23]

Second, if one reads between the lines of this account, it is possible to see a further attempt at rationalisation being made. A few members, the website goes on, felt dissatisfied with this and after reflection realised that the prophecy had in fact occurred, although not in the literal sense that they had been expecting. The year 1976 had been designated as the 'Revelation Year of the Father' and as God can neither lie nor make a mistake, they concluded that Shiva must have been 'revealed' to the world in some other way. In this way, the 'Revelation Year of the Father' became spiritualised; it no longer referred to the end of the kalpa, but instead referred to the year in which Shiva would be 'revealed' to the world in His new, permanent corporeal 'chariot': Virendra Dev Dixit. Those who accepted this vision, either left or where expelled from the University and went join Dixit in forming what became known as the Advance Party.

Indeed, going further one may note another example of rationalisation within the Advance Party. On the original shivbaba.com website that I accessed in July 1998, the date for destruction was given as 2001 (see Walliss, 1999, p. 382; Walliss, 2000a). However, on the new Shivbaba.org website, this date has been moved back to 2008. Similarly, the date at which it is claimed that the Brahma Kumaris will merge with the Advance Party has also been postponed by four years. Both timetables, however, presented 2036 as the beginning of the 'Golden Age'. When I asked the Advance Party the reason for this revision I was told that it was the result of human error. In their excitement and over-enthusiasm, the Advance Party miscalculated the date. The dates 2001 and 2008, I was told, were 'never given to [the Advance Party] by Shiva, but instead 'were just educated guesses made by the students...who were doing research on godly sermons'.[24] On this basis, one could perhaps speculate on what might happen within the Advance Party when their revised prophecy (hopefully) does not come to pass. Will they, like the Jehovah's Witnesses, set further dates based on new calculations or, like the University, reject the 'date-consciousness' of the literal millennium in favour of a more metaphorical one? Would further rationalisation and postponement of the date of destruction lead to a schism within the group, with some members either breaking away to form a more radical group, leaving completely or perhaps leaving to rejoin the University?

All this is of course, whilst interesting, still speculation. However, if the account presented on the Advance Party's website were true it would potentially explain much concerning the University's recent history, such as why its internationalisation programme intensified in the 1970s and 1980s, and why Dixit and the Advance Party left the University in 1976. Nevertheless, there is, as far as I am aware, no way of independently corroborating the information presented on the Advance Party's website and so any conclusions made on this matter will have to remain at best tentative. On a slightly more concrete level, looking to the future rather than into the past, one could speculate on the significance of 2008 for the University, the date given by the Advance Party for the apocalypse, or 2037, its one hundred year anniversary. One could also consider how it might cope following the deaths of the few members who remain from its early years such as Dadi Janki or, perhaps more importantly, the death of Dadi Gulzar, the official medium for the incorporeal Lekhraj (Whaling, 1995). My own sense is that the millennium, like the University itself, is reflexive, malleable and constantly open to revision.

Notes

[1] http://www.bkwsu.com/about/phil5f.html (accessed November 2001).
[2] Within the Brahma Kumaris' theodicy, the 'Advance Party' are the group of pure souls who arrive on the earth at the start of the Golden Age to prepare the way for the other souls. The break-away group's use of this name is therefore seen within the University as somewhat impertinent and they therefore refer to them instead as the 'Shankar Party' or the 'Shankars'. For the sake of simplicity and without wanting to step down on either side of the confrontation, I will use the term 'Advance Party' in this chapter.
[3] http://www.shivbaba.org/opl.htm (accessed November 2001).
[4] http://www.shivbaba.org/misconcept-2.htm (bold in original) (accessed November 2001).
[5] http://www.shivbaba.org/introduction.htm (accessed November 2001).
[6] http://www.shivbaba.org/contrast.htm (point 6) (accessed November 2001).
[7] Ibid. 'An Introduction to the Advance Knowledge'.
[8] Ibid. 'An Introduction to the Advance Knowledge'.
[9] Avaktya Murli delivered on the 31st of May 1977. http://www.shivbaba.org/point2.htm (point 3) (accessed November 2001).
[10] http://www.shivbaba.org/point4.htm (point 4, emphasis in original) (accessed November 2001).
[11] http://www.shivbaba.org.contrast.htm (point 36) (accessed November 2001).
[12] I found this quote on the Advance Party's previous website – www.shivbaba.com – in mid 1998. The page that it was posted on ('Churning Points 5') has since been revised and the quote removed.
[13] Email from 'ShivBaba21' (dated 3.8.98).
[14] 'Open Letter'.
[15] This quote was also found on the previous version of 'Churning Points 5' posted on shivbaba.com.
[16] http://www.shivbaba.org/summary1.htm (bold and underline in original) (accessed November 2001).
[17] http://www.shivbaba.org/misconcept-2.htm (bold in original) (accessed November 2001).
[18] 'SUMMARY-ADVANCE KNOWLEDGE (FOR BKS ONLY)'.
[19] Raja Yoga multimedia CD ROM published by the University in 1997 and offered free of charge on the BKWSU.COM website for a limited period in 1998.
[20] http://www.shivbaba.org/misconcept-5.htm (accessed November 2001).
[21] 'Misconceptions in Godly Knowledge-5'.
[22] 'Misconceptions in Godly Knowledge-5'.
[23] 'Misconceptions in Godly Knowledge-5'.
[24] Email from Dr. Anil Maheshwari (dated 6.12.01).

Conclusion

In Search of Post-Traditional Religiosity

In chapter one I introduced the two versions of the detraditionalisation thesis. As will be recalled, the radical version of the thesis – put forward by Beck, Bauman and Giddens – claimed that within the contemporary world there has been a shift in authority from 'without' to the voice that came from 'within' the individual. Thus, for example, Giddens argued that within what he termed Late Modernity, the individual's sense of self-identity could no longer be conferred authoritatively, but, rather, became a reflexive project. Likewise, Bauman argued that postmodern men and women were expected, on the one hand, to act ethically and yet, on the other, denied a universal set of binding norms. Indeed, Bauman claimed that the opposite was the case; the postmodern habitat being characterised by not one but a multitude of equally feasible ethical codes suggesting – rather than demanding – that they be followed. Finally, Beck argued that the only way of coping with the consequences of life in the global Risk Society was the jettisoning of tradition, old sureties and ideas and for modernity to become truly 'reflexive'. Individuals can no longer be (allegedly) passive, but, rather, have to actively shape the modernisation process through their actions.

In this book, I have been arguing against this view, in favour of the alternative, 'co-existence' version of this thesis. This, again as I set out in chapter one, levelled three main criticisms at the radical thesis. First, according to this view, the past was not as tradition-dominated as the authors above would believe. As Adam (1996), Luke (1996) and even Giddens (1999) have argued, this idea is a fiction, representing instead 'a set of tacit presumptions about modernity...and the equally tacit epistemological presumptions of anthropological fieldwork' (Jenkins, 2000, p. 15). Traditions, according to this view, were never simply received passively (even) in the past, but were always open to some degree of questioning, revision and elaboration. Second, this view rejects the claim that the contemporary world is 'post-traditional' and that, as a result, contemporary individuals are completely autonomous. Rather, as Heelas (1996d, p. 9) points out, 'in practice – and despite the language of autonomy and choice – we are controlled by routines, rules, procedures, regulations, laws, duties, schedules, diaries, timetables and customs'. Similarly, whilst our voices of authority might indeed come from 'within', these are not created *ex nihilo*, but instead are acquired to some extent from established values and practices. Third, perhaps most importantly, the co-existence thesis holds that the process of detraditionalization does not occur in isolation, but rather intersects with processes of tradition-maintenance and (re)construction. Thus, as I argued in chapter two, in the case of the New Age Movement, one finds a complex situation where, on the one hand, there is the rejection of external voices of authority in favour of the (spiritual) voice that comes from 'within' the individual whilst, on the other, there is the drawing on of such voices as sources of inspiration and, more importantly, as sources of justification. Similarly, it may be seen that the world-ambivalence that I have discussed in the previous four chapters could in some sense be usefully reframed as a tension – or, perhaps, an ongoing dialogue – within the University between the forces of detraditionalisation and those of tradition maintenance and rejuvenation.

Tradition Persistence and Rejuvenation

Primarily, at the most simplistic level the Brahma Kumaris example demonstrates the persistence of tradition in the contemporary world as a source of moral and identity-conferring authority. For committed members, Raja Yoga serves as a voice of ultimate authority and provides the basis for both epistemology (the distinction between body and soul consciousness), ontological security and personal identity (the notion of *Om Shanti*), and metaphysical speculation. Moreover, one could argue that Raja Yoga serves, in a Durkheimian sense, to bind individuals together on the basis of their shared (soul-conscious) experience of the 'sacred' (Durkheim, 1961). Howell and Nelson (1998), for example, write of the 'strong sense of intimacy' at murli readings and how this is further consolidated through the serious member's pilgrimage to Mt. Abu and his/her meeting with the incorporeal Lekhraj through Dadi Gulzar.

During everyday life, during meditation and particularly at murli classes, Raja Yogis claim to be seeking to transcend their lower, body conscious selves and achieve experiential contact (yoga) with the 'sacred' both within themselves and as manifested through Shiva Baba. In doing so – whether individually or in a group – they are also expressing a solidarity based on remembrance and soul consciousness that distinguishes between insiders and outsiders, the 'chosen' and the 'forsaken'. The sacred – that is, soul conscious – community of committed Raja Yogis also serves to provide both a sense of individual purpose and identity, although this is largely a result of their membership of a 'community of remembrance'. Thus, a common narrative told by committed members is that before becoming involved with the University, they felt that they did not fit in or belong in society, or in specific institutions such as the church, or felt that their life had no purpose. However, through (re)discovering their 'true' identity they also (re)discovered their purpose. For example, Pam expressed the view that she was meditating and trying to become soul conscious not just for herself but also 'for the world' because, as she saw it, 'a certain number [of people] have to get their thoughts right in order that world transformation will take place'. Indeed, she held that 'towards the end' she and all the other Raja Yogis will be needed to 'give peace and harmony to everyone else in the world'.

Moreover, at another level the Brahma Kumaris example demonstrates both the re-invigoration and the ongoing re-creation of tradition, hence my utilisation of Mellor's (1993) notion of reflexive traditions as a hermeneutic tool to examine this malleability and two-way interaction or negotiation. Examples of this phenomenon within the University may be broadly classified into two main areas. First, the development and re-interpretation of Raja Yoga to suit a world-affirming 'cultic milieu' (*elaboration*), such as the ongoing globalisation, New Age-ification and instrumentalisation of the original, world-rejecting theodicy; the changing status of Lekhraj and the *Avakyta* murlis; and the searching for signs heralding the 'end' in both the inner (psychological and group) and outside world. Second, techniques to negotiate world-ambivalence and dissonance (*consolidation*), such as the negotiation between 'frontstage' and 'backstage' areas of the University; between world-rejection and affirmation; between East and West; and between conservative and progressive. In addition there is the tension engendered between this negotiation and the critique of the University provided by the Advance Party and – at both the institutional and individual level – the methods utilised to discredit, marginalise or even deny the existence of the latter schismatic group. Likewise, within the Advance Party one finds the ongoing (re)interpretation and elaboration of Raja Yoga to suit their own purposes as well as, I would argue, an ongoing attempt to rationalise and spiritualise a series of failed prophecies.

Detraditionalisation

This is not to say, however, that despite the persistence of tradition as an external voice of authority, in some instances such traditions are not becoming for some individuals more and more a site of personal reflexivity and *bricolage*. In the context of the Brahma Kumaris, the instrumental and eclectic users described in chapter five demonstrate this phenomenon clearly. For both of these membership types, Raja Yoga becomes both privatised and decontextualised and seen predominantly as a means to an end. Thus, instrumental users will describe the reasons for their initial and continued involvement with the University in terms of how the meditation or the atmosphere at their local centre has helped to alleviate the symptoms of physical ailments or helped them to find a successful means of coping with stress or self-esteem issues. Similarly, for eclectic users, Raja Yoga serves as one 'tool' amongst maybe many that they will try out and then possibly discard in their spiritual quest. Indeed, both have little or no interest – or indeed, in some cases, awareness – of the normative aspect of Raja Yoga. 'Margaret', it will be recalled, characterised her involvement with the University and a range of other groups and techniques as 'dipping into things' rather than membership *per se*. Indeed, during our telephone conversation prior to the interview she expressed the view that she felt that she was not really the 'type' of person that I wanted to interview as she had to a large extent given up even minimally attending the University's events. She had, she said, taken what she liked from the University and now wanted to 'dip into' other things. Likewise, 'David', an instrumental user, had been attending for over five years when I interviewed him and yet expressed little or no knowledge of, or interest in, the 'spiritual side' of Raja Yoga.

This situation is made all the more interesting when it is considered, as noted in chapter five, that the majority of those attracted to the Brahma Kumaris and New Age activities in general fit almost exactly the socio-demographics of those one would expect to be involved in conventional religiosity (females, professionals and those in the older – mid-life onwards – age group). When considered in relation to falling church attendance figures (see, for example, Bruce 1995), this could perhaps add support to the view of the religious Establishment that the New Age and NRMs like the Brahma Kumaris are drawing individuals away from organised religiosity (see Bunting, 1996a). This would appear to have some level of validity when related to the case of the spiritual searchers discussed previously whose membership of the Brahma Kumaris grew out of a disenchantment and then disengagement with Christianity. However, at another level it may equally be argued that they may represent what Featherstone (1991), drawing on Bourdieu (1996 [1984]), refers to as the 'new petit bourgeois', not least in regard to their predominant occupational backgrounds in the provision of 'symbolic goods and services'; the creative and helping professions. This emergent social group, Featherstone argues, is characterised by an obsession with the 'art of living', with the pursuit of 'expressive and liberated lifestyles'. Members of this social group

> are fascinated by *identity*, *presentation*, *appearance*, *lifestyle*, and the endless quest for *new experiences*...Indeed, their awareness of the range of experiences open to them, the frequent lack of anchoring in terms of a specific locale or community, coupled with the self-consciousness of the autodidact, who always wishes to be more than he/she is, leads to a refusal to be classified, with *the injunction to resist fixed codes* as life is conceived as *essentially open-ended* (ibid., p. 44, emphasis added).

One could therefore argue that the 'invisible religion' (Luckmann, 1967) of the New Age is the religiosity of this social group *par excellence*. In both there is the emphasis on shaping identity as a project, on novel experiences and the rejection, on one level at least, of the 'fixed codes' of tradition. Bourdieu in fact goes so far as to list some of the practices adopted by this social group and includes such New Age activities as the esoteric, extra-terrestrials, parapsychology, PSI and telepathy, Transcendental Meditation, yoga and Zen (ibid., p. 370). Indeed, one could go further and argue that as a result of the high costs involved in participating in many New Age activities it is often only these 'reflexivity winners' (Lash and Urry, 1994) who have sufficient financial resources to dedicate themselves to these pursuits. As Steve Bruce (ibid., p. 114) has wryly noted 'unmarried mothers raising children on welfare tend to be too concerned with finding food, heat and light to be overly troubled by inner lights'.

However, what is particularly noteworthy in regard to the University is that although its events are run on a non-fee basis, those who attend are the very people who would in principle, given their incomes, be able to attend if a fee was levied. One cannot therefore argue that a significant segment of the population, the unemployed or manual workers, do not attend the University's events for financial reasons – a claim that could be made in regard to organisations or events that charge large sums for attendance (see Bourdieu, 1996, p. 217). Rather, more pertinent factors may include such things as interest (itself a reflection of cultural capital), levels of self-regard, limitations on free-time or even, following Bourdieu, different orientations toward the body and self-identity stemming from one's place in the job market (ibid., pp. 212-13). For example, drawing on Bruce again,

> it is a lot easier to imagine that, appropriately adjusted, the self is a powerful autonomous agent if your work offers autonomy and some opportunity for creativity than if you are part of a large semi-skilled manual labour force and pressingly aware of how little you can affect anything (op. cit., p. 113).

It is also perhaps noteworthy that the great majority of the courses run by the University in the UK at the present time address issues concerning the experiential, identity, the effective 'presentation of self' and, in particular, methods of finding fulfilment in – or at least of not being over-stressed by – life as a professional in whatever sector. The *what do you need to achieve the good life in the rollercoaster 'Nanosecond Nineties?'* and *what do extremely busy people need to achieve success without stress?* series of seminar-workshops and audio cassettes are a case in point. Indeed, Mike George, the Raja Yogi responsible for both these courses, has recently developed a management training programme entitled the *Brahma Kumaris Self Management System.* According to the literature this aims to help 'those who have to lead others during a period of transformational change' in

> **Integrating** the different priorities and responsibilities of your life – Work, Family, Health and Fitness, Community and Personal Self Development;
> **Clarifying** your focus in life – Your Personal Purpose, Values and Vision, Life Goals and Directions;
> **Learning** how to focus your mental energies and develop the will power necessary to bring about the changes you want in your behaviour and habits;
> **Developing** the authentic communication skills, clarity and self-esteem necessary to inspire and empower others (Brahma Kumaris Self Management Systems, n.d.).

Conclusion: In Search of Post-Traditional Religiosity

Of course, the Brahma Kumaris example detailed in the preceding pages represents just one manifestation of contemporary religiosity. The question could therefore be posed of whether the hermeneutic tool that I have deployed could be usefully applied to other manifestations of the religious life – past as well as present. Is reflexivity, as Barbara Adam (1996) suggests, 'ontological to all of humanity'? Whilst a detailed, comparative examination of this issue is beyond the scope of the present study, my answer at a theoretical level would have to be an affirmative. As Adam (ibid., p. 139) notes, 'irrespective of the strictness of the rules that regulate social life, there is always room to redefine situations and act in the light of experience and new knowledge'; in other words, to be reflexive. Despite some continuities in, for example, the belief in a specific deity or eschatology, no tradition – even an 'invented tradition' – has remained static since its beginnings either because of internal schism, external pressures to change or develop or through it being passed on to succeeding generations who necessarily reinterpret their inheritance (see Shils, 1981, pp. 213-61). Indeed, as Shils has argued, one aspect of possessing a tradition is to engage in such processes of modification precisely because it is never wholly adequate:

> There is something in tradition which calls forth a desire to change it by making improvements to it. There is an unceasing striving in the strongest minds for 'better' truth, for greater clarity and coherence, for adequacy of expression of the perceived and imagined (op. cit., p. 214).

Likewise, 'the creation and legitimation of reflexive subjects through *Gesellschaft* cannot happen in a vacuum...[but rather] inevitably requires a fixed set of conventions, a stable set of rules which regulate cultural and social life...namely "traditions"' (Luke, 1996, p. 111). If a tradition were completely reflexive, open to chronic, ongoing revision, it would arguably have no stable core element capable of being passed on. As has been noted, despite inter-generational reinterpretations, schisms or re-evaluations in the light of external criticism or new evidence, all traditions contain within them a largely stable element; an element that is seen by its adherents as its fundamental essence in spite of such changes and developments.

In other words, the tradition/reflexivity dynamic should be seen less as a dualism – an 'either/or' – and more of a dialectic – an 'and' or 'with'. Any attempt, as in the radical detraditionalization thesis, to analyse this dynamic from the former position is therefore, to draw on the work of Adam again,

> unsuitable for encompassing conditions where there is an interpenetration and coexistence of tradition and self-conscious construction, of rational control and endless damage-limitation exercises to cope with unintended consequences, of expanding knowledge and increasing uncertainty, as well as possible variations in between (op. cit., p. 141).

In this way, to sum up, I would argue that the study of contemporary traditions needs to address three important issues. First, the need to move beyond the either/or of the radical detraditionalisation debate (i.e. tradition or reflexivity) and instead look at the 'and' – the interactions within contemporary traditions. Second, the need to look at both the changing nature of tradition *per se* in the contemporary world and, more specifically, the changes and developments within particular traditions through detailed ethnography. Finally, perhaps most importantly, the need to examine – again at the empirical level – the continuing appeal of certain traditions for individuals and, by extension, social groups. These issues, I have argued, are not adequately addressed by the radical detraditionalists. Rather, tradition is used as something against which modernity can be compared. In contrast I would argue that a true sociology of contemporary traditions needs to concern itself with, firstly, both the reflexive and static elements of its subject matter and, secondly, the continuing, if not growing, appeal of a variety of traditions to contemporary individuals.

Bibliography

Adam, B. (1996), 'Detraditionalization and the Certainty of Uncertain Futures', in Heelas, P., Lash, S. and Morris, P. (eds.), *Detraditionalization: Critical Reflections on Authority and Identity*, Blackwell, Oxford, pp. 134-48.

Alberge, D. (1998, October 29), 'New Age Brings Search for the Spiritual', *The Times*, p. 14.

Anderton, B. (1990), *Life Cycles: The Astrology of Inner Space and Its Application to the Rhythms of Life*, Quantum, Slough.

Babb, L.A. (1982), 'Amnesia and Remembrance in a Hindu Theory of History', *Asian Folklore Studies*, vol. 41, no. 1, pp. 49-66.

Babb, L.A. (1984), 'Indigenous Feminism in a Modern Hindu Sect', *Signs: Journal of Women in Culture and Society*, vol. 9, no. 3, pp. 399-416.

Babb, L.A. (1986), *Redemptive Encounters: Three Modern Styles in the Hindu Tradition*, University of California Press, London.

Barfield, D. (1954), *History of English Words*, Faber and Faber, London.

Barratt, D.V. (1996), *Sects, Cults and Alternative Religions: A World Survey and Sourcebook*, Blandford, London.

Basham, A.L. (1967), *The Wonder That Was India: A Survey of the History and Culture of the Indian Sub-continent Before the Coming of the Muslims (Third Revised Ed.)*, Sidgwick and Jackson, London.

Bauman, Z. (1987), *Legislators and Interpreters: On Modernity, Post-modernity and Intellectuals*, Polity Press, Cambridge.

Bauman, Z. (1990), *Thinking Sociologically*, Blackwell, Oxford.

Bauman, Z. (1991), *Modernity and Ambivalence*, Polity Press, Cambridge.

Bauman, Z. (1992a), *Intimations of Postmodernity*, Routledge, London.

Bauman, Z. (1992b), *Mortality, Immortality and Other Life Strategies*, Polity Press, Cambridge.

Bauman, Z. (1992c), 'Survival as a Social Construct', *Theory, Culture and Society*, vol. 9, no. 1, pp. 1-37.

Bauman, Z. (1992d, November 13), 'The Solution as Problem', *Times Higher Education Supplement*, p. 25.

Bauman, Z. (1993), *Postmodern Ethics*, Blackwell, Oxford.

Bauman, Z. (1995), *Life in Fragments: Essays in Postmodern Morality*, Polity Press, Cambridge.

Bauman, Z. (1996), 'Morality in the Age of Contingency', in Heelas, P., Lash, S. and Morris, P. (eds.), *Detraditionalization: Critical Reflections on Authority and Identity*, Blackwell, Oxford, pp. 49-58.

Bauman, Z. (1997), *Postmodernity and its Discontents*, Blackwell, Oxford.

Bauman, Z. (1998), *Work, Consumerism and the New Poor*, Open University Press, Buckingham.

Bauman, Z. (1999), *In Search of Politics*, Polity Press, Cambridge.

Bauman, Z. (2000), *Liquid Modernity*, Polity Press, Cambridge.

Bauman, Z. and Tester, K. (2001), *Conversations with Zygmunt Bauman*, Polity Press, Cambridge.

Baumeister, R. (1986), *Identity: Cultural Change and the Struggle for Self*, Oxford University Press, New York.

Baumeister, R. (1987), 'How the Self Became a Problem: A Psychological Review of Historical Research', *Journal of Personality and Social Psychology*, vol. 52, pp. 163-76.

Beck, U. (1992), *Risk Society: Towards a New Modernity*, Sage Publications, London.

Beck, U. (1994a), 'The Reinvention of Politics: Towards a Theory of Reflexive Modernization', in Beck, U., Giddens, A. and Lash, S., *Reflexive Modernization: Politics, Tradition and Aesthetics in the Modern Social Order*, Polity Press, Cambridge, pp. 1-55.

Beck, U. (1994b), 'Self-Dissolution and Self-Endangerment of Industrial Society: What does this Mean?', in Beck, U., Giddens, A. and Lash, S., *Reflexive Modernization: Politics, Tradition and Aesthetics in the Modern Social Order*, Polity Press, Cambridge, pp. 175-83.

Beck, U. (1998), 'Politics of Risk Society', in Franklin, J. (ed.), *The Politics of Risk Society*, Polity Press, Cambridge, pp. 9-22.

Beck, U. and Beck-Gernsheim, E. (1996), 'Individualization and "Precarious Freedoms": Perspectives and Controversies of a Subject-Oriented Sociology', in Heelas, P., Lash, S. and Morris, P. (eds.), *Detraditionalization: Critical Reflections on Authority and Identity*, Blackwell, Oxford, pp. 23-48.

Beckford, J.A. (1985), *Cult Controversies: The Societal Response to New Religious Movements*, Tavistock, London.

Beckford, J.A. (1992), 'Religion, Modernity and Postmodernity', in Wilson, B.R. (ed.), *Religion: Contemporary Issues*, Bellew, London, pp. 11-23.

Beckford, J.A. (1996), 'Postmodernity, High Modernity and New Modernity: Three Concepts in Search of Religion', in Flanagan, K. and Jupp, P. (eds.), *Postmodernity, Sociology and Religion*, Macmillan, London, pp. 30-47.

Beckford, J.A. (2000), '"Start Together and Finish Together": Shifts in the Premises and Paradigms Underlying the Scientific Study of Religion', *Journal for the Scientific Study of Religion*, vol. 39, no. 4, pp. 481-95.

Berger, P.L. (1990), *The Sacred Canopy: Elements of a Sociological Theory of Religion*, Anchor Books, New York.

Bourdieu, P. (1996), *Distinction: A Social Critique of the Judgement of Taste*, Routledge and Kegan Paul.

Bowman, M. (1993), 'Reinventing the Celts', *Religion*, vol. 23, pp. 147-56.

Bowman, M. (1995), 'The Noble Savage and the Global Village: Cultural Evolution in New Age and Neo-Pagan Thought', *Journal of Contemporary Religion*, vol. 10, no. 2, pp. 139-49.

Brahma Kumaris World Spiritual University (n.d.), *When we Change... The World Changes*, Leaflet.

Brahma Kumaris Self Management Systems (n.d.), *Brahma Kumaris Self Management Systems Presents Self Managing Leadership: A Self Management Programme for Leaders*, leaflet.

Brahma Kumaris World Spiritual University (1988), *Meditations and Jewels of Knowledge*, Brahma Kumaris World Spiritual University, London.

Brahma Kumaris World Spiritual University (1995a), *Living Values: A Guidebook*, Brahma Kumaris World Spiritual University, London.

Brahma Kumaris World Spiritual University (1995b), *Practical Meditation* (4th Edition), Brahma Kumaris World Spiritual University, London.

Brahma Kumaris World Spiritual University (1996), *Visions of the Future*, Brahma Kumaris World Spiritual University, London.

Bruce, S. (1995), *Religion in Modern Britain*, Oxford University Press, Oxford.

Bunting, M. (1996a, November 12), 'Neo Paganism "a threat to society"', *The Guardian* (Home Page), p. 9.

Bunting, M. (1996b, December 16), 'Shopping For God', *The Guardian* (section 2), pp. 2-3.

Button, J. and Bloom, W. (eds.) (1992), *The Seeker's Guide: A New Age Resource Book*, Aquarian/Thorsons, London.

Cabot, L. and Cowan, T. (1990), *Power of the Witch: A Witch's Guide to her Craft*, Michael Joseph, London.

Campbell, B.F. (1978), 'A Typology of Cults', *Sociological Analysis*, vol. 39, no. 3, pp. 228-40.

Campbell, C. (1972), 'The Cult, the Cultic Milieu and Secularization', *A Sociological Yearbook of Religion in Britain*, 5, pp. 119-36.

Campbell, C. (2001), 'A New Age theodicy for a new age', in Woodhead, L. and Heelas, P. (eds.), *Peter Berger and the Study of Religion*, Routledge, London, pp. 73-84.

Capra, F. (1992), *The Tao of Physics*, Flamingo, Fort Lauderdale.

Carrette, J. (1999), *Foucault and Religion*, Routledge, London.

Carrette, J. and Bernauer, J. (eds.) (1999), *Religion and Culture by Michel Foucault*, Manchester University Press, Manchester.

Carr-Gomm, P. (1992), *The Elements of the Druid Tradition*, Element Books Ltd., Shaftesbury.

Castells, M. (1997), *The Information Age: Economy, Society and Culture, Volume II. The Power of Identity*, Oxford, Blackwell.

Chander, J. (1983), *Adi Dev: The First Man*, Brahma Kumaris World Spiritual University, Singapore.

Chander, J. (1988a), *The Eternal World Drama*, Brahma Kumaris World Spiritual University, Delhi.

Chander, J. (1988b), *Science and Spirituality*, Om Shanti Press, Delhi.

Chryssides, G.D. (1999), *Exploring New Religions*, Cassell, London.

Chunn, L. (1995, July 31), 'Mary Butler is a Computer Programmer from Bradford seeks Enlightenment', *The Observer* (*Life* Section), p. 20.

Cohn, N. (1993), *The Pursuit of the Millennium: Revolutionary Millenarians and the Mystical Anarchists of the Middle Ages*, Pimlico, London.

Cook, E. (1994, April 4), 'Our Mother, Who art in Heaven', *The Guardian* (G2T), p. 9.

Cush, D. (1996), 'British Buddhism and the New Age', *Journal of Contemporary Religion*, vol. 11, no. 2, pp. 195-208.

Davie, G. (1994), *Religion in Britain Since 1945: Believing Without Belonging*, Blackwell, Oxford.

Dawson, L. (1997), 'Creating "Cult" Typologies', *Journal of Contemporary Religion*, vol. 12, no. 3, pp. 363-81.

Dawson, L. (1999), 'When Prophecy Fails and Faith Persists: A Theoretical Overview', *Nova Religio*, vol. 3, no. 1, pp. 60-82.

Dilner, L. (1997, May 14), 'Portrait: Warning - This man can seriously affect your health. For the better. At least, that's what he says', *The Guardian* (G2T), p. 4.

Douglas, M. (1995a), *Natural Symbols: Explorations in Cosmology*, Routledge, London.

Douglas, M. (1995b), *Purity and Danger: An Analysis of the Concept of Pollution and Taboo*, Routledge, London.

Drane, J. (1991), *What is the New Age Saying to the Church?* Marshall-Pickering, London.

Durkheim, E. (1952), *Suicide*, Routledge and Kegan Paul, London.

Durkheim, E. (1961), *The Elementary Forms of the Religious Life*, Allen and Unwin, London.

Eco, U. (1990), *The Limits of Interpretation*, Indiana University Press, USA.

Eco, U. (1992a), 'Interpretation and History', in Collini, S. (ed.), *Interpretation and Overinterpretation*, Cambridge University Press, Cambridge, pp. 23-45.

Eco, U. (1992b), 'Overinterpreting Texts', in Collini, S. (ed.), *Interpretation and Overinterpretation*, Cambridge University Press, Cambridge, pp. 45-67.

Featherstone, M. (1991), *Consumer Culture and Postmodernism*, Sage, London.

Ferguson, M. (1982), *The Aquarian Conspiracy: Personal and Social Transformation in the 1980s*, Granada, London.

Festinger, L., Riecken, H.W. and Schachter, S. (1964), *When Prophecy Fails: A Social and Psychological Study of a Modern Group that Predicted the Destruction of the World*, Harper Torchbooks, New York.

Finke, R. and Stark, R. (1988), *The Churching of America, 1776-1990: Winners and Losers in Our Religious Economy*, Rutgers University Press, New Jersey.

Fornäs, J. (1995), *Cultural Theory and Late Modernity*, Sage Publications, London.

Foucault, M. (1991), *Discipline and Punish: The Birth of the Prison*, Penguin Books Ltd, London.

Foucault, M. (1997), *Madness and Civilization: A History of Madness in the Age of Reason*, Routledge, London.

Garnham, N. (1982), 'The Information Society is also a Class Society', in Bannon, L., Barry, U. and Holst, O. (eds.), *Information Technology Impact on the Way of Life: A Selection of Papers from the EEC Conference on the Information Society Held in Dublin, Ireland, 18-20 November 1981*, Tycooly International Publishing Ltd., Dublin, pp. 284-92.

Gay, P. (1977), *The Enlightenment: An Interpretation - The Rise of Modern Paganism*, WW Norton and Company, London.

Gellner, E. (1992), *Postmodernism, Reason and Religion*, London, Routledge.

Giddens, A. (1990), *The Consequences of Modernity*, Polity Press, Cambridge.

Giddens, A. (1991), *Modernity and Self-Identity: Self and Society in the Late Modern Age*, Polity Press, Cambridge.

Giddens, A. (1994a), *Beyond Left and Right: The Future of Radical Politics*, Polity Press, Cambridge.

Giddens, A. (1994b), 'Living in a Post-Traditional Society', in Beck, U., Giddens, A. and Lash, S., *Reflexive Modernization: Politics, Tradition and Aesthetics in the Modern Social Order*, Polity Press, Cambridge, pp. 56-109.

Giddens, A. (1999), *Reith Lecture no. 3*. http://www.news.bbc.co.uk/hi/english/static/events/reith_99/week3/lecture3.htm.

Giddens, A. and Pierson, C. (1998), *Conversations with Anthony Giddens: Making Sense of Modernity*, Polity Press, Cambridge.

Goffman, E. (1969), *The Presentation of Self in Everyday Life*, Allen Lane, London.

Goffman, E. (1971), *Asylums: Essays on the Social Situation of Mental Patients and other Inmates*, Penguin Books Ltd., Harmondsworth.

Goodwin, J.A. (1994, May 7), 'Real Lives: A New Dark Age', *The Guardian* (Weekend), p. 32.

Greer, P. (1995), 'The Aquarian Confusion: Conflicting Theologies of the New Age', *Journal of Contemporary Religion*, vol. 10, no. 2, pp. 151-66.

Gross, D. (1992), *The Past in Ruins: Tradition and the Critique of Modernity*, University of Massachusetts Press, Amherst.

Hall, J.R., Schuyler, P.D. and Trinh, S. (2000), *Apocalypse Observed: Religious Movements and Violence in North America, Europe and Japan*, Routledge, London.

Hay, C., O'Brien, M. and Penna, S. (1994), 'Giddens, Modernity and Self-Identity: The Hollowing out of Social Theory', *Arena Journal*, vol. 2, pp. 45-76.

Heelas, P. (1981), 'Introduction: Indigenous Psychologies', in Heelas, P. and Lock, A. (eds.), *Indigenous Psychologies: The Anthropology of the Self*, Academic Press, London, pp. 3-18.

Heelas, P. (1993), 'The New Age in Cultural Context: the Premodern, the Modern and the Postmodern', *Religion*, vol. 23, pp. 103-16.

Heelas, P. (1994), 'The Limits of Consumption and the Post-modern "Religion" of the New Age', in Abercrombie, N., Keat, R. and Whiteley, N. (eds.), *The Authority of the Consumer*, Routledge, London, pp. 102-15.

Heelas, P. (1996a), 'Detraditionalization of Religion and Self: The New Age and Postmodernity', in Flanagan, K. and Jupp, P. (eds.), *Postmodernity, Sociology and Religion*, Macmillan, London, pp. 64-83.

Heelas, P. (1996b, October 5), 'Face To Faith: New Age comes of age in Spiritual Disneyland', *The Guardian* (Feature), p. 18.

Heelas, P. (1996c, October 12), 'Face To Faith: New Age that offers infinite variety of inner truths', *The Guardian* (Feature), p. 17.

Heelas, P. (1996d), 'Introduction: Detraditionalization and its Rivals', in Heelas, P., Lash, S. and Morris, P. (eds.), *Detraditionalization: Critical Reflections on Authority and Identity*, Blackwell, Oxford, pp. 1-20.

Heelas, P. (1996e), *The New Age Movement: The Celebration of the Self and the Sacralization of Modernity*, Oxford, Blackwell.

Heelas, P. (1998a), 'Introduction: On Differentiation and Dedifferentation', in Heelas, P., Martin, D. and Morris, P. (eds.), *Religion, Modernity and Postmodernity*, Blackwell, Oxford, pp. 1-18.

Heelas, P. (1998b), 'New Age Authenticity and Social Roles: A Response to Steve Bruce', *Journal of Contemporary Religion*, vol. 13, no. 2, pp. 257-64.

Hobsbawm, E. (1983), 'Introduction: Inventing Traditions', in Hobsbawm, E. and Ranger, T. (eds.), *The Invention of Tradition*, Cambridge University Press, Cambridge University Press, pp. 1-14.

Hogg, C. (n.d), *Ruling Power*, Audio cassette.

Howell, J.D. and Nelson, P.L. (1997), 'Structural Adaption and "Success" in the Transplantation of an Asian New Religious Movement: the Brahma Kumaris in the Western World, Part 1', *Research in the Social Scientific Study of Religion*, vol. 8, pp. 1-34.

Howell, J.D. and Nelson, P.L. (1998), 'Demographic Change and Secularization in an Asian New Religious Movement: The Brahma Kumaris in the Western World, Part 2', Pre-publication manuscript.

Jary, D. and Jary, J. (1995), 'Review Article: The Transformations of Anthony Giddens - The Continuing Story of Structuration Theory', *Theory, Culture and Society*, vol. 12, no. 2, pp. 141-61.

Jenkins, R. (1996), *Social Identity*, Routledge, London.

Jenkins, R. (2000), 'Disenchantment, Enchantment and Re-Enchantment: Max Weber at the Millennium', *Max Weber Studies*, vol. 1, no. 1, pp. 11-32.

Kane, P. (1995, January 4), 'In Thrall to New Age Thrills', *The Guardian* (G2T), p. 12.

King, R. (1999), *Orientalism and Religion: Post-Colonial Theory, India and 'The Mystic East'*, Routledge, London.

Kinsley, D.R. (1993), *Hinduism: A Cultural Perspective*, Prentice Hall, New Jersey.

Kranenborg, R (1999), *Brahma Kumaris: A New Religion?* http://www.cesnur.org/testi/bryn/br_kranenborg.htm.

Lasch, C. (1991), *The Culture of Narcissism: American Life in an Age of Diminishing Expectations*, WW Norton, New York.

Lash, S. (1994), 'Reflexivity and its Doubles: Structure, Aesthetics, Community, Reflexivity', in Beck, U., Giddens, A. and Lash, S., *Reflexive Modernization: Politics, Tradition and Aesthetics in the Modern Social Order*, Polity Press, Cambridge, pp. 110-73.

Lash, S. and Urry, J. (1994), *Economies of Sign and Space*. Sage, London.

Lash, S. and Wynne, B. (1992), 'Introduction', in Beck, U., *Risk Society: Towards a New Modernity*, Sage Publications, London, pp. 1-8.

Lovat, T.J. (1997), 'Patterns of Religious Separation and Adherence in Contemporary Australia', *Religion and the Social Order*, vol. 7, pp. 97-116.

Luckmann, T. (1967) *The Invisible Religion: The Problem of Religion in Modern Society*, The Macmillan Company, New York.

Luhrmann, T.M. (1994), *Persuasions of the Witch's Craft: Ritual Magic in Contemporary England*, Picador, Basingstoke.

Luke, T.W. (1996), 'Identity, Meaning and Globalization: Detraditionalization in Postmodern Space-time Compression', in Heelas, P., Lash, S. and Morris, P. (eds.), *Detraditionalization: Critical Reflections on Authority and Identity*, Blackwell, Oxford, pp. 109-33.

Lyon, D. (1993), 'A Bit of a Circus. Notes on Postmodernity and the New Age', *Religion*, vol. 23, pp. 117-26.

Lyon, D. (2000), *Jesus in Disneyland: Religion in Postmodern Times*, Polity Press, Cambridge.

Lyotard, J-F. (1984), *The Postmodern Condition: A Report on Knowledge*, Manchester University Press, Manchester.

Manda, Sister (1994, January 8), *Co-Operation, Love and Peace*, Audio cassette.

Manohan, Dadi (1996), *History of the Brahma Kumaris World Spiritual University*, three audio cassettes.

Marx, K. and Engels, F. (1996), *The Communist Manifesto*, Orion Books Ltd., London.

May, T. (1998), 'The Discontented Epoch: Freedom and Security in Bauman's Postmodernity', *Theory, Culture and Society*, vol. 15, no. 1, pp. 117-31.

McGovern, M. (1996, October 6), 'Sunday Times Science Editor Awaits Flat Earth', *The Observer* (REA Page), p. 1.

Mellor, P.A. (1991), 'Self and Suffering: Deconstruction and Reflexive Definition in Buddhism and Christianity', *Religious Studies*, vol. 27, pp. 49-63.

Mellor, P.A (1993), 'Reflexive Traditions: Anthony Giddens, High Modernity and the Contours of Contemporary Religiosity', *Religious Studies*, vol. 29, pp. 111-27.

Melton, J.G. (2000), 'Spiritualization and Reaffirmation: What Really Happens when Prophecy Fails', in Stone, J.R. (ed.), *Expecting Armageddon: Essential Readings in Failed Prophecy*, Routledge, London, pp. 145-57.

Meštrović, S.G (1998), *Anthony Giddens: The Last Modernist*, Routledge, London.

Moir, J. (1993, August 4), 'Summer Lives: The Heal Thing', *The Guardian* (G2T), p. 8.

Morgan, P. (1982), 'From a Death to a View: The Hunt for the Welsh Past in the Romantic Period', in Hobsbawm, E. and Ranger, T. (eds.), *The Invention of Tradition*, Cambridge University Press, Cambridge, pp. 43-100.

Nietzsche, F. (1998), *On the Genealogy of Morals: A Polemic* (Trans: Clark, M and Swenson, A.J.), Hackett Publishing Company, Inc, Indianapolis/Cambridge.

O'Donnell, K. (1995), *New Beginnings*, Brahma Kumaris World Spiritual University, London.

O'Donnell, K. (1996), *Pathways to Higher Consciousness*, Eternity Ink, Sydney, Australia.

O'Flaherty, W. (1973), *Asceticism and Eroticism in the Mythology of Šiva*, Oxford University Press, London.

Palmer, M. (1993), *Coming of Age: An Exploration of Christianity and the New Age*, The Aquarian Press, London.

Palmer, S.J. and Finn, N. (2000), 'Coping with Apocalypse in Canada: Experiences of Endtime in La Mission de l'Espirit Saint and the Institute of Applied Metaphysics', in

Stone, J.R. (ed.), *Expecting Armageddon: Essential Readings in Failed Prophecy*, Routledge, London, pp. 211-31.

Parsons, T. (1978), *Action Theory and the Human Condition*, Collier Macmillan, London.

Peake, M. (1980), *Titus Groan*, Penguin Books Ltd., Harmondsworth.

Perry, M. (1992), *Gods Within: A Critical Guide To The New Age*, SPCK, UK.

Peters, T. (1991), *The Cosmic Self: A Penetrating Look at Today's New Age Movements*, Harper Collins, New York.

Philips, F. (1997), 'Age of Aquarius', *Prediction*, vol. 63, no. 11, pp. 24-6.

Rose, N. (1996) 'Authority and the Genealogy of Subjectivity' in Heelas, P., Lash, S. and Morris, P. (eds.) *Detraditionalization: Critical Reflections on Authority and Identity*, Blackwell, pp. 294-327.

Rose, S. (1998), 'An Examination of the New Age Movement: Who is Involved and What Constitutes its Spirituality', *Journal of Contemporary Religion*, vol. 13, no. 1, pp. 5-22.

Rustin, M. (1994), 'Incomplete Modernity: Ulrich Beck's "Risk Society"', *Dissent*, vol. 41, pp. 394-400.

Schmalz, M.N. (2000), 'When Festinger Fails: Prophecy and the Watchtower', in Stone, J.R. (ed.), *Expecting Armageddon: Essential Readings in Failed Prophecy*, Routledge, London, pp. 233-50.

Shils, E. (1981), *Tradition*, Faber and Faber, London.

Shilling, C. (1997), *The Body and Social Theory*, Sage, London.

Shubow, R. (1988), *The Voyagers: A True Story of a Race of Beings Far More Intelligent than Us*, Brahma Kumaris World Spiritual University, London.

Skultans, V. (1993), 'The Brahma Kumaris and the Role of Women', in Puttick, E. and Clarke, P.B. (eds.), *Women as Teachers and Disciples in Traditional and New Religions*, Edwin Mellen Press, New York, pp. 47-62.

Slater, H. (ed.) (1988), *A Book of Pagan Rituals*, Robert Hale, London.

Smart, N. (1995), *The World's Religions: Old Traditions and Modern Transformations*, Cambridge University Press, Cambridge.

Soares, J.A. (1997), 'A reformulation of the concept of tradition', *International Journal of Sociology and Social Policy*, vol. 17, no. 6, pp. 6-21.

Stark, R. and Bainbridge, W.S. (1979), 'Of Churches, Sects and Cults: Preliminary Concepts for a Theory of Religious Movements', *Journal for the Scientific Study of Religion*, vol. 18, no. 2, pp. 117-33.

Stark, R. and Bainbridge, W.S. (1985), *The Future of Religion: Secularisation, Revival and Cult Formation*, University of California Press, Berkeley.

Stillerman, S. (ed.) (1998), *Wings of Soul: Emerging Your Spiritual Identity - The World and Wisdom of Dadi Janki*, Brahma Kumaris World Spiritual University, London.

Storm, R. (1991), *In Search of Heaven on Earth: A History of the New Age*, Aquarian Press, London.

Sutcliffe, S. (1995), 'Some Notes on a Sociology of New Age and Related Counter Cultural Religiosity in Scotland', *Journal of Contemporary Religion*, vol. 10, no. 2, pp. 181-4.

Symonds, J. (1973), *The Great Beast: The Life and Magick of Aleister Crowley*, Mayflower Books Ltd., St. Albans.

Taylor, C. (1989), *Sources of The Self: The Making of Modern Identity*, Harvard University Press, Cambridge, Massachusetts.

Thompson, D. (1996), *The End of Time: Faith and Fear in the Shadow of the Millennium*, Sinclair-Stevenson, London.

Thompson, E. (1994, May 1), 'Room of our Own', *The Observer* (Magazine), p. 44.

Thompson, L. (1995, January 22), 'Laura Thompson Embarks on a Holistic Overhaul of her Inner Life', *The Observer* (*Life* Section), p. 78.

Turner, B.S. (1999), *Religion and Social Theory: Second Edition*, Sage Publications, London.

Van Hove, H. (1996), 'Higher Realities and the inner self: one quest? Transcendence and the Significance of the Body in the New Age Circuit', *Journal of Contemporary Religion*, vol. 11, no. 2, pp. 185-95.

Vattimo, G. (1999), *Belief*, Polity Press, Cambridge.

Vitz, P.C. (1977), *Psychology as Religion: The Cult of Self-Worship*, William B. Eerdmans Publishing Company, Michigan.

Wallis, R. (1974), 'Ideology, Authority and the Development of Cultic Movements', *Social Research*, vol. 41, pp. 299-327.

Wallis, R. (1984), *The Elementary Forms of the New Religious Life*, Routledge and Kegan Paul, London.

Wallis, R. and Bruce, S. (1989), 'Religion: The British Contribution', *The British Journal of Sociology*, vol. 40, no. 3, pp. 493-520.

Walliss, J. (1998), *Reflexive Traditions: New Religious Movements and the "Negotiation" of Identity*, presented to the BSA Sociology of Religion Study Group Annual Conference, Durham, 9th April 1998.

Walliss, J. (1999), 'From World Rejection to Ambivalence: The Development of Millenarianism in the Brahma Kumaris', *Journal of Contemporary Religion*, vol. 14, no. 3, pp. 375-85.

Walliss, J. (2000a), 'Responding to Late Modernity: The Brahma Kumaris as a "Reflexive Tradition"', University of Sheffield, unpublished thesis.

Walliss, J. (2000b), 'The Brahma Kumaris', in Barker, C. and Tyldesley, M. (eds.), *Sixth International Conference on Alternative Futures and Popular Protest: A Selection of Papers from the Conference, 25-27 April 2000, Volume II*, Manchester Metropolitan University, pp. 148-60.

Walliss, J. (2001), 'The Problem of "Tradition" in the Work of Anthony Giddens', *Culture and Religion*, vol. 2, no. 2, pp. 81-98.

Walter, T. (2001), 'Reincarnation, Modernity and Identity', *Sociology*, vol. 35, no. 1, pp. 21-38.

Walter, T. and Davie, G. (1997), 'The Religiosity of Women: Understanding a Paradox', unpublished manuscript.

Walter, T. and Waterhouse, H. (1999), 'A Very Private Belief: Reincarnation in Contemporary England', *Sociology of Religion*, vol. 60, no. 2, pp. 187-97.

Washington, P. (1993), *Madame Blavatsky's Baboon: Theosophy and the Emergence of the Western Guru*, Secker and Warburg, New York.

Weber, M. (1965), *The Sociology of Religion*, Social Science Paperbacks/Methuen and Co Ltd., London.

Weber, M. (1970), 'Science as Vocation', in Gerth, H.H. and Mills, C.W. (eds.), *From Max Weber: Essays in Sociology*, Routledge and Kegan Paul, London, pp. 129-56.

Weber, M. (1989), *The Protestant Ethic and the Spirit of Capitalism*, Unwin Hyman, London.

Whaling, F. (1995), 'The Brahma Kumaris', *Journal of Contemporary Religion*, vol. 10, no. 1, pp. 3-28.

Williams, R. (1979), *Keywords: A Vocabulary of Culture and Society*, William Collins Sons and Co Ltd., Glasgow.

Wilson, B.A. (1969), 'A Typology of Sects in a Dynamic and Comparative Perspective', in Robertson, R. (ed.), *Sociology of Religion: Selected Readings*, Penguin Books Ltd., Harmondsworth, pp. 361-83.

Wilson, B.A. (1970), *Religious Sects: A Sociological Study*, Weidenfeld and Nicolson, London.

Wolffe, J. (1993), 'The Religions of the Silent Majority', in Parsons, G. (ed.), *The Growth of Religious Diversity, Britain from 1945: Volume 1. The Traditions*, Routledge, London, pp. 307-46.

Wroe, M. (1995, April 2), 'DIY Spiritualists Challenge America's Old-Time Religion', *The Observer* (News), p. 18.

York, M. (1991), 'The New Age and Neo Pagan Movement', *Religion Today: A Journal of Contemporary Religion*, vol. 6, no. 2, pp. 1-3.

York, M. (1994), 'New Age in Britain: An Overview', *Religion Today: A Journal of Contemporary Religion*, vol. 10, no. 1, pp. 71-82.

York, M. (1995), *The Emerging Network: A Sociology of the New Age and Neo-Pagan Movements*, Rowman and Littlefield, Lanham, MD.

York, M. (1999), 'Invented Culture/Invented Religion: The Fictional Origins of Contemporary Paganism', *Nova Religio: The Journal of Alternative and Emergent Religions*, vol. 3, no. 1, pp. 135-46.

Zohar, D. (1991), *The Quantum Self*, Flamingo, London.

Yukav, G. (1998), *The Dancing Wu Li Masters*, William Morrow, New York.

Zygmunt, J.F. (2000), 'Prophetic Failure and Chiliastic Identity: The Case of the Jehovah's Witnesses', in Stone, J.R. (ed.), *Expecting Armageddon: Essential Readings in Failed Prophecy*, Routledge, London, pp. 65-85.

Index